UNDERGROUND WOMAN

In the series
Labor and Social Change,
edited by Paula Rayman and Carmen Sirianni

UNDERGROUND WOMAN

My Four Years as a New York City Subway Conductor

MARIAN SWERDLOW

TEMPLE UNIVERSITY PRESS

PHILADELPHIA

Dedicated to

Steve

and in memory

of Mark

Temple University Press, Philadelphia 19122
Copyright © 1998 by Temple University.
All rights reserved
Published 1998
Printed in the United States of America

TEXT DESIGN: Judith Martin Waterman

CATALOGING-IN-PUBLICATION DATA

Swerdlow, Marian, 1949–
        Underground woman : my four years as a New York City subway
conductor / Marian Swerdlow.
                p.   cm.
        ISBN 1-56639-609-3 (alk. paper). — ISBN 1-56639-610-7 (alk. paper)
        1. Subways—New York (N.Y.)   2. Swerdlow, Marian, 1949-   .
3. Railroad conductors—New York (N.Y.)—Biography.   I. Title.
HE4491.N65S94   1998
388.4'28'092—dc21
        [B]   97-45187
                                                                      CIP

CONTENTS

Acknowledgments   *vii*

Introduction   1

More Than Door Openers   7

Woodlawn   20

Crew Room Cowboys   38

Health and Safety   59

Greatness   71

Hell on Wheels   90

Rejection   101

Lackluster   119

Greater Greatness   128

Miscellaneous   139

Coworkers   147

Characters and Cronies   169

Riders and Conductors   181

Transit Worker Wit and Wisdom   193

Why I Left   212

The More Things Change . . .   231

Afterword   *241*

Glossary   *251*

ACKNOWLEDGMENTS

Many people encouraged me to write a book about my experiences working on the New York subways. Pierre Bouvier and Al Swerdlow stand out in my mind.

Steve Downs, Marjorie George, Alan Lefkowitz, Charlie Post, Al and Bertha Swerdlow, and Josephine Teng read the manuscript, in full or part, and made helpful suggestions. I am deeply grateful to them. Joanne Foti contributed her whimsical subway map, grappling with the concept of "Brooklyn Bridge" as a station underground instead of a span over water. I also specially appreciate the efforts of Michael Ames, acquisitions editor at Temple University Press, who discerned promise in the initial eight-hundred-page manuscript and nudged me along as I trimmed and shaped it into its current form.

I also thank the many friends who helped me survive my four years in transit. Although I cannot name them all, I am especially indebted to Ruth and Chuck Hoffman, Alan Lefkowitz, Jim Murphy, Anne Sherry, Anita Waters, and the late Jessica Atlas.

Steve Downs gave me indispensable help in the preparation of the Afterword to this book.

UNDERGROUND WOMAN

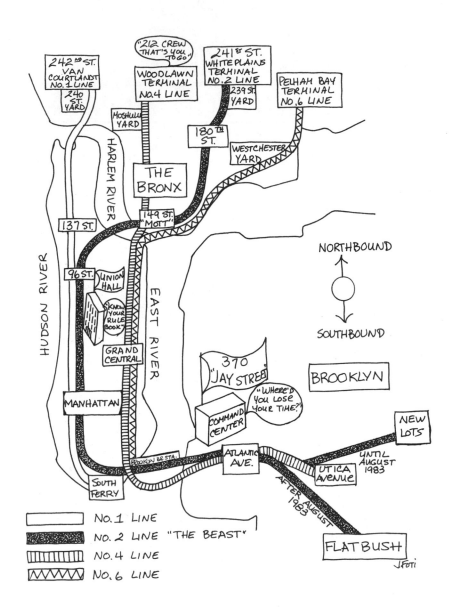

DRAWN BY JOANNE FOTI

INTRODUCTION

I was born in the South Bronx, in 1949. My family lived there until we moved to the northeast part of the same borough when I was almost ten years old. I attended city public schools and graduated from the High School of Music and Art.

My parents were leftists. I was unaware of that until my mid-teens, by which time, I myself had been radicalized by opposition to United States intervention in Southeast Asia. While I was a student at Bard College, my involvement in the women's liberation movement deepended my radicalism.

These early political experiences shaped my view of labor unions. I saw that there were unions whose policies supported racism, sexism, and imperialism. Yet I always believed that the rank-and-file members of these unions could be persuaded to support equality and peace, because these were the policies consistent with their own interests as working people.

After my graduation from college in 1971, I went on to graduate studies in the sociology department at Columbia University in Manhattan. I worked in a copy shop and then as a part-time college instructor. The rank-and-file upsurges of the 1970s, which convulsed the United Mine Workers, the Teamsters, and the Auto Workers, among other unions, further refined my view of the labor movement. There was clearly a dichotomy between the membership of these unions and their leadership.

In the late 1970s, I met and eventually married a fellow sociologist. Jim was an active supporter of the union reform movement in the United Mine Workers, the Miners for Democracy. Those experiences taught him that electing honest reformers was not enough to change a union. The rank and file had to maintain their own organization and activity. He passed this lesson on to me. Jim left graduate school and became an organizer for local 1199 of the Health and Hospital Workers Union in New York City. After a few years in nonelected staff positions, his views changed. He became suspicious of the rank and file and committed to "top–down" union leadership.

This same decade saw the "fiscal crisis" of New York City. Under the pretext that the city was "bankrupt," a coalition of realtors and financiers seized direct fiscal control of the city and imposed austerity. Politicians and union leaders fell into line. The result was a terrible decline in the quality of life for most New Yorkers. Among the most grievous and long-lasting effects, free tuition at the public City University was eliminated, the subway fare rose from twenty to thirty-five cents, thousands of city employees were laid off, and others saw their pay delayed or frozen.

The fiscal crisis was also the pretext for foisting four years' worth of bad contracts on the transit workers. A hiring and promotion freeze was imposed. A two-year pact (1976 to 1977) granted no wage increases whatsoever. In 1978, during a time of double-digit annual inflation nationally, a new contract granted a raise of 6 percent over two years, plus a cost-of-living adjustment of 29 cents an hour. The combination of these contracts and the rate of inflation resulted in New York City transit workers' losing about one-third of the purchasing power of their wages between 1973 and 1979. These events were the immediate causes of the New York City transit strike of April 1980.

For the six thousand transit workers who operated the subways, the austerity had insidious effects upon working conditions as well as pay. To save money, the Transit Authority discontinued all routine preventive maintenance of facilities. Trains, tracks, roadbeds, and elevated structures received little or no inspection, cleaning, or care. The results were a growing number of accidents and a steady decline in service and working conditions. Unmaintained tracks caused increasing delays and ultimately derailments. Because the number of track cleaners was cut, rubbish accumulated on the roadbeds and sometimes smouldered or flamed.

Train motors and other moving parts were not checked, and faulty equipment was not fixed unless trains broke down in use. This meant the trains had to be taken out of service and the riders ordered off. Waiting times for trains lengthened, and fewer trains meant more crowded trains. Even when a malfunction did not necessitate a train's removal from service, it might slow the train's movement, jam a door, or even close a car. Nonfunctioning windows, fans, and heaters made riding and working on trains more uncomfortable and unhealthy. These conditions were inconvenient and aggravating for both riders and workers. They led to rider hostility toward the subway workers, whom riders assumed were to blame for the poor conditions.

But problems for workers surpassed discomfort; they meant real danger. In July 1981, a motorman was killed in a collision that was caused in large part by broken signals. In 1982, a motorman was killed on a work train when communication equipment failed. Subway workers suffered hundreds of nonfatal but often serious injuries as a result of austerity.

The decline in pay and working conditions was combined with the conviction among many transit workers that the leaders of their union, the Transport Workers Union Local 100, had not fought on their behalf. Although the national rank-and-file upsurge of the seventies had already crested and was losing strength, it provided inspiration for a reform movement in the T.W.U. In November 1979, the incumbent Local 100 president, John Lawe, was reelected in a four-way race, but he failed to win a majority of the votes cast. Furthermore, almost half the seats on the local Executive Board were won by candidates from various opposition slates.

The T.W.U. contract was set to expire on March 31, 1980. Pressured by the opposition and its support among the membership, President Lawe refused to accept the Transit Authority's offer, and the local struck. The impact on the city was tremendous. Carrying on everyday activities—shopping, working, visiting, going to a movie—became increasingly difficult. Traffic clogged all streets. The effects reached into almost everyone's life.

For me personally, it was dramatic proof of the potential power of organized workers. I had known it, intellectually, but now living the reality changed the way I wanted to live my life. Since the fiscal crisis, New Yorkers had been dealt a series of blows and defeats by the wealthy and powerful, which we had been helpless to resist. In the strike, I saw what I believed to be a force strong enough to reverse our retreat and even win new victories.

After eleven days, some of the union's demands were met. The settlement amounted to a raise of approximately 20 percent over two years and an end to the permanent two-tier pay structure begun in 1978. The settlement, however, was not a complete victory. Under the Taylor Law, New York's legislation governing collective bargaining by public employee unions, public workers who strike are subject to personal fines. Transit workers were fined two days' pay for each strike day. The fine was deducted from their paychecks; thus offsetting the gains of the contract for a full year. The penalty created an atmosphere of defeat and hopelessness among the rank and file, which pervaded the opposition as well. Taking advantage of the demoralized silence of the dissidents, the Lawe leadership was able to persuade many members to blame the opposition for the cost of the strike, while taking credit themselves for its gains. Some of the reformers were hounded out of the system. Others were co-opted by the union leaders. Still others took promotions and became supervisors. It is the remnants of these forces that I refer to in my story as the "old opposition."

I had no first-hand knowledge of this. My impression of the strike and of the transit workers remained one of strength and triumph. My marriage had hit the rocks, I was on my third attempt to write a dissertation proposal my department would accept, and I was looking for a way to support myself.

In October 1980, while crossing the plaza at Lincoln Center, in front of the Metropolitan Opera House, it occurred to me that I could get a job with the Transit Authority. From that moment on, I was completely determined to do so. It seemed practical, and it had political value as well. I wanted the experience of being a union activist. I wanted to contribute to the rank-and-file upsurge.

More subtly, but perhaps most compellingly, I felt a need to break away from my life as it had been and perhaps even from my identity. I saw my life up to then as too safe, intellectual, and insular. I had lived at a remove from the events I considered central and important. My goal of being a college teacher seemed a continuation of this, and I was eager to change that completely.

In December 1980, my thesis proposal, a study of collective bargaining among registered nurses, was finally accepted, and I began my research. In July 1981, the Transit Authority opened filing for the job of subway conductor. In January 1982, my husband and I separated. That August, "Transit" called me for a job.

By the time I was appointed subway conductor, I had been keeping a personal journal for several years. Soon after I started working for T.A., I stopped writing in a bound journal and began using looseleaf paper instead. That way, I could carry several individual sheets with me in the pocket of my uniform shirt. I wrote between stops as I was working. Those writings are the basis for the narrative that follows.

In writing this narrative, I wanted to present my experiences to readers who shared my view that the people I worked with, and their lives, are important. New York City subway workers have an enormous potential clout. Organized and united, they have the power virtually to shut down the largest city in the United States.

Hell on Wheels, the rank-and-file newsletter, the inception of which is described here, still exists. It has become the newsletter of a reform rank-and-file caucus, "New Directions," which garnered almost 45 percent of the votes for president of the at the end of 1994. Some of the people described in this book are still prominently involved in New Directions. They have an extremely strong influence on this potentially powerful group of workers.

I found that subway workers and the activists among them belong to many races and ethnic backgrounds. They have more education than I had assumed and they possess a wit, worldliness, and sophistication that I found both distinctive and appealing. Predominantly male, they often conformed to gender norms, but they also departed from them in unforeseen ways. My relationships with people I met on the job, who became my friends and lovers, gave me my closest look at workers' lives, although that is certainly not why I became involved with them.

I was among the first women to work as subway operatives in an almost completely male workplace, which affected the way workmates, supervisors, riders, and union officers viewed and treated me. This treatment in turn affected my ability to handle my job and its conditions, including my union activities. I believe that my experiences are, to a significant extent, representative of those of thousands of women who have entered "nontraditional" jobs, especially in "blue-collar" occupations.

I reject the notion that my close associates and I were not "typical workers," because I do not believe there is one "type" of worker. I have tried to show that, among subway workers, I was an example (albeit, perhaps, an extreme one) of a layer of educated, sophisticated, and often politically liberal or even radical workers.

In almost all cases, I have changed the names of the people with whom I worked. We rarely used, or even knew, each other's first names. Nicknames came from last names. I have chosen pseudonyms with the same ethnic character as the originals. Since most of the workers with English or Scottish surnames were black, I have tried to mention the exceptions. I also have tried

to write in the tradition of a genre that I have always enjoyed: narratives
written by workers themselves, with little or no analysis of the formal academic type. The earliest example I have found is Richard Henry Dana's *Two
Years Before the Mast*, originally published in the 1840s. Robert Tressell's
The Ragged Trousered Philanthropists is a thinly fictionalized story of British
construction workers written around 1906 and finally published posthu-
mously about fifty years later. More recently, there have been Satoshi Kamata's
Japan in the Passing Lane (1982) and Maynard Seider's *A Year in the Life of
a Factory* (1984). Singlejack Books in San Pedro, California, now apparently
defunct, also put out a wonderful series of "little books" in 1980, with titles
like *Night Shift in a Pickle Factory*, *Longshoring on the San Francisco Water-
front*, and *Foundry Foreman, Foundryman*. Some of the selections in James
Green's 1983 anthology, *Workers' Struggles, Past and Present*, also fall into
this select group, such as John Lippert's "Shop Floor Politics at Fleetwood."

There are many monographs in the field of the "sociology of work"
which mix academic analysis with vivid accounts of workers, their work, and
their attitudes. My favorites in this category include Ruth Cavendish's *Women
on the Line*, Alvin Gouldner's *Patterns of Industrial Bureaucracy*, Laurie
Graham's *On the Line at Subaru Isuzu*, Tom Juravich's *Chaos on the Shop
Floor*, and William Kornbloom's *Blue Collar Community*. This varied body
of work has inspired me, and I have sought to contribute to it by writing my
own story.

MORE THAN
DOOR OPENERS

I arrived at the New York City Personnel Office the day filing opened for the Civil Service Examination for Bus Operator and Conductor. Even though the office still had not opened for the morning, hundreds of people were already waiting in a line extending for blocks. It was July 1, 1981, and good unskilled jobs were already hard to find. Most of the people on line were young black men, but just about every kind of New Yorker was represented. I had expected that, as a woman, I would encounter hostility from fellow filers. Instead, I found camaraderie.

The written part of the test was given two months later. It was mainly reading comprehension, with a few questions about rules of the road, which as a conductor I would need only if I drove to work. There were some judgement questions, also some about bus operation. Everyone wanted to do as well as possible, since one's score determined when one would be called for the job.

Although I got only one answer wrong on the exam, it was more than a year before I was called. I was scheduled for a physical test on August 3, 1982. I was especially apprehensive about the physical. I asked every conductor I met about it during the week before the test. None could recall taking it.

On August 3, I arrived at 370 Jay Street, Transit Authority Headquarters, carrying eight pages of forms I had filled out with information including my every address and job for the past twenty years. I had my birth certificate and my social security card with me.

They did give me the physical, and it was rough, but I passed it. The next stop was a huge grey room filled with desks. The guy in a tie who went over my application noticed my education: "You won't be a conductor long. You'll be up on the thirteenth floor with the bosses."

Training began on August 10. We reported to a former elementary school in South Brooklyn.

There were about fifty of us. I was surprised that so many of us, around half, were white. There were about half a dozen women. The atmosphere was friendly, with everyone asking everyone else, "What division are you in?" "Where do you live?" "What were you doing before this?" We were now on the payroll at the starting rate of around $7.35 an hour.

The first day, we were assigned to either the "A" or the "B" Division of the subways. The "A" Division is the I.R.T.; the "B" Division is the B.M.T. and the I.N.D. Each of us was given a pass and a pass number, a badge, a flashlight, and a set of keys, and we swore an oath of office.

My title was "conductor," one of the two-person crew of a train. The other worker, who drove the train, had the title of "motorman." Until around 1980, all motormen were in fact men; by 1985, the title had been changed to "train operator," but drivers of both sexes continued to be called motormen.

The union reps came to our classroom, distributed literature, and collected membership cards. Thus we became members of Transport Workers Union Local 100.

Our instructor regaled us with numerous stories of conductors whose trains left without them, and his special delight was stories of employees getting "clipped," or hit by trains. "Don't extend your arm out the window"; then he described how a conductor had his arm torn off by a signal. I was getting the idea these calamities were weekly occurrences, which shook me up. I scribbled into my notebook:

fatality

fatality

During the question period, I asked how many transit workers were actually killed on the job each year. The instructor paused to think. "Three last year," he said finally, "only one so far this year." I knew of two during the previous year. The best known fatality was Jesse Cole, a motorman, killed in a collision. His train had rear-ended another standing just inside the tunnel entrance on the New Lots line.

The instructor concluded, "Walking the track, you should be a little afraid. It's something people never get used to and never like. And that's good." If fear was good, I reflected, I was going to be sensational.

One day, our instructor explained the signal system to us. He said that any train that failed to stop for a red signal would be "tripped." As long as a signal was red, a little arm in front of it, called the "trip arm" would be raised. If a train passed the red signal, this arm would hit a part of the car next to the wheels called the "trip cock." This in turn would automatically activate the train's emergency brakes and stop the train. Our instructor said that if the power goes out on the signals, the trip arms come up automatically.

I came to attention. I thought of the accident that killed Cole. The power on the signals had been out. According the article I'd read in the *New York Post*, however, that section of the railroad didn't have the feature the instructor described. Instead, it claimed, there was a seventy-year-old system in which the stop arms froze in position if the power stopped.

I raised my hand, "The system you described, it's not on every part of every line, is it?"

He insisted that it was.

I continued, "What about the collision last summer that killed the motorman?"

"He didn't follow instructions, didn't heed the signals."

"But what about the trip arms?" I persisted, "Did they fail?"

The class grew restless. I suddenly felt afraid that I'd asked too many questions.

But the instructor turned more reflective and less defensive, "Everything was against the poor guy. First of all, it was a bright, sunny day. His leader was standing just inside the portal. Second, there'd been trouble on the line. The signals had been dark for days previously. Every trip all week, he'd stopped and called in that the signals were dark, and had been told to proceed according to thirty-seven Nancy" (that is, rule 37(n): "Proceed at restricted speed and with extreme caution, at a speed that will permit a stop within half your range of vision."). "He was going downgrade. The train ahead of him had experienced brake problems and had stopped. He never even saw it, because there was no brake application, and he was still in the cab. Once you dump it" (that is, apply the emergency brake), "you might as well leave the cab."

At the end of the day's notes, I scribbled in my notebook:

> 200 ways to get killed by a train
> 1,000 ways to hang a conductor

We were introduced to the world of signals and communications, automatics and interlockings. The most important signal for a conductor is the conductor's indication board, a zebra-striped board about eight inches wide and at least four feet long, located in the middle of the station platform, facing the train. It is usually six or seven feet off the ground, fixed to a wall, or suspended from the ceiling. If the motorman makes his stop properly, so that the entire train is in the station, the conductor's position is directly opposite this board.

Like most riders, I'd never thought much about this aspect of train operation. I think I believed the doors would not open unless all the train's cars were in the station, rather like elevator doors that will not open between floors. A comforting notion, but not an accurate one. It sometimes happens that the motorman overshoots the station, not stopping until a door, or perhaps even a car, is facing tunnel or sky instead of platform. Sometimes it happens because the brakes fail, sometimes, because the motorman fails. Here is where the conductor really earns the paycheck. If the conductor is not directly in front of the board, the conductor is not supposed to open the doors. Of course, there are a few conductors who will throw open the doors the instant the train stops, with nary a glance to make sure they are where they should be, but there are few who have not goofed in this way once or twice.

We also learned about holding lights. These were three amber bulbs set overhead near the edge of the platform. When they were illuminated, it meant keep your doors open. But it could also have meant close your doors. It depended on where you were. If you were at a terminal, the dispatcher turned these on to tell you to close the doors and give the motorman the "proceed" signal of two long buzzes. At a "gap" station, along the route, however, the lit bulbs meant hold your doors. To make matters more complicated, the same station could be a terminal on some trips and a gap station on others. This system has been made more reasonable only recently, by adding new green bulbs at any station used as a terminal. The green ones go on to give the signal to start, and the amber ones still serve as the signal to keep the doors open.

We were taught a series of buzzer signals used for communication between motorman and conductor. Like the words "yes" and "no," they are ambiguous in meaning and change in context. A long buzz means stop. But what is to be stopped has to be inferred from experience and the situation. Two buzzes mean proceed, usually referring to whatever you have previously been told to stop. A motorman who overshoots the station is supposed to give the conductor a long, long buzz, which means don't open the doors.

When we had been measured for our uniforms, the guys from the uniform center told me, "Try one of the ladies' caps." They were soft, beretlike caps.

I said, "I want the one with the visor," the traditional flat-topped-visored one.

"Yeah, that's right. You have a choice."

A conductor came in to tell us the uniforms had arrived. Full of excitement, I went into the ladies' room to try it on. I was disappointed to find no mirror. One of the white women in my training class, who was going to "B" Division, also came in. The first thing she did was jeer at my hat.

"You're just jealous," I said.

She told me she didn't like the instructor's attitude. "It comes through by way of all his anecdotes and illustrations. Women are airheads, distracting men. He's always saying, 'And if the conductor is talking to some *chick* or something . . .' It sends me up the wall! And he picks on the ladies in the class, like when he asked you what some signal meant, and you opened the book, and he said, 'You won't have that book in the tunnel. Didn't you read the book last night?'" I shrugged it off. Most motormen and conductors were friendly to us "students."

After a couple of weeks at the old school building, we were assigned to report to the yards for "School Car," for instruction on equipment. Because the equipment for the "A" and the "B" divisions is different, the class was divided at this point. The twelve of us destined for the I.R.T., "A" Division, were sent to the yards at 239th Street in the Bronx.

Seven black people, two Hispanics, and three whites made up my class. Two of us were women. The other woman was Leah Goss. She had once worked for the Revenue Department of the T.A. Although small, she was as strong as I. She had trained as a gymnast in her teens and practiced karate. She was pursuing a master's degree in forensic psychology at John Jay College of City University.

The friendliest member of the class was Laurence Brown, a big, strong man in his middle twenties. He had been studying to become a computer programmer at City University, but dropped out and tried a variety of jobs. His last one had been orderly in a psychiatric hospital.

The yard, with its ribbons of tracks and third rails, frightened me. On my way there, on the first day, I was very much afraid that I would fall in the yard. Some people are so terrified of heights, I recalled, that they finally jump just to end the fear. Minutes later, Goss and I were picking our way among a veritable maze of third rails. We had inadvertently taken the longest way through the yards.

Motor Instructor Booth was our main School Car instructor. Unlike the instructor in Brooklyn, Booth treated the men and women in the class exactly the same, never making any special reference to the presence of women. He was a patient and attentive teacher. Booth told us, "Any monkey can open and close the doors. We're going to make more than door openers out of you. We're going to make you conductors."

Booth told us, "In a station, you must hold your doors open for ten seconds and then close with safety. There will be curved stations where you cannot see the front or the rear of the train. There, hold them open for twenty seconds. Then, you must observe the platform for three car-lengths as the train is leaving the station. Conductors don't like sticking their heads out, because people on the platform deliberately hit them. But the 'beakies'"— T.A. undercover inspectors—"look for observing the platform, especially. And it is part of your job."

"Observing the platform" is a misnomer, since you actually are supposed to have your eyes on the train. The purpose of this exercise is to make sure you are not dragging someone stuck in the doors, and someone who is stuck in the doors is not going to be on the platform. The conductor, however, usually does end up watching the people on the platform—to make sure no one is waiting to take a swing at him or her (or to check out attractive individuals on the platform).

On the last day of School Car, we went to Westchester yard. I walked into the yard and, after a while, I realized I was lost. I stopped and looked around slowly: I had walked right past the tower. Picking my way back among the tangle of tracks and third rails, I was angry at myself and nervous.

"Are you lost?"

"Why didn't you go that way?"

I looked at the switchmen who had addressed me. What kind of answer could they expect to those questions? I felt furious, but still less angry than scared and humiliated. I was scared I would be killed, literally. And I'd already heard enough to know that any accident I suffered would be a humiliation—not only for me but for every woman on the job. Such an acident would be used to discourage women from taking the job, and thrown in the face of any woman who tried.

"Can you type?"

"Can you type?"

I had been asked that question a hundred times already. "If you can type, you can go down and work at Jay Street," the T.A. headquarters, "for a conductor's salary."

We learned to fasten down a trip arm, throw a switch, put an emergency brake on a work train, and climb up ladders directly over the third rail. These tasks brought sharply home to me how weak and small I was. I started to feel very sad and inadequate. I got through it because, although I was not good, I was minimally competent and, more important, my instructors and classmates neither criticized nor ridiculed me.

The next part of our training was "road break-in." Each of us made one trip or more on each I.R.T. line under the tutelage of a regular conductor. I began with the No. 1 train, the Broadway local. I was assigned to job 211, with Conductor Eddie Good.

As soon as the rush hour ended, Good let me operate the doors. As I worked nervously, he repeated, "One: See the indication board. Two: Insert the key into the control panel. Three: Turn the key and flip the handles."

Sometimes Good would talk and distract me, and I'd get confused. I announced the wrong stop a couple of times. I almost reopened the doors after the indication light was on. Eddie kept repeating, "Board. Keys. Handles." I preferred the handles to the buttons on newer trains.

The only thing that really got to me was Eddie's moving in to correct me or, worse, taking over when I made a mistake. I wanted to correct myself, to draw conclusions, and to learn from my own mistakes. The worst part came when he explained to me why I was wrong after I'd already realized it myself.

Eddie repeated, "Safety comes first." But he also told me, "You play little games with yourself to make the time go. See how fast you can make the run." He called out "Popito!" to the little old man at the newsstand at 157th Street. He flirted with the token clerk at 23rd Street.

On my third and final trip, I found out Good had been a conductor for only three months. I was impressed by how well he knew his job and how good he had been at teaching me.

During the week my class was breaking in, a motorman was killed while flagging a work train. According to scuttlebutt, John Ahern fell off the work train. *Not* following the rules. You never walk across a moving flat car. *Carelessness.*

I heard other suggestions, though: that the crew was using a buzz box, a piece of equipment that allows crews to send and receive buzzes and light signals only, and the motorman heard two buzzes, assumed it was his flagman, and moved the train. But the flagman was still down on the track.

I was convinced that the equipment and the schedules were the culprits. Ahern's crew was in a hurry to get to their worksite. A buzz box is not a reliable means of communication. Still, a lot of the workers blamed the carelessness of the victim. It was more comfortable psychologically. Each worker wants to think that if he or she is careful, it won't happen. But then denial becomes complicity in the problem.

"The worst thing about this job is the riders." I heard this, in one form or another, from dozens of transit workers during break-in. "The public, you have to deal with the public." "The riders, you can't do enough for 'em."

I had my first bad experiences with riders. As my train left the station I was given the finger and I was cursed at by people who had missed the train. There were, however, many more smiles and encouraging words. As one of the first women conductors riders had seen, I got raised fists and cries of "right on!" These almost always were from women or black men. A casually dressed woman, perhaps my age, extended her hand, saying, "You're just great. We need more like you." I peeled off my filthy work glove and shook her hand.

"Well, 95 percent of 'em's all right," allowed one of my break-in conductors, Sand. "It's the standing that's the worst part," he added. "When you go home, just forget everything that happened," Sand advised me, "I take a nice hot bath." Sand told other workers, "She's not afraid of the job. You wouldn't think it. She looks kind of timid and quiet. But she's not afraid of the job."

Nevertheless, when I'd get home, I'd feel as if I were in a boat in a storm. I would have to lie down and sleep for an hour.

My earliest report during break-in week was four-thirty at Woodlawn. My motorman's first reaction when he saw me was, "Can you open the doors with such small hands?"

"It doesn't take big hands to turn the key," I shot back.

I made some mistakes. When my break-in conductor dozed off, I went to the wrong side at the Bowling Green station. He woke up before the train stopped and shouted at me. "I wouldn't have opened it when I didn't see the conductor's board," I reassured him.

"I hope not," he said.

In the crew room at Flatbush, the other conductors teased my break-in conductor when he asked to borrow a shoe brush, "You didn't ask for the shoe brush when you had men students. Now you have a lady and you want to get proper." "You didn't go through these changes for the men."

He ribbed back, "Don't listen to him. Never listen to anything he says. . . ."

The chop-busting went on incessantly and everyplace. At best, the crews could be real artists of put-down, eschewing heavy and direct insults for subtle teasing with a pretense of objectivity.

Leah Goss told me that while she was at the Lenox terminal, the dispatcher called the crew room, "Someone told me you have a woman in there."

"He must have felt foolish," she smiled.

It gave me a glimpse of what a woman had once meant in the crew room, and to some extent still meant.

Tubbs, my break-in conductor on the Pelham line, was the first to ask me to go out. I was flattered. "You wouldn't be sorry," he added, insinuatingly.

I demurred, but I tortured myself as to why I didn't want to go. Was it because he was so much older? Was it because he was black? I didn't yet realize how little it meant to these guys to ask me out and be turned down. They just took a shot at it, and the stakes were low, if there were any stakes.

Tubbs was good company. He had a thousand gory stories, mostly about "riders buying the farm." "When I had just gotten started," he told me, "a man jumped, or was pushed, in front of my train. Five cars went over him, and when the train stopped, the body was right under my operating position. I was looking right into his face. His arm and his leg had been sliced off, but he was still alive. I was new. I needed a few days off, but the motorman just put another notch in his brake handle."

Tubbs told me that recently a kid had shot a man on his train. "The man just put his hand up and because it was a light gun, just a .22, he stopped the bullet with his hand. I could have grabbed the kid's arm and held it so the gun pointed to the roof. But what if the bullet had ricocheted and hit a rider? The T.A. would have told me, 'That's not your job.'

"The name of this job is 'Cover Your Ass.' Note the defect on the car defect sheet. Write it down in your little notebook. Sometimes the job can be scary, like the curved stations, where you can't see the ends of the train, you just can't. Remember, after the indication lights go on, the motorman will start the train, so you must not reopen the doors. If the doors open while the train is moving, even if it can't move far, that will upset the riders and make the motorman very angry."

During break-in, I was usually overwhelmed by tension. Looking back later, I was moved by the optimism and humanism these men tried to impart to me in the face of an unrewarding and punishing job.

At the end of break-in, my class was reunited at the training school in South Brooklyn. We compared notes.

"The Flushing line sure is nice."

"It's got the best equipment."

"The best crew rooms."

"Did you notice it's the one that doesn't go through any burnt-out ghettoes?"

"And no graffiti."

"They've got the dogs that guard the yards. . . ."

We got the final exam of our training, and we got our schedules. I was given midnight reports on the Eastern-Queens division and Wednesday and Thursday as regular days off. Midnight reports meant my jobs began anytime from 10:30 P.M. to 4:30 A.M. As a new hand, I would be "extra-extra," working in place of people who were out sick, those recently retired, promoted, or resigned. Eastern-Queens included the Nos. 4, 6, and 7 lines and platform jobs.

The midnight hours really freaked me. I was worried about being able to sleep during the day. On that coming Monday, which was Labor Day, I had a platform job. Having to work a holiday made it painfully clear to me that my life wasn't my own any longer. Of course, I told myself, that's a condition of life for almost all people everywhere. The paycheck is supposed to make it all alright. But that didn't work for me. I wanted the paycheck, but I had forty hours a week to put in on "the property." I wanted the job to be better. And I believed it could be. For the rest of the week, I would be working days. I would have Saturday off, and then go to work early Sunday morning, on the midnight shift.

I was "road qualified," ready to work solo. I felt more than ready, not nervous at all, but eager.

One afternoon, in the crew room at Woodlawn Terminal, I was being barraged as usual by questions from the curious crews.

"How do you like it?"

"Are you married?"

"What does your husband think of this?"

"How many in your class?"

"How many women in your class?"

"Can you type?"

"I heard that a whole class at the school went out to lunch and none of them came back. Was that your class?" This story was repeated periodically, but always as a current event, the whole time I was with the T.A. I even heard it from supervisors and union reps.

One guy smirked at me, "This is a pretty hard job for a woman."

He was outrageously attractive, tall, broad-shouldered, and muscular, with salt-and-pepper hair and beard. The word that came to my mind was "hunk." But his smirk annoyed me. "No harder for a woman than for a man," I retorted.

"Oh, yeah? You like the job? you do, do you? What's today's date? September 10? By October 10, I'll bet you won't."

I was sufficiently dazzled to ask around about him. "I know him," a conductor told me, "I worked with him last pick. He taught me a lot. He's got several degrees. He's French. He comes from a wealthy French banking family, but he won't take a cent from them." I imagined a woman with platinum hair in a long silk negligee, waiting for him with a cocktail shaker each night after work. Way out of my price range, I decided.

It was my first midnight road job. The dispatcher at Van Cortlandt terminal told me that after my second trip, I'd be doing a "put-in" with my motorman. This meant we would be preparing a laid-up train for passenger service. This aroused my deepest fear: crossing the tracks on the elevated structure to reach a train laid-up in the middle. I pictured myself trying to climb over the third rail and stumbling on the wood protection board above it. I pictured myself trying to keep my footing, leaping between the widely spaced ties. And I was going to have to do this in darkness and exhaustion.

I was preoccupied with this during the beginning of my second trip, when I heard raucous noises in my car. A bunch of kids were partying, filling the air with loud music and the sickly sweet smell of dope. They were hanging between the cars as I dutifully observed the platform at 215th Street. "Hey, it's a girl!" they exclaimed gleefully. I shut myself in the cab.

As we started moving again, I heard an awful banging around in the car. I said to myself, "I'm supposed to be observing my operating car between stations, not locking myself in the cab. If there's vandalism, I'm supposed to know about it." So I peeped out. I saw two passengers, a kid and a husky white-haired man, scuffling in the middle of the car. I dived back into my cab. A barrage of popping noises split the air. I assumed the worst and crouched down in the cab. I reached up and locked the door with shaking hands.

The train stopped. We were in the 207th Street station. I heard shouts, "I've been shot!" Someone was banging on my cab door, "Call the police! Someone's been shot!"

I got up. I had no P.A. I pressed the buzzer, a long buzz, short buzz, long buzz, short buzz, the call for assistance. I was just opposite the token booth, so I yelled to the clerk, "Call the police! There's been a shooting! Call the police!"

My cab was still locked, and the train doors were still closed. Was there still a gunman threatening people? Did they want to flee the train? "Should I open the doors?" I shouted.

"No, No!" "Keep 'em closed!" I heard voices call.

I held them closed. I was still locked in my cab, looking out my cab window on the dark, deserted platform and the token clerk's booth.

Then a figure appeared from between the two last cars of the train. It climbed out and onto the platform. Two more figures followed. They walked down the platform, towards me and toward the exit. Now I could see they were three stocky black kids. They were exclaiming, "Oh, man. Someone's been shot." "Shit, I'm getting out of here. He's been shot, man." As I watched, motionless and helpless, they disappeared off the platform and into the anonymity of the night.

As soon as they were gone, I opened my cab and stepped out. Opposite my cab sat a large white man with blood on the front of his shirt. In his hand, he cradled a small revolver. "He shot me," he said to me, "but I got the gun away from him."

"It looks like you're going to be alright," I said.

The passengers drifted back into the car. "There's another guy shot in the next car," they informed me, "He looks bad. He's lying on the floor."

I couldn't think of any rule in the book that required me to go take a look, so I didn't. I walked up to the first car. The motorman was still locked in his cab, and wouldn't open it even for me.

I went back to my position. The riders were restive, "Why isn't the train moving?" "Shouldn't we get them to a hospital?" I told them that we were waiting for an ambulance.

A rider suggested instead we continue to the 168th Street stop and drop them off at Columbia-Presbyterian Hospital. "This is not an ambulance," I answered.

At last the police came. They asked if I would come in their car for an "area search" for the other "alleged perpetrators." I hadn't seen much, but I was eager to get off the train and avoid doing the put-in.

Later I learned that both men had survived.

I slept like the dead that day. When I got up to go to work that evening, I wanted only to get back into bed, to burrow into a familiar, safe place, and hide. I was being forced out into a dangerous and unpleasant world. That night I had a platform job. But I couldn't stop thinking that some dark morning, sooner or later, I would be out on the structure someplace, doing a put-in.

I was on midnights for four more weeks. Sometimes I worked platforms, but mostly I was on a train. I had a stabbing, and a couple of times male riders threatened and harassed me in sexual terms. I had a tough time sleeping days, and after a couple of weeks, I was so exhausted I was falling asleep between stops standing up.

Finally, during my days off, when I called the crew dispatcher to find out what my Thursday job would be. He said, 'You wanted to get off midnights, didn't you? You wanted P.M.s?," that is, jobs that begin in the afternoon.

I practically danced with delight. I thanked him effusively. I bet I was the first person to tell the crew dispatcher that he was "a prince."

Only one other person in my training class had been put on midnights. He had quit after a week.

WOODLAWN

The air was crisp-cold liquid, the light was golden. The sunsets glowed rosy pink. It was October and I was on P.M.S.

At Woodlawn, there was a concrete patio with benches behind the bumper block where the tracks end, leading to the crew room. I enjoyed sitting on this "veranda" and listening to the other employees. Everyone was friendly. Conversations began with someone mentioning something that happened on the job recently. Each of the others would then add his story on that subject.

Someone mentioned a code twelve-nine, a man under, that happened over a weekend.

Someone else said, "I know a motorman hit a guy southbound. Command Center tells him, 'You can take three days on compensation.'

"'Nah,' he says. He felt he didn't need it. Northbound, he hits another one. No shit.

"He gets on the radio, 'Gimme my six!'"

If I mentioned I'd been on the board six hours, without picking up a job, someone would be sure to tell me how once, when he was on the board, he had been sent out on a job after seven and three-quarters. Or some similar horror story.

I loved it. I felt immersed in the legends of the railroad. To me it was a railroad, and the railroad was a romance.

I was up at Woodlawn, on the board, lazing around the veranda. A new sight caught my eye. Another woman conductor. What struck me was that she, like me, had chosen the traditional conductor's hat with the visor. She was a tall white woman with very long brown hair. She was talking to another conductor, a young black man. Was he breaking her in? Was she breaking him in? Was she newer than me, or more senior? I tried to catch her eye.

Finally, I succeeded, and she gave me a conservative little wave.

Later, she settled herself on the veranda. She took out *Women's Day* magazine and appeared to become absorbed. Slowly, we struck up a conversation. Her name was Jasmin Joyce: "Call me Joyce. That's what they called me on the force." She had been a police officer. "I'm gonna go back to that. I can't stand this job."

As we were talking, a familiar figure was coming down the platform toward us. It was the mysterious French motorman, scion of the wealthy banking family. In a plaid flannel shirt and a worn army field jacket, he looked even more rugged and handsomer than my memory of him. As he came near us, I leaned forward, "It's been a month, and I still like the job."

"You do, do you?" he laughed, and vanished into the crew room.

A second later, he peered out of the door, "Did we make any stakes on that bet?"

"No, and I've been kicking myself ever since."

"Would you like to make some retroactive stakes?"

My heart was thumping audibly. "What would you like to give me?" I flirted.

"Dinner?"

"Sure!"

He wrote down his phone number on the back of an overtime slip, "I shouldn't give this to you," he said, "you might use it to put in for overtime."

I looked at the name. Mark Goniea. He pronounced the last name for me, "Gone-yay. Like, 'he's gone! Yay!'"

That night, I called him. "I'm glad you called me," he said, "refreshing for a change."

"They told me at work that you come from a wealthy French banking family."

He laughed. "My grandfather had a bank in River Rouge. But we were hardly wealthy. My father worked for a federal agency."

"I got the impression you were from Paris."

"No, I was born in River Rouge, Michigan, and I grew up in Dearborn. My father's family was from Quebec." So his degree was from Michigan State, not from the Sorbonne.

We talked more than an hour, until he had to go to work. "Listen," I told him, "I have a very early job tomorrow. I'll be off about seven. We could get together for dinner then."

He was pleased, "I'd have been crushed if I'd had to wait a week to see you." He told me he'd been following me on the assignment sheets. He'd heard about the shooting on my train.

I was ecstatic. He was obviously wild about me. And I'd come along at just the right moment; he'd just broken up with someone. I accepted all this as part of the romance of the railroad. Things were falling into place, storybook perfect. I felt no more wary than at a happy ending of a novel. It surprised me no more than the appearance of the brave, resourceful hero at the opening of a romance.

The next day was another beautiful portrait of autumn. As the day dissolved in a rainbow sunset, I rode down to the Upper East Side, to the mammoth building where Mark lived. He was fussing in the kitchen, "Shall I open a bottle of champagne?" He cut some hard cheese and opened a box of biscuits. "You get my last wine glass," he told me, pouring his own wine into a tumbler. He bustled around, shaking his head and laughing nervously.

Finally, we sat down beside each other. He lit his pipe. "I'm very nervous," he said, between puffs, "if I didn't keep the pipe in my mouth, my teeth would be chattering."

I found it so appealing, seeing this huge arrogant man so shaken. I was flattered and I was intrigued. I put one hand on his shoulder, feeling the rough texture of his sweater. "What are you so nervous about?" I asked gently.

"Being here with you like this. I don't know." He really seemed stymied.

His pipe smelt lovely. I was aware of his still hidden, coiled body. I placed my other hand on his arm. As though he could bear it no longer, he sprang toward me, embraced me, and pressed his lips to mine.

We finally did get out to that meal I'd "won" on our "bet" around midnight. As we walked through the deserted streets, I felt safer than I ever had before. A giant had his arm around my shoulders.

He told me the story of his life, and it was pure romance. He'd been a sailor, owned a yacht, and taken the wealthy on cruises. Then he got eager for easy money, and became a smuggler, using his sailboat to run guns for the Sandinistas and marijuana for domestic consumption. With the proceeds, he bought a chain of diving-gear stores and a Porsche. Then a couple of his associates got overconfident and didn't pay off the Coast Guard. One associate was found "floating in the bay without a face." Mark decided to go legit.

Alas, a messy divorce left him penniless, and he shipped out. He ended up working as a civilian diver for the Navy.

He'd also found time to work in a truck factory and sabotage military trucks, to be stationed on a spy ship off the coast of North Vietnam, and to work as a psychologist in a mental hospital. It was a marvelous tale. Some of it was even true.

I didn't hear from him for a week.

Then he called and started apologizing and calling himself "a rat."

"What are you apologizing for? So you didn't call? What else?"

Finally he got it out, "I don't know when I want to go out with you again. This whole thing has gone much too fast for me. I want to be your friend and see you casually." He took a deep breath. "I'm very confused and very scared. I don't see my therapist until Tuesday. I know I want to be friends. . . ."

"What do we have in common that could make us friends?"

"I know you're very angry. I'm very scared of getting involved again. I want to go slowly with you. Just see you casually. It would be easy for us to see each other and just start rolling around on the floor together. I want to go slowly. You're a very needy person, and you have voids I just can't fill."

"Who asked you to? If you want to go slowly, fine. I need to learn to go slowly, too. But I might want real closeness. I think that's what you're afraid of."

"It might be. I'm very scared. Getting involved is very frightening. Aren't you scared?"

"You're not giving me a chance to be scared. You keep rejecting me."

"I'm not rejecting you. I want to see you. I just don't know when."

"It would be easier for me if you just came right out and said that you don't want to see me again."

"But that's not the case. I promise I'll call you. I just can't say when."

I was completely crushed. I had fallen in love. I was obsessed. Henceforth, my moods and my actions revolved around seeing Mark, speaking to Mark, trying to interpret his moods and his words. He held me at bay, rarely seeing me except on the job. There, "on the property," he constantly tried to persuade me to have sexual "quickies" with him in nooks and crannies of the Woodlawn terminal. Occasionally, I'd be invited for an afternoon visit to his home, but soon it would be "kick-out time." He kept me at a distance, but he kept me.

A friend of a friend, who was a member of the "old opposition" in the union, called one evening to tell me, "The union is holding classes for shop stewards. It needs people to hand-collect the dues since it lost the dues checkoff. You should send in an application."

My opportunity came quickly. In the Pelham Bay crew room I crossed paths one late afternoon with my union rep, Vinnie Torrelli, whose proper title "Vice Chairman, Conductors, A Division." Vinnie (called "Turn Around" because he was wont to interject "I'm going to turn around and . . ."), pink-faced and, to his chagrin, tubby, was holding forth as he also was wont to do, "Wear the tie, fellers, the supervision's cracking down . . . an' be on your train two minutes before your interval. . . ." He responded to my request for the steward class application with enthusiasm, "Dammit, Christ, I know I had those forms somewhere," rummaging through his attaché case. I knew only one other worker who carried an attaché case, and he loaded it with nothing but the fruit he ate for lunch.

He was unperturbed by the absent form. "I'll make you a steward!" he raved. "Lemme give ya the lowdown," he hushed his voice confidentially. "The important thing is ya come to the union meetings. Ya vote the way they wantcha to, and ya put in a good word about the officers, in other words, ya puddup with alotta shit, forgive my French. But they take carrah their own. If you want an A.V.A, the union makes sure you get it. Supervision gives ya trouble, the union helps ya out. You sell the COPE [Committee on Political Education] tickets, you vote with the union, you're my steward, makes me look good. You vote against them, bad mouth the union, makes me look bad, understand?

"There's alotta assholes in the union, you'll see. But ya don't say nothing, ya see. I sponsored a guy last year, and he starts criticizing the union. Makes me look bad."

If you had asked me, a year before this conversation, my dearest ambition in life, I would have answered, "To be a shop steward in Local 100." However, I had envisioned a long, slow process of learning the ropes, of becoming known and respected by my workmates, and reaching my chosen pinnacle in an election. This sordid process was a bitter antidote to my fantasies.

Still, I saw it as a valuable opportunity. I believed that you had to be on the inside to change things, that small groups of insiders, the palace guard, are the only ones in a position to change things. You get yourself elected, make furtive alliances with like-minded others, and perfectly time the break, the right moment for denunciation.

But there was a hitch. To get inside, you had to follow Vinnie's advice. You had to support a leadership that had the well-deserved distrust and scorn of the members, and your support was going to get you scorned and distrusted, too.

The conductor-tower division of Local 100, T.W.U., AFL-CIO held membership meetings every third Wednesday of the month, once at 10.30 A.M. and again at 6.30 P.M. The meetings began with the Pledge of Allegiance to the Flag, and then "a moment of silence for those among us who have passed on since the last meeting." Next came the officers' reports, and finally, "old and new business," during which the membership was allowed to take the floor.

In the front, behind a trestle table, would sit the officers and organizers. Facing them, attempting to improvise comfortable positions on the rows of grey-painted metal folding chairs, would be one or two dozen members.

Most of the members present were the regulars who get rewarded for their loyalty with such sinecures as "pick men" (those who were off the road half the year overseeing the pick) or perks like trips to conventions at vacation resorts. In addition, there were as usual one or two who were there for the first time or the first time in a long time, drawn by curiosity or a special personal problem or complaint.

The officers' reports were long and tedious. They celebrated the officers' accomplishments and often mocked the membership. Then there would be "old and new business," when members could take the floor. Any member with a problem would be told, invariably, to "write a G-2," a memo, and give it to a union rep. When the officers decided that this had gone on long enough, one would declare, "Motion to adjourn!" This was never voted upon, or even debated. It was accepted as the signal that the meeting was over, and those present streamed to the doors.

After the meeting, Vinnie took "his" three stewards out for lunch. "I take carrah my own," he reassured us, not for the first time. One was Harry, a big, sloppy white guy, an old friend of Torrelli's. He said to us, "You'll be surprised how much the union can do for you, if you'll just play ball with the union."

The other one, Billy, a young man born in Ireland, replied, "Depends what game the union wants to play."

Vinnie led us into a Japanese restaurant. "Ain't it something?" he commented. "First we kill 'em in Vietnam, and now we eat in their restaurants."

Soon, he got to reminiscing about the old days. "T.A. was a racket when I first got here, around '70. Now you see me going around, I tell the guys to wear the uniform, right? Because you gotta now, right? Back then, we never used to wear the uniform. You know one-eighty?" (The No. 5 line terminal.) "We had a country club, there, a country club. I had a job, I made one trip, then we sat around, we had hammocks up there, booze. We were on the property maybe twenty-five hours a week, working maybe five. . . ."

"No wonder the public hates us," said Billy.

"The service was better then," I said.

"One thing I gotta tell you, Marian," said Vinnie, "I don't believe women should be motormen or conductors. Because it's just a matter of time before one of these animals out there takes advantage."

I said, "Well, in an office you get a lot of sexual harassment. There's no getting away from it in our society. The boss says if you want to work here, you've got to sleep with me."

Torrelli said, "But in that case you have a choice."

"Yeah, lose your job!"

Billy said, "I guess it's a question of principle."

"Uh-huh," I said, "and the principle is, a woman should have any job she is willing to do and able to do."

A smoke condition in the tube had everyone in the Pelham crew room talking about fires. "It was on the elevated structure, on the Flushing line," began a plump, nearly bald, white motorman. "Bright, sunny day, spring. It was my last run before my R.D.O.S, so, you know, I'm daydreaming a little. All of the sudden, I see this giant, sparkling cloud of mist. And these rainbows, all these bright and beautiful rainbows! And I said to myself, 'Well, my time has come. They said it would be spectacular, and it sure is!' Then, it all disappeared. It was only the fire department, down in the street, hosing down a track fire."

"You better be glad about that," said a conductor, "because you can't afford to be dead."

"No, no way!" said the motorman, "I got two kids with my first wife, a kid with this marriage, I got a mortgage. Death benefit wouldn't even cover my funeral."

"Death benefit's a joke," said the conductor. "I told my wife, 'When I die, go to the undertaker and ask for the cheapest casket he's got. Then tell him you want the box it come in.'"

Another conductor said, "My wife won't even look at the sheet. She gets as far as 'In the event of . . . ,' and she say, 'Take this thing away.'"

I was called out on the platform to clean out trains. Between lay-ups, the flagman struck up a conversation with me. He was wearing a turtleneck and windbreaker, but I thought nothing of this, since flagging conductors often wore whatever they wanted. I asked him what his name was.

"Swanson," he replied, "but they call me lots of other things."

"Conductor Swanson?"

"Motorman Swanson. Restricted."

"Restricted? I hope nothing bad happened."

"Nothing happened to me. It happened to the guy I was working with. We had a work train at one-three-seven," the 137th Street underground yard.

"Yes, I heard about that. A motorman was killed, awful. You hear all sorts of crew room talk, but what really happened there?"

"Well, our diesel was on the middle track. There was a garbage train at the platform. Me and my conductor walked over the garbage train. The other motorman, he walked in front of it.

"My conductor and me got on the diesel. We got two buzzes from my partner, and I moved the train. Now they say that the buzzes I heard that night was from the garbage train. But I saw the light on the buzzer box, and my conductor did, too. But the motorman on the garbage train, he volunteered some stuff he didn't need to. He told them my partner did not have time to get on the flat. But that's not true, he had a lot of time. I'll tell you what it was.

"What it was, the man should not been on the job. He'd had a head injury, still had dizzy spells. But the T.A. doctor said that he was fit for duty. The T.A. clinic said go back to duty, go back to duty or you will not get paid. It was a crane car he was on. Most cars, they have gates this high, high as your waist. But the crane car, it got just a bar, you have to hold on to. So the man could just slip down . . . .

"But I *heard* the buzzer. I *saw* the light.

"Next thing I know, I'm B.I.E. I went down to walk around the train, and the wheels were right on top of him."

Not many days after that, I walked in on a fierce argument in the Woodlawn crew room. Spruce, a thick-set, very dark motorman from the Caribbean, was shouting, "If you take that train out of service, it is insubordination!"

His opponent was Lock, who was saying, "I have no intention of risking my life for this T.A."

"You will lose your job, man," warned Spruce.

"If they told me to stuff paper in the gap—"

"If Command Center tells you stuff paper, you stuff paper."

Another motorman explained to me, "There was a big gap in the rail. I reported it on the radio. They told me to go down on the tracks and stuff the gap with newspaper."

Lock's conductor, Lucey, said, "If my riders' lives are in danger, it's my responsibility, regardless of what they tell me on the radio."

"You do what Command Center tells you," repeated Spruce.

I butted in, "You should refuse an order if it poses a clear and immediate danger to your life. You may get into trouble, but in the end you can beat it. Even the Supreme Court has ruled on that."

"You heard the lady," said Lock.

"They don't care if you have that right," said Spruce. "Okay, you do that. You'll be in the street. It's like the service."

"No," I said, "it's not like the service. In the service, you're expected to risk your life. This is a job."

"Do you have a family?" Spruce challenged me. "I represent my family here. I put the bread in their mouths."

"All the more reason to protect your life. You can't put bread on the table if you're dead."

"You try sticking your neck out and you'll see what happens."

"I'm not saying stick it out. I'm saying to save it."

Spruce went on, "A conductor gets written up. Wasn't wearing the uniform. What does he expect? Everyone says they'll back you up. But then you're out there and you look around and everyone else is behind you—waaaay behind you."

This provoked general agreement. I said, "I'm not saying stick your neck out on the uniform. If it's something like that, we all have to do it together. A petition, a mass grievance, a bargaining demand. All I'm saying is that if your life is in danger, you have to protect it."

Spruce said, "Your life is in danger when you go out on the road, anytime you go down the road. No one's job is more dangerous than the motorman's. He's got to go out and walk around his train. You new people aren't used to this. I've been here thirteen years. Let me tell you about a situation and you tell me there wasn't danger to my life.

"I was coming into Flatbush terminal. You know there is a water condition there. I see the water on the roadbed is up real high. It is smoking, so I know it is up to the third rail and it's electrified. So I call Command Center and I describe the water. They told me, 'Discharge your riders through the first two cars and take the train on in.' The transit patrolman said to me, 'I wouldn't go through that water: it's electrified.' But Command Center said, 'What are we supposed to do with that train?'"

"Change ends and take it back out, obviously," I said. "The union ought to back us up. I know that they don't, but that's what a union's supposed to do."

"As long as the union officers are on the T.A. payroll, they'll never back us up. You don't bite the hand that feeds you."

This was a common explanation of the union's unresponsiveness, but it was based on a fallacy. Only the lowest officers were paid by T.A. The president, vice presidents, and organizers, who effectively run the union, were all on union salaries.

I came into the flagging shack shaking with anger. I interrupted the conversation between Jasmin Joyce and "Hey Babe" Black. "I got spit on!" I said.

"This is the first time?" asked Joyce.

"I've been spit *at* before, but not on. This time they connected. We were pulling out of a very dark station. I could see there were three little kids near the end of the platform, but they were so far away from the edge that it didn't occur to me that they could do anything to me. But as I got alongside of them, *splat*! The little bastards could spout like whales. It was all over my hat, even a little on my face."

"Well, it's never happened to me," said Black, "But if it ever did, I would pull the cord and chase them. I wouldn't let anyone hurt my dignity."

"Well, I don't feel my dignity was hurt."

Joyce tried to conciliate, "Well, it was an insult."

"No, it wasn't. It's only an insult—if I let it be!" I maintained.

Both Joyce and Black insisted: it was an insult.

I felt betrayed. "Do you think I have any less dignity, do you think I'm less of a person because I got spit on? Is that what you're implying?"

They were silent.

I was aggravated enough to consult a dictionary when I got home. Insult was defined as "an act or words intended to hurt feelings or self-respect."

So I had been insulted. I decided to try to render it an unsuccessful insult. My feelings would not be hurt. My self-respect would not be damaged. I would be indifferent. Wasn't indifference the best response? There was no rational reason for my self-respect to be vulnerable to kids acting like punks. That was all fine on a rational level, but reason could not overcome my growing feelings of hopelessness and devastation.

All at once it was winter. The Christmas season seized us and flung us into street filled with decorations and lined with windows filled with goods. My motorman commented, "I'm gonna take it slow going into some of the stations: it's the suicide season." A conductor in the Woodlawn crew room who carried a radio told us, "Token booth holdup in Brooklyn. That time of year. Kids want toys. Mama wants money. Papa wants money."

It was a crisp day, with the remains of the first snow glinting under a blinding blue sky. In the crew room, I was on the board. I had my steward's pin and wore it proudly. I had heaps of blank medical, dental and prescription forms. I was eager for the start of my stewards' classes. I didn't know a damned thing.

Mark Goniea came in and sat beside me to drink his coffee. "I told you," he said, disgusted, "I've been in a lot of unions, but this is the worst. I've never actually thought much about the corruption in this union. I've always just sort of wished it would go away."

Folks have been discussing the cold. Ever since the weather turned, complaints about B.O. (bad order: malfunctioning) cab heaters are constant. The motorman works where the train is coldest; the conductor is limited to a uniform of cheap and poorly insulated material to keep out the cold. No one mentions the union as a possible recourse.

Christmas on the road was ordinary and miserable: the stinking derelict who sits right at your position, the gleeful cries of "It's a lady!" the daredevil kids leaping between the cars as you pull out of the station.

As dusk fell, there was a code twelve-nine at Parkchester. The power was off up to Pelham Bay, so my last trip was dropped. After an hour or so, power was restored and arriving crews were showered with questions about the incident. "The guy wasn't badly hurt," a conductor told us. "He was conscious, just a cut on his head. But his down coat was ripped open and there's feathers all over the place. Looks like they hit a chicken."

"What are you looking so sad for? Aren't you lookin' forward to gettin' your new hat?" Conductors had been given the option of a new uniform hat for winter, a blue plastic helmet with flaps, lined in synthetic fur with the texture of lint, also in blue.

Crew room wisdom is that this new hat of ours is the contribution of a conductor on the "A" train. The "A" to "the Rock" speeds along a narrow isthmus in Jamaica Bay to Rockaway, surely the chilliest ride in the system in winter. Our resourceful hero exchanged the usual cardboard-fabric cap for one of the police hats with phony furry flaps. Toasty ears until unhappy encounter with hidebound supervision. Taken out of service for being "out of uniform," he eventually not only won his case but won for all of us the privilege of wearing this new furry hat, available at the uniform center for $7.00 cheap.

Soon many of us were sporting it, for it clearly answered a need. It was not, by a long shot, a handsome item—100 percent man-made materials and dyed a blue tint alien to the natural world—but it did the job of insulating the heat-squandering head. One conductor claimed the T.A. was making a killing on these, having obtained them as free souvenirs distributed at the funeral of Leonid Brezhnev.

Another requirement of a conductor's uniform was "dark brown or black shoes." This rule was nearly the undoing of "Hey Babe" Black. Through a combination of circumstances, he arrived at work on Christmas Day wearing red sneakers. Warned that the notorious Motor Instructor Prior was on the prowl for just such anomalies (the detrimental effects upon service of which cannot be underestimated), necessity gave birth to invention. Black removed his sneakers and socks, which by luck were black, and then put the sneakers on again, this time with the socks over them. And that was how Black worked Christmas.

The message on my answering machine was from natty Nat Nash, the union organizer. Did I have any collected dues to turn in? Alas, amid my fantasies of working-class triumphs, I'd managed to collect a grand total of three dollars.

Turning the bills over to Nat, I told him, "I was planning to wait until I'd had the stewards' classes before I really started tracking down dues. I don't really know enough to do much for the fellers. I feel kind of strange taking their money. Are the classes starting soon?"

"No, the union officers are all taken up with the dues collection."

"What can I do in the meantime to prepare for being a steward?"

"Read the rulebook. Read the contract."

"I don't have a copy of the contract."

"It isn't really a contract. It's an award . . . ," he mumbled, opening each drawer in his desk in turn and peering inside. At last he pulled out a glossy flyer, issued by the union, on highlights of the 1982 arbitrators' award.

I put it in my bag. When I read it, I was disappointed, because it had only a few items that applied to all T.A. hourly employees. It didn't answer any of the questions I heard on the road daily. I still believed that somewhere, like the Holy Grail, a basic contract must exist, setting out our rights, our grievance procedure, our pay conditions.

Approximately every six months, a subway division gets a new work schedule, a "pick." Before it can begin, motormen and conductors pick their jobs on the new schedule. This process also is called a "pick," and it lasts about six weeks. The workers pick in order of seniority, with the most senior picking first, from the greatest selection of jobs.

The week after Christmas, my turn to pick came, and I went up to Pelham Bay to do it. When I saw the pick board, my heart sank. There were fewer than fifteen jobs left. This was the garbage, the jobs no one on the I.R.T. wanted: late P.M.s on the No. 2 line, ominously nicknamed "the Beast." Dizzy with anxiety, homesick already for Woodlawn, I watched the pick man write my job on the pick slip. One thing I resolved, I would take the road. I was sick of hearing, "All the girls go down to Jay Street." Here was one who wouldn't.

The only place I felt relief from the anxiety that began when I picked was "on the property." With everyone asking, "Wudja pick?" and my answer, and the commiseration and consolation, "You'll be okay. Just don't look for trouble." "It's not really that bad. Every one talks about it, but. . . ."

The days of early January were hard for me. The long afternoon shadows and quiet cold hours have always inspired in me a kind of terror. I came up to Woodlawn well before my time to report, to shake my solitude, and to see Mark.

The few guys in the crew room greeted me, the familiar refrain, "Wudja pick?" When I answered, I was told, "I did it for years. It wasn't anything." Another conductor rejoined, "You liked 'the Deuce'? If you liked it so much, how come you're not back there?" He turned to me, "You'll get your knocks. And you'll come back here." His casual air was reassuring: there's life after White Plains.

"It's all a state of mind."

"What job you got today? Three-oh-eight? You're here early."

I felt someone touch the back of my neck and I turned around to see Mark. "I see you picked P.M.s on the No. 2. Why'd you do that?"

"There was nothing left."

"You're going to need something to protect yourself with over there."

"I know. I've been thinking about getting a gun."

"A gun is tricky unless you're able and ready to use it."

"That leaves me out. A lot of the guys carry knives."

"That's even worse. There's mace."

"I might be able to get some at a police supply store. That's what I'll probably do." I looked at my hands. "The job is really affecting me physically. Look," I showed him the bump on my left index finger, next to the thumb.

"From the keys?"

"No, I use my right hand for the keys. From opening the window of the cab. You have to squeeze the lock together to release it."

"Get gloves."

"I do wear gloves."

"Get thicker gloves."

"No glove is going to . . . I have to face it. This job is going to shape my body. For better or for worse."

The January conductors' union meeting was dragging to a close, with the customary "motion to adjourn" undebated and unvoted. I sauntered toward a conductor who had come from my training class, not because I wished to talk to him, but because the young white guy he was talking to had attracted my notice. His appearance set him off from the other fellers present. His work boots, flannel plaid shirt, wire rim glasses, and beard seemed more "student union" than "union hall." I'd liked the things he said in the discussion and the way he'd said them. He's interested in the union and he's attractive, I reasoned; one of those angles might pan out. So I proposed we go out for coffee. As we disappeared toward the elevator, Torrelli beckoned to me. I raised my index finger, "Just a second," and skedaddled.

His name was Dave Stone; he was from Detroit where he had been a chemical worker.

I asked, "OCAW?"

He explained that he belonged to a different union. "It was part of UAW, but broke away to return to the AFL."

"You know a lot about unions." I said.

"Everyone in Detroit knows a lot about unions."

I did not find that convincing. I asked him what his parents did. He told me his father taught law. Now the picture was coming into focus.

We found a nearby diner. Over lunch, we commiserated and laughed over the officers' remarks at the meeting, like George Nash's blaming the delays in crew room renovations on the fact that union labor is doing the work. From there, we went on to discuss the 1980 strike and the dissident movement in the union. We found ourselves very much in agreement on these matters.

"What do you think about doing in the union?" he asked me.

I hesitated. I didn't know him well enough to say anything, but I didn't want to strain our rapport by appearing to hold back anything. So I said, "What about you? What are your plans?"

He smiled and his eyes lit up a tiny bit, that is, to their maximum. "Well, I have my fantasies. Like a newsletter." He told me he'd gotten to know some people in track maintenance and that they had written a critique of the dissident leadership. He offered to mail it to me.

The lunch crowd was gone and the luncheonette was quiet. Our conversation began to slow down as we became more aware of time and of how long we had been talking. We were at that point when the length of the interaction becomes more significant than what is being said and we both were growing self-conscious. I asked if he would like us to get together again. He agreed without any hesitation, but after a pause, he added, "You mean, just to talk about the union, right?"

I couldn't say anything for a moment. Feeling very awkward, I explained, "Honestly, I would like to go out with you. But if that's not what you want, or you can't, like you're not in a position to, alright, that's fine, I'd still like to see you to talk about the union. I mean, there's no subject I'm more interested in."

"I'm living with someone," he explained.

"Okay, fine," I approved inanely, bobbing my head.

"You have a very direct approach," he said.

"Maybe it's the job," I apologized, "so many guys are very direct with me. Listen, are you sure you really want to meet, just to talk?"

"Oh, definitely. I feel the same sense of isolation as you do."

The Utica 7:38 to Woodlawn, with the 314 crew, going two behind, was pulling out of the 86th Street station. I was observing the platform, playing the moving target in the shooting gallery. She was strolling down the platform toward the exit, with a friend, out on a Saturday night, young, black, and giggly. She reached over almost casually and pushed her hand into my face.

No pain at all but my vision blurred. What's happened to me? I put my hand to my face and realized—my glasses. I moaned in dread and took them off and by this time we were almost out of the station. The right lens was gone, fallen off the train. The frame had broken too. The rules! What am I supposed to do? Can I get in trouble?

Over the P.A. I informed my motorman, "Motorman, I've been assaulted by a rider. My glasses are broken and I can't operate."

The train slowed to a halt. "What was that, conductor?"

I repeated it.

"Is he still on the train?"

"No. I was hit from the platform. And it was a girl."

I was shaken up and at a loss about what to do next. What would happen now. I was waiting to see what that mammoth machine, the T.A., would do in response to my misfortune.

"Conductor, we're going out of service at one-two-five."

So we discharged at 125th Street; the platform announcement was, "Injured conductor." The riders were not sympathetic. They stared stonily or cursed me. To them, I was no fellow human. I was a part of a machine supposed to get them to their destination. One girl offered me tape. "The lens is gone," I explained apologetically. A middle-aged man jestingly offered his glasses. Another rider snarled, "Next time carry an extra pair, stupid!"

I cleaned out the train. "The train is going back in service at Mott," my motorman told me. "They took the conductor off another train that went out of service. Motor Instructor Prior will meet you there."

Prior had a reputation as a stickler and a harasser, so I didn't feel great being entrusted to his care. He led me up to the tower, where he collected about a hundred forms while the cop got my story. Prior got off the phone and told me unhappily that Command insisted I go to the hospital. The desk wanted to cover the T.A. in case I went blind on the morrow. Luckily for me Prior had the sense to veto the cop's suggestion that we go to Lincoln Hospital, just upstairs, a last-resort municipal hospital. A Saturday evening emergency room in the South Bronx would have rivaled the antechamber of hell. We traveled by subway to Manhattan Eye, Ear, Nose and Throat instead. Lord knows I had no need of an ambulance.

To my surprise, Prior believed me when I explained that I wasn't wearing safety glasses because, despite my applying for prescription safety glasses three months ago, I had not received them yet. He was doing the paper work on the subway, "I hate paperwork! There's less paper work on a twelve-nine!"

When we found the hospital, the ER was like a bank at midnight. As we waited for the doctor, Prior asked me, "Do you have an extra pair of glasses at home? If you do, you can work tomorrow. Then go down to Jay Street first thing Monday morning before you go to work."

I decided I did not have a spare.

The doctor, a young man, asked me to describe what happened. He was surprised, "Oh, I'm sorry that they do that. I'm sorry that happened to you." He was the first person who had expressed any sympathy for me. "Is there any pain?"

"No."

"Then, why are you here?"

"My employer ordered me to come," I said apologetically, "But there is a real problem." I explained my acute myopia and my inability to work without corrective lenses. As quickly as I could speak, he was writing a note to the effect that I could not work until I was fitted for new glasses.

By a little after eleven, we were out of there. Walking down the damp Upper Eastside streets, we were an unusual pair, a well-dressed, pot-bellied black gent and a bedraggled woman in a blue uniform and glasses with one lens missing.

I was looking forward to four days off.

On the last day of the old pick, I saw Mark up at Woodlawn. I told him how my glasses had been broken. He grew agitated, like a parent with a child who has hurt itself, concern mingling with reproach, "Now you've learned your lesson about observing the platform!"

"What's the lesson?"

"Don't do it!"

CREW ROOM COWBOYS

From my first night, "the Beast" lived up to its name. My first trip included police action, a bum hanging on between the cars and pretending (at least I hoped so) to be losing his balance, and riders on the platform spitting copiously on my window as soon as the train started. This, it turned out, was all pretty standard for a trip on the No. 2. I gave up observing the platform when the train was moving. I watched as I closed the doors, but once I had indication, I zipped up the window fast as I could.

The White Plains crew room had recently been renovated. It was newer and more spacious than the one at Woodlawn. Outside it was snowing hard, while inside a bunch of workers were discussing the letter the T.A. president had issued, reiterating T.A. policy that employees could not carry knives or guns. Almost every subway worker carries one or the other. Knives are freely displayed, to show off or to cut a drinking hole in the lid of a coffee cup. The letter infuriated the crews.

"It's okay if they kill us, but not for us to defend ourselves!"

"They don't care nothing about us."

"The riders come first, then the equipment, then us."

By time we started on our second trip, the snow must have been six inches deep. There were switch problems at "the East," which delayed us forty minutes. When we got out on the structure in Brooklyn, we went into emergency coming into a station. My motorman got out and walked around the train. The snowdrifts had tripped the emergency brake. He got back in and recharged the brakes with air. We moved another car-length, and it tripped again. In this tedious fashion we came into the station, tripping and recharging for every fifty feet we traveled.

By the time we left the Brooklyn terminal, we were two hours late. We did okay, though, until a couple of stops before East 180th Street. There we stopped and stood. It was past midnight. Outside the blizzard was raging.

There were even thunderclaps, but they only blended with the universal howl.

I was exhausted and yearning for home. Looking out at the abandoned, snow-clogged city, I tried to fantasize that spring would come, that Mark would call me. And we would go walking together on a sun-filled afternoon, in air humid and intoxicating, his arm around my shoulders.

After an hour, we moved into the East 180th Street station. We could not go farther, because north of 180th Street the third rail had frozen. My motorman and I discharged the train, and he told me we'd been ordered to make another trip to Brooklyn. It was two hours past my clearing time.

"I'm not going! I'm exhausted!" I protested.

He shrugged, "When they turn you, they turn you."

"No way I can do it."

"Well, go tell the dispatcher."

I plodded up to the office and told the dispatcher I was too exhausted to operate safely. So he got on the squawkbox and ordered a midnight conductor on the train. In relief and triumph, I staggered down the platform to tell my motorman I was going home. But as I was talking to him, the dispatcher rushed over. "Command says you can be relieved, but you can't go home. You have to stay here. There's a 'snow emergency.'"

So I followed him back onto the snowy platform, defeated and frustrated. He told me, "You can go in the crew room and take a nap." As no one was being allowed to go home, and hardly any trains were going out, the crew room was packed with crews.

I walked straight to the back. There, in the dark behind the lockers, a motorman was fast asleep on a chair, his feet propped up on a bench. The rest of the bench was empty. It was all of twelve inches wide. It was hard. It was directly below the pay phone. Nevertheless, it was the most promising berth in the house. I placed my dufflebag under my head, a hard and lumpy pillow, and used my coat as a blanket. I wept a few tears of self-pity and drifted off to sleep.

Each time the phone rang, it woke me, but I was so exhausted that sleep quickly reclaimed me.

A dark, somber shadow was hovering above me, asking me questions I could not comprehend. As consciousness returned, I realized it was a conductor I knew, asking me how long I had been there. My watch said it was six. I decided to call it morning. Sitting up was an effort. I could feel every muscle.

All around me, the crowded crew room was swaying with a raucous holiday spirit. The dispatcher was wailing that Command hadn't answered him in an hour. "They're all trying to read the instructions manual for the new snowblowers. They can't figure out how to start 'em."

No food, but every one took that in stride, noting past hardships, "Remember '68?" "Remember '78?" and wondering how they would get home. . . . Exhume their cars.

A "snow emergency" means workers are held eight hours past their "clear," their scheduled finishing time. So at 7:11 A.M., I would be a free woman. But I would still have to be back at White Plains at 4:30 P.M., to work.

The supervision decided to use one train to send all the White Plains crews south to Mott and operate the No. 2 service from there. It looked like that might be the last southbound train for a while, so there was a last-helicopter-out-of-Saigon spirit to the boarding. The riders had spent the night right there on that train, unable to go farther north. Now they had given up trying to reach home and were planning to go to relatives, friends, or even back to work. They looked tired and resigned. Their patience astonished me. When the conductor announced we would go nonstop to Mott, riders and workers alike cheered wildly.

On the train was one of my School Car classmates, Perez, looking pale. He'd been operating almost sixteen hours and still had to report back to work in a few hours. The only thing the supervisors offered to do for him was let him have eight hours relief before coming back to work. "That gives me six hours at home to sleep," he sighed. Despite the freezing cold he had his coat unbuttoned. "I feel hot," he explained.

When I got home, via Grand Central, the shuttle and the "A" train, I called the crew office to ask whether I should try to get to White Plains, or just report someplace nearby.

"Where do you live, Marian?" they asked, "Can you get up to Van Cortlandt?"

I was thrilled—an early P.M. job a few minutes from home.

One afternoon, as we were coming into the Utica Avenue station, our train lost power. Opposite us stood the Woodlawn train, as dark as ours. Its conductor told me why the power had been pulled: a twelve-nine at Nevins Street. Passengers irate at the delay grew quiet when I explained. At last power was restored. Busy answering rider questions, I didn't catch the platform announcement. I closed up.

The Woodlawn motorman, chatting with his conductor, started laughing at me, "Keep it open! Open it up! You know better than that, now. You've been up there." I didn't understand his meaning, but I reopened.

He went on, "You should know that after an emergency, you need a special permission to proceed." I only shrugged, and he laughed again, "So when are you coming back to the motors?"

"Back?" I snapped, "I've never been to the motors!"

"Oh, I'm sorry. I thought you was Mary," he came over and touched my gloved hand, and now his laughter was at his own mistake.

The conductor had mistaken me for Mary Hansen. Mary had been one of the first women to become a motorman. She was a train buff as well as a very aggressive personality. There was also a lot of gossip about her sleeping with many different men. She didn't look a lot like me. Although we were both white, she was about a foot shorter than I and ten years younger. She had much lighter hair and very different features.

One day Mary committed a very serious mistake: her train took the wrong track, she tried to back it up and she got caught at it. Exactly how she did this, and why, and how she got caught were the subject of endless crew room tales. Backing up a train was not unheard of. Motormen did it occasionally, and some got caught. However, Mary's action was talked about far more and far longer than any other motorman's. It happened before I came to the T.A., and it was still being talked about when I left. Mary was busted down to conductor as a punishment, but eventually she was restored to motorman, or "got her handles back."

The announcement now came, and I closed up. I was sore. How literally every woman on the job was Mary! I reflected to myself, how literally her screw-up is seen as a woman's screw-up, as every woman's screw-up!

I was sitting in the White Plains crew room, hoping for another quiet and routine day like the previous one. Holland, a very senior and articulate motorman, was talking to a group of conductors. "I got a call in the middle of the night. The desk trainmaster asks me, 'When did you last see your conductor? Did you let him off at Gun Hill Road?' I said the last time I saw him was in the White Plains crew room. He said, 'Well, here's what happened, and they want you down at Jay Street tomorrow morning.'

"So I go down, talk to the union rep. 'Let's go over our story together. Here's what we tell 'em. Here's what we don't tell 'em. We don't lie.' That's my story. I must have written twenty G-2s.

"According to the witnesses, he was talking to a couple of ladies down by the token booth at the Gun Hill Road station. And he told them he'd let them know when the train was coming. So he called to them, and then he walked to the end of the platform and sat down on the edge of the platform, not with his legs over the edge, but with his back to the edge. Then, as the train came in, he must have had a dizzy spell or something—the second south motor clipped him, flipped him up, and the north seven went over him. Sliced off the back of his head.

"We went to the hospital, but they wouldn't let us see him. They wouldn't even let his family see him. But he didn't die 'til last month."

Luck was with me that day. We made only half a trip, south to New Lots. We deadheaded back. My motorman, DiGangio, "D.G.," put his radio in the bracket in the conductor's position. He and I were sitting and chatting away about taxes, unemployment, the state of the world, our usual subjects, when the train went into emergency.

Over D.G.'s radio, we heard the motorman of the train report to Command that a signal had "flashed" on him. Command asked for the number of the signal. So the motorman had to walk back through the train, out its back, down to the roadbed, to get the number. Command kept calling for him and calling for him. Finally, he got back to his position and answered. The console operator at Command Center came across sarcastic and disdainful, "What took you so long, train operator?"

And I thought, that tone of voice is harassment. You have to have a thick skin. *Have* to. That tone of voice says, "incompetent." Yet the roadbed is hazardous, even deadly. You hurry at the risk of life and limb. If you move cautiously, you can expect a cutting, mocking query. I'd never be able to restrain myself from snapping back.

The two following trains also went B.I.E. Clearly, the signal was B.O.

On Saturdays, my motorman was a woman, Lena Strong. Though she was very friendly with the fellers, she seemed leery of me, though sometimes friendly. She blew hot and cold. I couldn't figure it out. Was it because I was a woman? White? One night when I was working with her, three of my rear cars failed to open at 135th Street. I learned this happy news from riders who had missed their stop and came to me convinced that I was somehow at fault.

At the next stop, I got out to check. Sure enough, three of my rear five were tight as a drum. By sheer luck, a dispatcher came to the platform in time to witness the offending doors flying open spontaneously. Just in case, I still took the badge number of a patrolman who saw the whole episode. As Strong put it, "They never would have believed *us!*"

Equipment could make or break a conductor's day. If the P.A.s don't work, you don't have to make announcements, but you can't communicate with your motorman in case you have questions or need assistance. Nor can you tell the riders when you are rerouted or there is a delay or an emergency.

Even worse for me were problems with doors. I've had cab doors I couldn't open to get into to operate, necessitating a humiliating call for help and long delays as we sat in the station, doors shut, and the riders fumed about "lady conductors." Some subway cars models had doors that opened only out of the cab into the car. After each station stop, the conductor was required to step out of the cab. With the cabs that opened out, this was easier said than done. It was paramount to push it open cautiously and slowly, since probably some rider would be standing near it, if not leaning against it, and if you just swung it out, you'd swat some rider silly, which would do nothing to promote harmony or employee health. But it was almost impossible to prevent this, because the door's inside handle was just a tiny sliver, so you could only get a couple of fingers on it—not enough for me to control the door, especially with the train lurching to and fro.

But the worst threat was posed by cab windows that were stuck open. All the noise and dirt came right through, and in winter the cold as well. In the stations, once the doors were closed, an open cab window made me an easy target. This was especially hazardous in the rush hour, when leaving people on the platform who would very much prefer to be on the train cannot be avoided. It was very desirable to have something solid between the vengeful masses and my face.

I was growing to dread the daily vandalism: riders breaking into the cabs, playing with the switches to disable the doors, babbling obscenities over the P.A., even halting the train by knocking out the motorman's indication. Inevitably, the other riders took out their frustration with these inconveniences on the conductor, with taunts, threats, and target practice. Of course, the vandals themselves would become ringleaders. The very folks who stopped the train would be the loudest and most insulting harassers as I labored to "overcome the problem."

Saturday night, Strong and I had a slow-accelerating train. Even I could tell it just had no pick-up. I had a backward door that only opened out into the car, so I stayed inside my cab.

At 72nd Street, someone opened my door, "Hello. I need your name." It was the mechanic, an "R.C.I." a road car inspector. So there was a chance we would go out of service. I was worried they would send us to a trainyard way out in Brooklyn. Then, going into Chambers Street, I felt the train lurch to the right and saw the lights flicker, so I knew they were putting us on the local track to send us around the loop at South Ferry and back uptown. What a break!

Sure enough, the platform P.A. announced, "This is the last stop on this train." The riders were naturally annoyed, but still relatively cooperative. After making sure there were no riders left aboard the rear half of the train, I grabbed my stuff and headed to the motorman's position.

"I was calling for an R.C.I. since way uptown," Strong complained, "and Command Center wouldn't answer me. It's the same guy that I always have trouble with. I would know his voice anywhere. First he answered the train in front of me; they had loss of indication. Then he answered the train behind me; they had a slow train. So I kept calling in. Finally, he said, 'Alright, we've got your slow-accelerating train. Now clear the air!'

"So he doesn't say nothin', then he gets all nasty! So the R.C.I. comes on and now he says we've got three dead motors and one that's only taking one point of power. So they asked him would it make the underriver tube and he said, 'I wouldn't risk it.' So they took it out. But, honey, if they hadn't I would have had to, because if we'd had to stop it in the tube on the upgrade, I don't know if I could have got it started again.

"But the way that man talks to me! Every time! It makes me not want to call Command, you know? So nasty! He has an attitude. It's sexism."

"But I've heard good things about you from all sorts of men. That you're a good motorman. They respect your operation."

"Really? Well, that means a lot to me. I wish they'd say these things to me, now. Y'know, a friend of mine said, to me, 'Lena, I hear you're a hotrodder.'"

"You mean, you're fast."

"If I were a man, I'd be fast. But because I'm a woman . . . you know?"

At Grand Central, at the leaving end, we saw a big guy in standard motorman's gear: field jacket, cap, and radio. Strong stopped and asked me to open the door for him. But before I could, he keyed himself in.

He asked us if we were going to the 180th Street yard. We had been ordered to lay up our train in the 239th Street yard.

"You out of One-eightieth Street?"

"No. White Plains."

"Well, all of your side signs say, 'Dyre.'"

Strong and I looked at each other and just laughed, because wasn't that the frosting on the cake? But our guest took it more seriously. He said to Strong, "You are responsible for the signs in this car, you know."

She was immediately defensive, "There are flagging conductors. And the dispatcher sees what comes into the terminal. Still you're right that the supervision would hold me responsible."

This didn't appease him. He kept busting her chops and was growing vehement. I broke in, "You know, we did you a favor letting you on and now you come on and give us a hard time."

"You didn't let me on. Your motorman did."

"Okay," I turned to Strong, "Your mistake. Good night, mister," and I left the car.

After 180th Street, I came back up front and Strong said to me, "You know, he ended up cursing me and getting off long before One-eightieth Street. After you left, he asked, 'Who is that white bitch?' And I told him I agreed with you. So he called me a bitch and told me to stop and let him off. I said, 'Only too happy. You've got an attitude.'"

"I'm sorry."

"No, don't be. He had an attitude problem."

I was waking up early every morning to work on my thesis before reporting. By Monday, the last day of my workweek, I was always exhausted. One Monday, I felt nauseated to boot. I went to the Columbia University clinic, found out I had an infection, and was given tetracycline. I called Jay Street to say I would be out sick, but would resume on Thursday, right after my days off.

The dispatcher at the sick desk explained to me that I would have to call there every time I left the house until I actually returned to work, even on my days off.

"What if I visit a friend?"

"Just call and tell us where you will be and then call us again when you get home."

"What if on the way home, I stop at Macy's to buy a pair of socks?"

"That's a detail. You don't have to report that," the dispatcher said patiently, "But if you go to a nightclub for four hours, and the beakies catch you, you'll be in trouble." The beakies are T.A. undercover investigators. They can come to your home when you are out sick and check on you. There are even beakie doctors, to make sure you are really sick. They do housecalls. The name came from an early subway boss named Beake who started these practices decades ago.

"What about if I go to the movies?"

"Well, the movies, well, with the beakie situation, you don't go to the movies when you're out sick."

"Even though I'm going to report as soon as my R.D.O.s are over?"

"You are carried sick until your R.D.O.s are over and you report back to work."

By the end of February, the union got its dues checkoff rights reinstated, and few of the workers overlooked the fact that management came to court in support of the union's case.

For several months I had been pestering the union officers about starting the steward training classes they had promised. First, they had claimed that hand-collecting the dues kept them too busy. Once the dues checkoff was restored, OSHA training became the excuse. But finally, the chairman of the conductor-tower division, Ray Lacy, sat down and gave me private tutoring in the rudiments of stewardship. For nearly four hours, he explained disability, pay shortages, seniority, emergency A.V.As, and sundry other matters. No formal grievance procedure existed, it turned out, merely appeals of discipline. Lacy solemnly instructed me, "Never approach people and ask if you can help. If they want your help, let them come to you."

My Friday motorman, "D.G." DiGangio, was an older Italian-American who lived in Co-op City. He doted on his two grown daughters and his grandchildren. One week, there was a different train dispatcher at the south terminal, and he deadheaded us back to White Plains, which gave us time for lunch and allowed us to begin our second trip on time. Riding uptown, D.G. said to me, "The regular dispatcher is afraid to drop a crew, so the crews go out late from New Lots for hours. It used to be all the jobs had 'T.C.,' transferring cars, right before or after lunch. You really didn't do nothing. And even if you were late, you got some time to eat. And if that made the job longer than eight hours, well, that was built in overtime, a few extra bucks. So it was a decent job. But today—it's not safe to operate the way we operate. If we're not rested, how can you be patient with the riders? How can I be alert for what's in the road?"

The subways were in the headlines. There had been a rash of recent derailments. So the T.A. had created about sixty "red-tag zones" where the motorman had to move at less than ten miles per hour. D.G. said, "They should just have one long red-tag zone: White Plains to New Lots."

"This is all the bad maintenance since 1975, coming home to roost," said someone in the crew room, and no one disagreed.

"If they'd take all the money from the damned Westway," said one motorman.

"If they just wouldn't send ten million dollars to El Salvador" said his conductor.

The weather turned terribly hot by the last week of June. On duty, I was constantly thirsty. I had to chose between closing the cab window and suffocating, or opening it and letting in the filth and deafening noise. The cabs with the backward doors became like little ovens.

The red-tag zones turned our jobs into nightmares. The running time between White Plains and New Lots, 85 minutes on paper, became 120 minutes in reality. Crews were going out "three behind," three trains after the one they were scheduled for, all day and night. No one was getting a lunch break. Finishing one to two hours late was typical.

Saturday, after four hours on a hot train, I had barely a fifteen-minute break before my second trip. In the crew room, the flagman and the switch-man were absorbed in watching *Death Wish* on cable television. I was bolting my lunch while they watched the infamous rape scene. I was sitting with my back to the set, but even the sound track grew impossible for me to bear. Added to the stress of the job, it completely unhinged me. I charged from my seat and changed the channel.

"Hey, we're missing the best part!" one guy bawled and rushed to change it back.

I returned to the set, determined to get my way. The guy pushed me away, "If you don't like it, get the hell out of here!"

"It's my crew room, too! I have ten minutes to eat and I need some relief!" I howled. "That stuff is offensive to me, and it would offend you too if you were only a human being!" I went back to my table, threw my things into my bag, and staggered out the door, in tears.

Another guy came out after me. "I know how you must feel," he said, "but you shouldn't have just changed the channel."

The pick dragged torturously to a close. One day, D.G. and I went out of service with a slow train going north. As we took the train to the yard, he told me how angry he felt about the weeks of working lengthened days without breaks or lunch.

I said, "I think people are taking it lying down because they're waiting for next pick. But if things don't get better next pick, I think all hell will break loose. I think there should be a petition or something, asking for a different road schedule that reflects the track conditions and the state of the equip-ment, so we really do get our breaks and lunches and clear on time."

But D.G. had a different idea, "There should be a rule about going out more than one behind. As soon as they are more than one behind, they should just drop a crew."

Clearly, D.G. liked being dropped. Very indignantly, he told me about the special bubble-topped subway car "they" have to transport v.i.p.s around the system in, "And they sit there with bottles of liquor and drinks on a table, while if we have a trace of alcohol in our blood, we could lose our jobs! They could have the decency to hide it! It's—it's like there are two classes! It's not fair!"

On the last Friday of the pick, we were so late coming uptown on our first trip that he was sure that we'd be dropped. But they never even let us back in the terminal. They turned us at 180th Street. We had no chance to get our lunches, drink some water, or use a toilet.

A few days after that, I came into the crew room and recognized the woman on the radios. It was Sherry Eldridge, the conductor who'd been temporarily blinded when kids on the platform threw sand in her eyes. She told me D.G., had been hurt. He was B.I.E. on the structure coming out of the portal in the Bronx. He went out on the catwalk to check it out. Debris and waste from construction was scattered all over the catwalks. D.G. slipped on something and a spike drove into his face.

Concerned after a long wait, D.G.'s conductor went out and found him. He hauled him back onto the train. D.G.'s profuse bleeding frightened him so much that he broke the rules and operated the train himself into 180th Street to get medical assistance.

Two days later, I was quits with P.M.s and with "the Beast." I was working days on Broadway. The Broadway No. 1 line was the least affected of all the I.R.T. lines by the red-tag orders. So I was getting my breaks, eating my lunch, and going home on time. But in the rest of the subway system, all hell had in fact broken loose.

Monday night, on my way home, I saw the front page of the *New York Post*. In huge letters, it read, "Wild Men Driving the Subways." I bought it for a look.

The story was built around the ignorant comments of some overpaid consultant hired by the T.A. to look into the derailments. He took a subway trip, the first in his life, and the trains went so fast it scared him out of his meager wits. He declared that the motormen drove like cowboys. Why, he had seen them "put their foot all the way down on the accelerator." This was perplexing because no subway controls are operated with the feet, and the motorman accelerates manually by means of a device at waist level. It's hard to figure out what the guy actually saw. I was pissed, but I dismissed it as the sensationalism of the dregs of the New York tabloids.

To my surprise, the *Times* covered the comments very seriously the next day, "Speeding Motormen Called Factor in a Rash of City Subway Derailments."

I heard from Jasmin Joyce on the phone that, in response to the publicity, the T.A. had started taking a lot of motormen out of service for "speeding." I asked Vice Chairman Vinnie Torrelli what the union was doing about the motormen who were being scapegoated for this consultant's dumb remarks.

Tony made excuses for the union's inaction. "Well, you see, Marian, with these ray guns they're using, it's hard to dispute." I assumed he knew what the ray guns were. I certainly didn't.

I asked whether the union was doing anything about getting the running times and the work schedules changed so we could get our breaks and lunches. "Gee, I'll tell you, Marian, if all the fellas would just take their breaks, there'd be nothing they could do about it. But these guys got no balls."

"They're not going to do it unless they're organized to do it. They don't want their time cut. And the union reps aren't going to do it."

I called Dave Stone, the conductor from Detroit whom I had met at the January union meeting. Ever since then, we'd had lunch together after every union meeting and continued to agree on pretty much everything. As usual, Dave had good ideas. He said that our bylaws allowed a meeting to be called by half the elected officers, or 20 percent of the members, of a division.

I headed downtown. Platforms were mobbed with waiting riders. It was obvious that day that the trains were being driven slowly. Every one of them crept along. Motormen were following the C.Y.A. (cover your ass) imperative, and they were also making their anger and power felt.

That night, the union president, John Lawe, held a press conference. He called upon motormen to follow the rules. He was about a day behind the rank and file. T.A. management eagerly seconded Lawe, declaring there was no slowdown, that motormen were simply following the rules and exercising caution.

Wednesday, service continued to move at a snail's pace. The T.A. president publicly apologized for the consultant's remarks. The mayor proclaimed that motormen were "unsung heroes." However, word was going around the crew rooms that dozens of motormen had been taken out of service, given suspensions of as long as thirty days and even demoted from motorman to their previous title, such as conductor, token clerk, or cleaner.

I telephoned some of my friends still working "the Deuce." To them, a petition for a special union meeting sounded like a good idea. Dave and I wrote up a petition and sent copies to everyone we knew. It caught on like wildfire.

In a few days, Vinnie Torrelli, the union vice chairman who had made me a shop steward, came to see me at Van Cortlandt terminal. "I'm gonna turn around and tell you something, Marian, the higher-ups don't like the petition."

"I didn't expect they would."

"Marian, they aren't gonna like a steward taking around this petition."

"So what's gonna happen? Is someone gonna shoot me? No! So then what's the worst that could happen? I could lose my job? I could get another one."

"No, no, no. Marian you are well liked in the union. You could be going somewhere in the union. If you need a favor, if you get into a jam, if you need an A.V.A . . ."

"I don't want favors. I don't want privileges. Things will get better for all of us down here. That's the only way I want them to get better for me. If my friends aren't getting their A.V.As, then I don't want mine either. It's more important to me to speak my mind in this union than to go somewhere in it."

"Things aren't gonna get any better down here. They're gonna get worse."

"Well, then they get worse for me, too. But I'm gonna do everything I can to defend what we've got."

"Look, I used to think like you do," said Vinnie, "but if you stick your neck out for these guys, they'll turn around and stab you in the back. And if you go to the union, they'll just give you the runaround. I'm an officer and they're still giving me the runaround."

Dave and I took the petitions down to the union hall. We had 650 names. Executive Vice President Martin Lawson, invited the two of us into his office, along with Vinnie Torrelli, and a few other staffers.

Lawson perused the petitions, smiling slightly, then looked over at Dave and me, smiling slightly, "You know, I can't call a meeting like this, anyway. I'm not a divisional officer." Nevertheless, he felt called upon to pepper us with the reasons a meeting wasn't necessary or, for that matter, possible.

One of the reps said, "There's lots of overtime right now. The fellows out there are happy. I haven't heard any complaints, have you?"

Another rep said, "No, not one."

Dave gestured towards the sheets of signatures on Lawson's desk, "Those sure look like complaints to me."

Lawson said, "Tell them to write G-2s. If they aren't getting their breaks, and they aren't getting their lunches, have them write G-2s, and send them to me. I'll make sure the thirteenth floor gets them."

A rep said, "The boys would rather make the overtime."

That Monday, I took an A.V.A and went up to Woodlawn at daybreak to collect "no-lunch" grievances. Even I had begun to wonder whether the union bureaucrats were right and the crews preferred to earn the overtime. First, I tried announcing in the crew room that I was taking grievances. No response. Then, I tried approaching individuals and asking, "Have you been getting your lunches?" Almost all said no. At that point, I would say, "I'm here from the union, to help you grieve it." Nearly everyone wanted to grieve it. I asked them questions and wrote out their grievance on a G-2 form. Then, I handed it to them to read and sign. By the end of the morning, I had thirteen grievances.

The next day, I went up to the union hall and gave Vice President Lawson the Woodlawn grievances. He was very matter-of-fact about it, just as if he'd been the one saying people were pissed, instead of denying that anyone out on the road had a beef. He said, "We'll give them to the superintendent at our regular Monday meeting."

Whenever the new work schedule was different, the union held a special schedule meeting for that division. This was the only kind of union meeting that included both the motormen and conductors from the same division. The special schedule meeting in September was well attended.

The vice president mentioned he'd met with the superintendent and told him something had to be done about the I.R.T., such as a supplemental schedule or dropping or turning trains. He reported he had threatened, "if things don't change, we're going to go 'upstairs,'" above the superintendent's head in the chain of command.

Eventually, I got the floor. I recounted the way I'd gotten the Woodlawn grievances, and asked Lawson what he had done with them, "Will they be put into the grievance procedure? If necessary, will they be taken all the way to arbitration?"

Lawson answered that they were waiting to give T.A. a chance to try their suggestions. However, he added, "If things don't improve in a reasonable amount of time, we will put them into the grievance procedure."

I asked what his idea of a reasonable amount of time was.

"Oh, by the end of the month."

Will Washington, an organizer for the motormen division, addressed himself to me, "I had an opportunity to look at those grievances. I found they were all written in the same handwriting."

"The signatures are all different," I rejoined, stung by his implication.

"You will learn in your tender years with us, Miss Swerdlow, that it is better to let people do things for themselves. We have taken cases such as these to arbitration. The contract states that you will get lunch between the third and sixth hours. The nature of the industry is irregular. The arbitrator has ruled that the industry that we are in is the public's eminent domain. The arbitrator has ruled that eminent domain takes precedence over individual interests."

I asked for the floor to respond, "All summer long, I listened to the union organizers and the union officers saying that the only thing stopping them from doing something about our working conditions was that they needed G-2s, they needed the problem 'documented.' So, I don't want to pat myself on the back, but, I went up to Woodlawn and in only a few hours I got thirteen grievances. And many of the people I got them from said to me, 'These won't do any good. The union won't really do anything. Management won't change anything. But you have to speak your mind anyhow.' And now, listening to Mr. Washington, I'm coming to the conclusion that they were right in their view of things, and that it's me who's been a sap!"

At that, all hell broke loose. The officers and organizers fell all over each other squawking and gobbling. The chair gave the floor to Vice President Lawson, by far the coolest head of the lot.

"I think," he said suavely, "you may have missed what Mr. Washington was saying. That's understandable. What Mr. Washington said was that we cannot win in all cases. But it's very important to submit the G-2s because we win some and lose some."

"Miss Swerdlow," said Washington, "Your tenacity is admirable."

More than a month after I'd collected the no-lunch grievances at Woodlawn, I returned to find out whether anything had improved. One by one, as they came back from their runs, I asked the train crews whether things had improved and told them how the union officers had responded to their grievances.

I called Vice President Lawson down at the union hall and told him that things were just the same up at Woodlawn: no supplement with corrected running times or anything. In addition, I had two new no-lunch grievances.

He told me to send him the two new grievances.

I interrupted, "But what are you going to do with the grievances I've given you already?"

He actually seemed flustered, "Well, I've got to look them over, you understand. And I want to talk this over with management, you understand—"

"But you, we, you did that! You did that already! It was . . . it's been . . . six weeks!"

Lawson said, "Now we have to go to the Safety Committee."

This was November's "Delaying Tactic of the Month"! I thought to myself. "That should have been done in July!" I snapped, "You've waited four months."

"You expect us to spoon-feed the membership."

After six months at Van Cortlandt, I picked over to Woodlawn. It was a lower seniority line, and I could get better jobs.

The new pick started in January. One of my motormen was Riggs the Radical. He was a member of the ultrarevolutionary "Spartacist League." Riggs was a white guy from a poor rural background. He had fought in Vietnam and he likened that war to the situation on the railroad, "The U.S. big brass simply could not believe that we could be losing the war to what they considered a backward country with a primitive army. So they put the pressure on the officers at the front to give them the results they thought they should be getting. The front line falsified the enemy body count and created the illusion that we were winning.

"Now the T.A. brass refuses to believe the railroad cannot be run according to the schedule. So they put the pressure on the supervision, who fudge the sheets to make it look like only the G.O.s, the repair work, and the breakdowns keep the railroad from running on time."

I said, "Everything I see in history convinces me that when the people are ready, they move, and things change rapidly. However, between those moments, nothing much can really be accomplished. You can't make people move, and you can't do much when they aren't moving. So what can revolutionaries do, in a period like this?"

In reply, he spoke of "building a new leadership for the union" and mentioned how his organization had run a campaign for office in the last race for union president.

I said I didn't think you developed leadership by running in elections once every two years. You have to develop leadership on the job.

One morning, "Turn Around" Vinnie Torrelli bounded into the crew room, eager to sign people up for COPE payments, contributions to the union's political action fund. He was instantly besieged by his constituents, who were aggrieved by their lack of lunches or breaks and their late clears. Vinnie babbled about a supplemental work schedule being in the works.

One day Mark called me to tell me that there was indeed a supplemental work schedule with new longer running times: he had actually seen it. I was disgusted. So we finally had the schedule with realistic running times that we had needed for over six months. But it was being imposed upon us. Rather than picking, we would be assigned jobs, with different starting times, different numbers of trips, and even different reporting places from the jobs that we had picked. It was a complete violation of our seniority rights.

When I got to work, confusion reigned. "First we pick. Then they change all the jobs. And they're giving us nine extra minutes of cab time each way."

As far as I could see, the supplement would accurately reflect the time each trip took. It added extra time, "penalty time," to each job, and on paper took three minutes off the lunch break. The important thing, though, was the longer work day would also include time for real lunch periods and breaks.

The crews were all bitching and moaning about "more cab time." But the only difference was on paper. We were already spending that time on the trains. The bad part was that the longer working day was becoming codified.

I went up to the dispatcher's office to see the supplement and my heart sank. The beautiful job I'd picked—two trips to Atlantic and a half-trip to Bowling Green—had turned into two to Atlantic and one all the way out to Utica Avenue. Another conductor was just as upset as I was. "I picked a later job so I could take my kids to school!"

I asked Dave Stone, the conductor whom I'd worked with on the petition for a special union meeting, how he thought I should approach the question of the right to pick on the supplement. "Present it as something you could do something about if you were organized," he said.

At the next union special schedule meeting, I spoke, "People only very recently picked. And now they have something different foisted on them. A conductor picked a late job to take his kid to school and now he has an early report. Someone else picked an early job because he has a class in the afternoon. A little extra pay doesn't make up for your life being messed up. As things stand now, the T.A. can assign anyone of us to any job at any time, just by printing it up and calling it a 'supplement.' We need to get contract language that restricts the T.A.'s license to impose just any supplement at any time."

(In 1996, a limit was achieved in an arbitration suit brought by a rank-and-file activist. The arbitrator said that, after a couple of months, the T.A. must allow workers to pick their jobs on the supplement.)

"I propose stipulating that no supplement can add a trip to any job, shorten lunches or breaks, or change reporting or clearing time."

Will Washington, one of the motorman division union reps, was on his feet instantly, "Miss Swerdlow, if you expect these kinds of rights, get out of the industry. You are in the public domain. When you work for the public, you are in the public domain."

A motorman was recognized. "Will, we all know about the public domain and eminent domain, and all the other domains. But why should we let them do this to our seniority rights?"

Washington answered, "You fellers wanted a supplement. Didn't you ask for a supplement?"

The supplement with the new running times went into effect. My cushy Thursday job turned into what my motorman called "a workhorse."

The supplement had changed Jasmin Joyce's job, too. Now she reported forty minutes earlier and finished almost an hour later. This meant she had to travel to work during the evening rush hour. And by the time she traveled home, the No. 4 was running local, so it took her a half-hour longer to get home. After four days of this, she was totally exhausted.

The supplement affected everyone else on the No. 4 line, as well. One conductor told me he'd picked two to Utica and on the supplement he had gotten two to New Lots, about thirty-six minutes more cab time, "I'm going to put in for extra service," he said.

"Sure, but that's not the answer," I said.

"No, it's not."

Riggs the Radical was moving into high gear. He had taken it upon himself to organize a work-to-rules on the No. 4 line.

He gave out a sheet of rules and urged everyone to "work to the rules." I felt threatened and competitive. What if Riggs organized the terminal after I had concluded the terminal was not yet ready to be organized? I called Dave, who had become my political mentor.

"Riggs feels that a terminal can be organized simply by the determination of a few leaders," I observed to Dave. "I tell him people move when they are ready to move. He says if we take that attitude, someone is going to haul off and smack the dispatcher, mistakes are going to be made, and it doesn't have to be that way. I answer that it is inevitable that workers make mistakes, they learn from these mistakes and that learning is necessary."

Dave said, "I agree with you—and with Rosa Luxemburg. How did she put it? One mistake that the masses learn from is worth a hundred leaders. But there's something you're missing. Some people go into motion sooner than others. You can't suck a movement out of your thumb, but you can work with people who are earlier in moving."

"Where's that group that comes into motion earlier?"

"Well, for example, there are the people who helped us circulate the petition for the special union meeting last summer."

"That's true, but that was a pretty minimal involvement. They invested their time commensurate with their belief it could have immediate payoff. Are there any people in T.A. we haven't met who are willing to invest their time for results at best long term and at least dubious?"

"I don't know," said Dave, "and I don't know what makes people make that kind of commitment. The only thing we can do now is to keep trying to do the things we have been trying to do. Maybe if something can get going around this binding arbitration thing, maybe from that we can get a contract committee under way. But you know," he said ironically, "I have great dreams." He also thought conditions would get much worse: swing shifts and one-person train operation.

I said, "The people on the job don't believe one-person operation is

possible. T.a. will try it and it will be a disaster. That way they don't have to
do anything."

As it turned out, almost everyone was dismissive of Riggs' scheme. They
didn't think the union would back a slowdown, and didn't think a work-to-
rules alone would have any impact on service. As Mark Goniea put it, "If
everyone followed the rules on Riggs' sheet, nothing would happen, nothing.
T.a. wants us to follow the rules. If we want to mess things up, we have to
look for ways to slow things down, and use the rules to cover ourselves.
That's what the union would not support. Of course, the union will support
us if we follow the rules. But it won't make any impact. A slowdown—that's
different."

The next day, when my motorman and I were scheduled to make our last
trip, there was no train for us. The train that was supposed to come in after
ours, which we were supposed to go out on, was nowhere near the terminal.

We were scheduled to go out at 2:04 p.m. Two o'clock came and went,
and there was nothing, nothing coming up. My motorman, who was in the
dispatcher's shack, said no one could figure out why that train was so late.
There were no problems on the road, no reported equipment problems.

At almost ten after two, a train appeared on the horizon. The motorman
was Riggs. It hit me that he had been "working-to-rule."

It worked out well for my motorman and me. Riggs was sent right back
out and we were dropped. We lounged on the veranda like great lazy lizards.

Riggs' attempts to organize the terminal to "work-to-rule" petered out. In
a few months, we began picking again on a schedule with the new running
times. Eventually, the No. 4 line began to get new equipment, the R-62s, and
we were actually exceeding the new running times.

But what crews were left with was a sense that, when their rights were
abused and taken from them, their union leaders and staff representatives
had been nowhere in sight. What they didn't yet have was a clear alternative.

HEALTH AND SAFETY

Two motormen had fallen through the catwalks on the No. 4 line's elevated structure.

The catwalks are narrow walkways on either side of the "structure," or elevated tracks. Motormen have to walk on them when they go to pick up "lay-ups," empty trains being stored when they aren't needed for service. They also use the catwalks when the emergency brakes of their trains are activated for an unknown reason. The train's striking something is usually the cause, so the rules call for walking around the outside of the trains to determine its cause.

Luckily, neither man had fallen completely through to the street. One was Ken Freeman, who was part of the union's "old opposition." "Ken's lucky he's such a big guy," said motorman "Brandy" Brandfield, the switchman. "He was too big to go all the way through, and his chest and arms stuck. He was about six inches from the third rail, but he managed to pull himself out. Tore up his knee, though." Brandy was one of Woodlawn terminal's most senior men and its spokesman of sorts. His concern carried some weight.

"The sad truth is," Brandy went on, "no one's going to do anything until someone falls into the street and gets killed. Then we might get the family to sue the union, or the T.A., or both. It's probably a bad idea to sue the union."

"Probably," I agreed, "but the whole point of workers' comp is that you can't sue your employer. The truly best thing, and mind you I don't think we're at the point where we could pull this off, is to shut down the terminal. If there's any place that could be done, it's Woodlawn."

"Yes," said Brandy proudly, "a lot of people say that about this place."

I called a motorman who was one of the leaders of the "old opposition." He told me there was already a contract to have the catwalks repaired.

"What's being done in the meantime to make sure the motormen know they have a right to refuse to walk on a dangerous part of the catwalk?"

"Ken," one of the motormen who fell through, "is telling people."

I called Ken Freeman. He told me the union would back up anyone who refused a dangerous order.

"May I tell people that?"

He said, "I know how you feel. But it's a complicated issue. And it's the motormen who have to walk around the train. So I don't think they want to hear it from a conductor."

"Fine. So you should tell them."

He said that he had, and that forty-five people had signed a G-2 about the condition of the catwalks. I asked him about requesting a Public Employee OSHA inspection. He had already asked for one.

One early December dawn, I set off for Woodlawn. My main purpose was to follow up on the no-lunch grievances, but as I rode in the lead car, I was studying the catwalks through the window of the storm door. Their disrepair was horrifying. Cracked or charred planks made every inch treacherous. At the terminal, I asked a senior motorman whether anyone had been up there to inform people that the union would back motormen who refused to walk on unsafe catwalks.

"The union's wrong on that one," he said.

"But people have a right to refuse a dangerous order," I protested.

"Any part of the structure is dangerous," he said. "You have to go around your train. You can take all day, but you have to go around it."

Vice Chairman Torrelli, who had made me a steward, came bounding in to the Woodlawn crew room, "Fellers! I'm here to turn around an' sign yuhs up for COPE!" the union's political action fund.

Motorman Brandfield, who had been sitting impassively, suddenly thundered, "What about the structure, Vinnie? The union had better put up a sign saying, 'Don't walk where there's danger. Refuse to walk unsafe catwalks. The union will back you up.'"

Everyone shut up and looked toward Vinnie, awaiting his response. His members' militancy affected Torrelli. He looked truly unhappy, "Fellers, I'm your rep. But a rep, I'm findin' out, has to walk a very thin, fine line. If I don't get along with the organizers, when I want to turn around an' do something for one of you, it's no dice; they're gonna turn around an' stonewall me. So I gotta try to make the organizers happy. Vote their way. Talk their way. Drop the stuff they don't wanna touch. But then if I do all that, the guys turn around an' don't want any part of me. Any favor I ask for, I gotta deliver somethin'. Like you fellers tell me you don't like COPE. Okay, but if you don't buy COPE, and I come ask for somethin' for this terminal, the V.P. gonna turn around an' say, the hell with them, they didn't buy COPE." "COPE" was the Union's Committee on Political Education fund, which in actuality used to give donations to political candidates. If you buy COPE, you choose an amount to be deducted from each paycheck, in addition to your union dues, to go to this fund. Most unions have a similar fund.

I interrupted, "It works the other way too, Vinnie. If the union got us something good, we would be more willing to buy COPE."

This met with approval from the crews.

Torrelli was so fired up he marched right to the telephone to call Vice President Lawson with Brandfield's idea for the sign.

He came back crestfallen. Lawson had given him the runaround, told him to ask the staff rep, Washington, whether the union was allowed to do that.

"Look, Vinnie," I told him, "there's two ways you can get what you want from the organizers. You know one: be on their good side. The other is to get them over a barrel by building your own base of support."

Wednesday was the union meeting. Before it began, I was in the hall talking with Vinnie, "What happened when you asked Washington about the sign for the crew room?" I asked.

"He said it couldn't be done. The workers would take advantage of it. They'd use it as an excuse not to do their jobs."

"Oh, you know that's bull, Vinnie. I don't accept it. Washington is basing that on his idea of the workers. It's insulting, and I think it's false. Even if the sign were put up, most motormen and conductors would still be scared to refuse. Someone is going to end up a hamburger on Jerome Avenue. And now that's going to be partly our fault, too."

Vinnie looked nervous, "I got an idea, Marian. We'll all go walk the catwalk from Burnside to one-six-one [161st Street, where the tunnel begins]. We'll make a list of all the dangerous spots and post it in the crew room."

So on my days off, I went up to Woodlawn to meet Torrelli. He was telling anyone who'd listen about what he and I were about to do, and Motorman Brandfield was telling Vinnie about all the worst spots with the manner of a man recommending the best sightseeing attractions to tourists.

Vinnie and I decided not to go all the way down and got off the downtown train at 167th Street. We decided to cross to the east side of the structure, so we could walk on the catwalk next to the uptown tracks. I made it as far as the middle of the downtown track. Then I just couldn't figure out how to proceed. There was no place to plant my feet. I didn't see how I could step over the third rail, which was right in front of me. I tried to turn back, but I couldn't see any way to get back either. The next train was inching over the horizon, only a station away.

"Vinnie!" I hollered. It was not my shining moment. Vinnie, who was already at the uptown platform, picked his way to me and helped me back to the downtown platform.

We went downstairs to the station mezzanine, and crossed to the other side the way the riders do. Then we commenced our walk uptown, toward Burnside Avenue, on the catwalk.

The catwalk consists of four planks, each about six inches wide, spaced about four inches apart. The whole thing is about three feet wide. About every four feet, a tie perpendicular runs beneath the planks. On the outer side, there is a guardrail. Sometimes the third rail runs along the inside. With this construction, if one of the planks is damaged or missing, there is a gap eighteen inches wide, wide enough for a leg to go through.

In the areas where Vinnie and I walked, an easy step was rare. The planks were rotten, charred, splintered, even completely missing. In some places the guardrail was loose as well, even swinging back and forth. Many of the planks were not fastened down, but rested on the ties, popping up like a see-saw if you stepped on one end. Others rested on top of other planks, so that, in darkness or in snow, they'd be easy to trip over.

I was taking pictures and then I wrote down in my notepad where each picture had been snapped. We moved slowly. The weather was damp and cold. By the time we reached Burnside, I was worn out, cold, and unnerved. We took the train from Burnside back to Woodlawn, where we were greeted heartily by the crews who'd witnessed our trek.

Vinnie and I went to a luncheonette to get some hot food, to sit down, and to plot our next move.

"I'm going to request an inspection by P.E. OSHA." P.E. OSHA is the Public Employee Occupational Safety and Health Administration. It administers the state's version of OSHA for its public employees.

"Marian, gimme a chance to try to do this my way. By going with you today, I think I've earned that."

"What's the point?" I laughed. "In your place, I'd just go ahead and put up the sign. Let the union try to refuse to defend someone."

"Marian, you gotta understand. I wanna be made." He meant, appointed as a staff rep.

The photos came back, clear and damning. I noted the location of each on the back. I took them with me to work.

The terminal was hectic because Superintendent Ford was due on a "state visit." The train dispatcher was snapping at everyone to get their ties on and their pullover sweaters off. Mark and I walked back to the crew room, where His August Highness was expected momentarily.

When Superintendent Ford at last appeared, I went up to him and launched into my spiel about the catwalks, flipping my photos to drive home my message. I asked for a bulletin informing all employees that they have a legal right to refuse to walk any part of the catwalk in such poor repair.

Superintendent Ford seemed impressed, "Can you get me a copy of these pictures? I'll see what I can do."

"This set is for you," I said, "keep them."

After Ford's visit, we came back to find a crew of porters from as far away as 86th Street scrubbing down the crew room with ammonia. The crews were jubilant over the news that the dispatcher, whom they detested, had been written up for the condition of the crew room.

The next day they were less gleeful. Signs were up in the crew room exhorting us to keep our quarters clean. A sign on the door announced that we were no longer allowed to keep our meals warm on the heaters or radiators. These messages were signed, "T/D Stein and by order of President Gunn." The narrow rack above the heater that we had used to keep our food warm had been removed. Making our lives less comfortable could be accomplished overnight.

The next day, the signs were gone and the lunches back on the radiators. This was direct action by the working class.

I came back to Woodlawn after my days off, and as I walked into the crew room, "Brandy" Brandfield told me he had heard that the dispatcher had gone so far as to throw out the lunches he'd found on the heaters. But Brandy wasn't going to do anything until he found someone actually missing his meal, just in case it was only a rumor.

A midnight motorman gestured toward the trash barrel, overflowing as it always was, and said, "Why can't they give us an additional trash can?"

Another added, "That's what draws the insects, not the food on the radiator."

I began to tell two conductors about giving Superintendent Ford the pictures. One, a very senior man, said, "You won't get anything from Ford. He belongs to T.A."

"Then, I'll ask for an OSHA inspection."

"That's the only way."

The other conductor was even newer than I. He said, "Our morale is bad, and this makes it worse. Don't they understand? They aren't going to get any more productivity out of us."

The senior man said, "There's a temper to the times. The Supreme Court rules now that a company can get rid of its unions by declaring itself in bankruptcy. There isn't any future for unions."

Saturday, Vinnie Torrelli was up at Woodlawn on his day off to make overtime pay. In front of the crews, I gave him a set of the photos of the structure to give to Vice President Lawson. I repeated my intention of asking for a P.E. OSHA inspection.

"A word to the wise," said Vinnie to me, looking worried, "That would be one thing that could get T.A. really mad. I'm gonna turn around and tell you, they'll make trouble for you if you push this thing."

I said, "You're the union rep, warning me not to exercise my rights. If you don't use them, you lose them."

A motorman said, "But there's a lot of people who used their rights who aren't around anymore. They can get you any time. We are all breaking the rules, all the time."

"If they can frighten us out of using our rights—"

"How long have you been on the job?"

"A year and a half. That makes me just like a whole lot of other people on the job who've been around a year and a half. And I've had other experiences with management and unions."

"T.A. is unique."

"No, T.A. is not unique. A boss is a boss. They all want you quiet. Most want you scared."

One motorman was nodding at what I was saying, but that was all the support I got. Everyone else listened silently. I went down the road wondering whether I'd done the right thing.

The next day was another big day at Woodlawn, even bigger than the day of Ford's state visit. T.A. Head David Gunn himself was paying us a call. A crew of porters was not just washing, but polishing, the crew room floor. There were no paper towels in the rest room, the one trash barrow was filled to the ceiling, yet the floor was shining. There were carpenters on the platform mending the decrepit bench that had been broken for at least as long as I had been a conductor. Things could get done fast, when management made them a priority.

When I got to work on Saturday, there was a notice on the conductors' board that conductors should not carry their keys on chains because of the danger of electric shock.

Humph, I thought, tell me news, not history. Besides, my keys are on a rope, not a chain.

At Boro Hall, southbound, I was deep in a fascinating magazine article. I glanced up and saw a motor instructor. He said, "I could take you out of service."

I guiltily tried to hide the magazine.

He pointed to my rope, "Did you hear that a conductor got killed last night? He was dragged by the chain on his keys."

I was startled. "I saw a notice on the board. But it said the danger was from electric shock. It said no chains."

"No, nothing that attaches to your body."

I was pretty shook up.

The first story that went around at Woodlawn was that a "B" Division conductor had been outside his train, closing it down with his key so it could be laid-up. He couldn't get his key out, and since it was attached to him, he'd been dragged to his death.

Dave Stone, who was "B" Division, knew the guy's name, Rogers. He said it had happened "on the midnights" at Mott Avenue, and they don't lay-up anything from there during those hours.

On Sunday, a new story was being told at Woodlawn. A conductor was trying to open his closed-down train, again from the outside. But why would the train be closed, and not open, when the conductor was on the platform? Who closed it and why? What made it more mysterious was that this had happened at a terminal. Motormen leaving a terminal in passenger service must wait until they hear two long buzzes from their conductor before releasing the brake and moving the train.

Dave gave me a reason the motorman may have moved without two long ones in this instance. On some "B" Division equipment, if neither the buzzer nor the intercom works, the conductor sometimes uses a different signal: turning his key in the door control panel to flicker the motorman's indication light.

Monday, on my first trip, I heard yet a third story from a conductor still in School Car. He'd heard the victim's key chain got caught in the pentagraph gates, the gates between the cars. This did not explain why the conductor was outside the closed train or why the train moved without the conductor aboard.

This incident created a general atmosphere of dread among the crews, and I felt it even more sharply than most. As I worked, I felt constantly apprehensive. I was especially afraid when I had to close down my train from the outside by standing on the platform and reaching my key inside the cab window. This was supposedly how Rogers had been killed. Unfortunately, this was the way I had to do it at Utica Avenue terminal.

So, by Utica Avenue, I was feeling anxious. But I announced the last stop and got off the train. A lot of riders refused to get off. I was annoyed. I didn't want to see all of them go down the relay track, the U-shaped track on which the empty train is moved from the upper level to the northbound lower level. I shouted into the cars, "Last stop, last stop!" They still sat. I gave up. I reached in and shut it down. Then I saw where I was. Franklin Avenue, the stop before Utica. I had been so scared about closing down my train, that I'd jumped the gun.

I watched my train go off without me. It was strange, like watching my clothes walking down the street without me. Luckily, a No. 3 was on the local track. I got on and rode it to Utica Avenue. There the platform conductor had opened up my train. I explained that I had gone to the rear to check a rider's report that the car was filled with smoke.

From Riggs the Radical I got the Spartacist League's explanation of Conductor Rogers' death. He'd been pushed by white racists, because he was black. It fit with their idea that the number-one issue for transit workers at that time was racist terror. It was the most frightening of the theories I'd heard.

Four days after Rogers's death, T.A. put out a bulletin forbidding trains from leaving a terminal in passenger service unless there was some working means of communication between motorman and the conductor. This came close to an acknowledgment that T.A. had permitted practices that were dangerous and may have caused or at least contributed to Rogers' death.

Dave knew the motorman, Norland. "It's a small detail, yet in a way it's the crowning irony. Both Norland and Rogers were working on their days off. Norland was a good motorman, very safety conscious. He and Rogers were friends. After the accident, he tried to put in his papers, [that is, resign]. But T.A. wouldn't accept them. They have him on indefinite suspension. They are also considering involuntary manslaughter charges, because they say the train dumped [that is, the emergency brakes were automatically activated] twice and he didn't go check."

"How do they know it dumped?"

"There were skid marks on the rails."

"Couldn't those have been made by something else?"

"Well, there's a story that Norland stopped twice because he heard screaming. That would also explain the skid marks."

Before the conductors' union meeting began, people were sitting around talking about Rogers's death. One conductor objected, "We're all just Monday morning quarterbacking."

Then Vice President Lawson came sauntering in. "I had to go to a funeral last week, and I'm upset because the man didn't have to die." We were silent, expectant. We were waiting for the facts. Lawson went on, angrily, "And you conductors are still doing it!"

The meeting was small. Almost everyone there was a union flunky. They sat cowed, like third-graders being scolded by the principal. At last, I called out, "What is it we're doing?"

"Jumping between the cars on a moving train! You all take shortcuts, doggone it. The motorman who didn't want to wait until he got to a clearance area. And now this conductor. It's because you're all doggone lazy! That's right, lazy!"

I couldn't believe my ears. A conductor was dead. Instead of the union giving us the facts, the union is blaming us and insulting us. In a rage, I broke my pen in half and threw the pieces across the room.

Lawson was speechless for a moment. Then he continued in a calmer vein. But he still couldn't resist complaining that Rogers's beneficiary card was all screwed up, and that was an inconvenience for the union. "Just stupid, doggone stupid." I was outraged that Lawson acted as if his having to go to that funeral was the worst part of the accident. He was also miffed that "no one ever told me," that conductors were signaling motorman by flickering the indication. Without waiting for the floor to be opened for discussion, he left the room.

I followed him out and gave him a copy of the grievance on the catwalk conditions. "I'm very angry about what you said," I told him, "I don't know many motormen or conductors who take unsafe short cuts, but when they do, it's because they don't get breaks or lunch, or they get late clears, or they're harassed or pressured. But it's not because they're lazy."

"In your opinion, a conductor can do no wrong," he said sarcastically.

"In yours, a conductor is always wrong," I shot back. "Maybe you worked with lazy people. I don't."

"I don't want to go to any more funerals."

"And I don't want to die for T.A. and have my union blame me for it!" I pointed to the grievance, "If you really want to spare yourself a funeral, do something about this. Because sooner or later, someone's going to die. And if you say, 'No one ever told me,' you'll be lying."

It was my last trip before my R.D.O.S, so I was in good spirits. Then, as I was opening up at 176th Street, there was an explosion. A tongue of flame shot out of the panel on the wall of my cab over the circuitry. Smoke billowed out.

I got on the P.A., "Motorman, there's been an explosion in my cab. I'm coming up front." I was not too dazed to forget to remove my illegal earplugs, which had probably just saved the hearing in my right ear.

My motorman, Lock, had known something was wrong even before hearing me on the P.A. because the train lights went off. He looked out of his cab to the platform and saw people streaming off from the middle of the train. I explained to him what had happened. He said, "I'll check it out. You go up there and call Command on the radio."

I told Command Center I had a ringing and pain in my right ear. "Discharge, conductor," they told me, which was the order for me to get the riders off the train.

I waited an hour and a half for a motor instructor to escort me to the hospital. He took me to Manhattan Eye, Ear, Nose and Throat, the same hospital I was taken to after my glasses had been broken by a rider. I was becoming a regular. The doctor there determined I had suffered some hearing loss, "probably temporary."

After my days off, I reported to the T.A. clinic. Because of the note from the doctor, they put me on "light duty" for a week. For the first two days, they had me working platforms, where my main job was answering rider questions. Since I was (probably temporarily) partially deaf, I was perfect for the assignment.

During the week I was on light duty, I woke up one morning to find a message from Jasmin Joyce on my machine, "It was 'Lucky' Lewis who derailed. Mark Goniea was stuck in Brooklyn."

Of course, at Woodlawn the next morning, it was all anyone talked about. I heard right away that both the conductor and the motorman on the derailed train were taken for blood alcohol tests. The past exploits of Lucky Lewis were recounted. While still a new motorman, he was on a B.O., a "bad order," that is, a malfunctioning train, which had to be operated from the second car. A motor instructor was giving him instructions by radio from the lead car. "Keep comin', keep comin'," said the motor instructor. And Lucky Lewis did. And Lucky Lewis' train ran right into the rear end of a laid-up train. More recently, while Lucky Lewis had been operating out on the elevated tracks, the wall of an abandoned warehouse had collapsed on his train.

The T.A. investigation later concluded that the derailment was the fault of the contractor who had laid the new tracks in that area.

The next week, I reported back to the clinic. I saw the same doctor. He sent me down the dark corridor they used for the eye tests. "Turn to your right," he directed, "Put your left finger in your left ear." I did so. "Put your left finger in your left ear," he repeated.

"My left finger is in my left ear."

"Oh, I couldn't see it. Now repeat the numbers I say after me."

I did. By passing this improvised test, I was off restriction.

My next paycheck was short. T.A. hadn't paid me for the day my cab blew up. I thought of the old work song about drillers building a railway tunnel, "Drill Ye Tarriers":

> Last week a premature blast went off
> And a mile in the air went big Jim Goff.
> Next time payday came around
> Jim Goff a dollar short was found.
> When he asked what for, came this reply,
> "You were docked for the time you were up in the sky."

How dangerous are subway operative jobs? Close to the end of the time I worked in transit, I had to see someone in labor relations. The Labor Relations Office handled all the cases of Workmen's Compensation and differential pay for leave due to on-the-job injuries suffered in Rapid Transit Operations. As I was waiting, I asked the clerk, "How many conductors and train operators would you estimate come in here each week with job-related injuries?"

She thought about it a fair while before telling me that there were probably about forty train operators and forty conductors there every week, "and half again as many who report the injury, but don't take any time off, because they can't afford to wait to receive the pay."

I reflected that, after I had been injured in February, I hadn't received my differential pay for that day until May.

I did a little fast figuring. That made 120 reported injuries a week. That meant each subway operative averaged one reported injury a year. It also meant a train operator or conductor had a better-than-even chance of losing time due to a job injury during any given year.

One day that spring, my motorman told me that they had started fixing the catwalks.

GREATNESS

When I had been forced to pick "the Beast," my greatest fear was that I'd get killed. My second greatest fear was that I wouldn't have any way of getting home after finishing work past midnight. But close after that, had been the fear of losing touch with the man nicknamed "the Great Goniea." So when Mark called me about a month into the pick and asked me over I was delighted. I was also annoyed by how delighted this made me.

When I told him how beautiful he looked, he responded with a Bronx cheer.

"You don't know how to take a compliment," I complained.

"I take it like a man!" and he laughed heartily at his own witticism.

He told me, "On a building I passed, I saw carved in stone, 'Knowledge Is Power.' But I think knowledge is a curse. The more you see and know, the more the world and people disappoint you, and the more you realize how little you know. It's a blessing to be stupid and self-satisfied. I met a woman in a bar who told me she wanted money, power, and recognition. I could hardly help laughing out loud."

"What do you want?"

"Happiness."

"Do you feel intelligence makes it harder to be happy?"

"Definitely."

We saw each other on and off for a month; then he went to the Caribbean on vacation. I waited eagerly for him to come home. He had been deliberately vague about his date of return, so I telephoned his home over and over again to see if he was back yet. All I got was his answering machine. Since I wasn't sure whether he would call back if I left a message, I didn't leave one.

When I finally reached him, he was very cold. He answered all my questions about his holiday in a manner that was at best civil. Finally, he burst out, "It's crazy, calling me over and over again and not leaving a message. You know I screen my calls."

"Maybe I don't want to be screened."

"We might as well hang up. I think we've said all we have to say to each other."

"No, I haven't. I feel like I've been set up! If I were sure you'd call me back, wouldn't I leave a message? But I have to sit here not knowing if you are home but don't want to speak to me, or not home. You say this is a casual relationship. If it were, we could just make calls, casually. You know it isn't casual."

"You don't have to take it."

"Take it? I'm screaming at you."

"You never have to speak to me again."

"You know I want to speak to you again. And I know you want to speak to me again—don't you?"

"Are you fishing?"

"Fishing? Hell, no. I know you like me. Sometimes you like me well enough."

"Okay," he suddenly sounded very tired, "it's alright. Or it's as alright as it ever has been."

Monday night, at the end of my week, I came home and found this message from Mark on my answering machine: "Damn straight I'll leave a message. Please do not call. Please do not call. Your crazy phone calls, where you hang up! Please, forget my phone number. Don't call me any more. Thank you."

I was shocked and indignant. I had not dialed his number once since our last, unpleasant talk. I cried myself to sleep. The next morning I called Mark and left a message on his machine, declaring my innocence and begging him to call me. I cried on the subway. I cried through my haircut. I cried in the restaurant eating dinner. I came home, left another message for Mark, and cried some more.

I left two more messages. Then I gave up.

I picked the next day. I got A.M.s on Broadway. Only seven more weeks on "the Beast." For a few days I was euphoric. Soon I settled down to my usual depression and obsession with Mark. Jasmin Joyce invited me over for dinner and tried to cheer me up, "He's going to call you. He thinks you're wild about him and would do anything to pick back there."

She bet me three dozen home-baked cookies that Mark would call me before the pick ended.

The pick ended.

I won the cookies.

I now was working at Van Cortlandt.

Joyce and I came up with the idea of my sending a book to Mark for his birthday. Joyce said, "He'll have to thank you. So he'll probably call."

He did call. It was the first time we had spoken in four months. After he had thanked me, he asked why I'd done it.

"Above and beyond the fact that I thought you'd enjoy it, I didn't want things between us to be hostile."

"I have a confession to make," he said, "I do find you attractive, physically and mentally. But you have such a dark and gloomy side to you. And that has such a profound effect on how I see my life that I'm quick to push it away. How can I say it? People are attracted to the flame's personality, but so are moths and vampires. Sometimes I get that queasy feeling that you are potentially damaging to me."

"All I'm asking for is friendship."

"I don't trust your motives."

"You big idiot! If you were here, I'd pull your hair!"

"If you pull my hair, we'd go to bed together."

"Oh, no, there's no way I'm going to bed with you!"

"Then how could you pull my hair?"

"I'd just climb up on a stepladder and pull it!"

I called Joyce to tell her she was right.

"Too bad we didn't bet on it," she observed. When I had recounted the conversation, she said, "He called you up with the idea of going to bed with you. That's what all that stuff about your motives was about."

"What a jerk I am. How come I didn't see it?"

"Well, you've had an offer."

Not long after that, I had to go up to Woodlawn terminal to post some leaflets. I checked the schedule and found Mark would be out on the road while I was there. But I was walking up the platform when a train, the first in almost an hour, finally came in. The motorman was Mark. As he went by me, he turned toward me, laughing. He was ordered to the yard for a put-in. I offered to come with him. As we walked, he said, "I'm still irritated with you. I agree we could be friends, but the sexual part enhances it." And he took my hand in his.

"Yes," I agreed, and he put his arm around me and I nestled comfortably under his immense shoulder as we walked. It felt good to press against his warm body.

At Christmas, Mark gave me a pair of gold earrings, elegant, dainty love knots. Joyce had boasted about how much her lover's gift to her had cost. Mark said, "You can gloat over your friend. These are worth a lot more than sixty dollars." Still, he refused to believe how much I loved them and kept reassuring me that I could exchange them.

But on New Year's Eve, he called me, "This time I truly am sorry. You are a very dangerous person, literally, to screw around with."

"What's wrong?"

"You know what's wrong!" he charged. "I have painful urination. It's your fault. It could be clap. It started right after I was with you. I had painful urination."

"Mark, I couldn't give you the clap in twelve hours."

"Stop being logical about my mad! Why is it that every time I go to bed with you, I have a problem? It's like our bodies are at war!" He got down to the punch line, "I don't think we should see each other tonight. We're both too angry at each other."

The new pick was posted, and the crews began picking jobs in order of seniority. It took weeks to reach a rookie like me, but my turn was getting closer. I was trying to decide whether to stay at Van Cortlandt or pick over to Woodlawn.

I got a call from "the Great One."

"I still have the clap, given to me by you," he greeted me, "although maybe it isn't the clap." He allowed it might be a urinary tract infection, or even a kidney stone, "but the lab lost my specimen. In any case, get a pencil and write down these numbers. Thursday and Friday, two-nineteen on the No. 4; Saturday two-thirteen on the No. 4—"

"What are those?" I interrupted him.

"Those are my jobs. And you are allowed to pick one and only one."

"Who are you to tell me what to pick? What if I pick all five?"

"I'll book sick for the whole pick! I'll quit!"

"How flattering to have such an effect on you. Actually, I'd been planning to pick a two-tripper on Thursday and Friday with Motorman Medgars and late jobs on Saturday and Sunday."

He gave a hurt little laugh, "How about that? You're not going to pick with me at all. How about that?"

"I can pick better jobs than you've got. Besides, you don't seem to want to work with me, 'allowing' me to pick one job with you!"

"Oh, no," he sounded crestfallen, "I think it would have been fun to work with you."

I picked with him on Thursdays and Fridays. Our first Thursday together, we met in the crew room. He greeted me, "Hello, Miss Swerdlow." I took this as sarcasm. We began our first trip "one behind," which meant that we were the last morning train going out to Utica. The crew on this interval was scheduled to "deadhead," that is, ride back to Woodlawn, instead of operating back in service.

I had a student, a former machinist from Long Island. I said to him, "You watch. When we get to Utica, the motorman is going to say that you were a faster conductor than me."

Sure enough, as the three of us were deadheading back to Woodlawn, Mark said to me, "Funny thing is, he's a better conductor than you are."

"You see that!" I cried to my student. "Say that again! Didn't I tell you?" To Mark, I snapped, "I told him you'd say that to me." I was hurt and furious.

The student conductor said, "Well, that's how me and my wife began. We used to fight all the time. Now we've been married nine years. Who knows? A year from now, you two might be married."

Not likely, I thought. But I got a kick out of the idea.

By the time we got up to the Bronx, we were more kindly disposed toward each other. I confessed to him that I'd been nervous about working with him. "Well, you knew I was going to give you a hard time," he said.

"Why do you have to give me a hard time?"

"It's my nature."

However, it was on the final trip uptown that Greatness shone its brightest. Our train was creeping up the East Side. Mark was doing an excellent job of keeping the riders informed through his P.A. announcements. He explained the delays and announced the resumption of West Side service. After one informative announcement, he felt compelled to continue, "And while I have your attention, riders, I have a few thoughts I would like to share with you. . . ."

I cringed.

"Since every other nut and religious kook gets on the trains to peddle their wares and to proselytize, I would like to say a few words to all those inconsiderate slobs who hog the seats and annoy their fellow riders by spreading their legs all over the seats. Please keep your knees together. No one wants to have your big sweaty legs leaning all over them. Thank you."

I was burning with embarrassment. Is there a clinical term for this kind of madness, I wondered. However, my student and the riders were smiling with amusement.

One day when we were southbound at Boro Hall, a man got on my train and asked me, "Who's that up front? I didn't get a good look. Is it the Great Goniea?"

I nearly died. "Yes, it's Goniea. But tell me, how did you know that's his nickname?"

"That what we all call him at Command Center. That's on good days. Other days, he's called 'Cryin' Goniea.' He puts everything on the radio. He'll put a burnt-out lightbulb on the air."

One day at Union Square, the riders swarmed over to my position, "There's a fire!"

"The bottom of the train is on fire!"

"It's smoking underneath the train!"

I peered out and I saw grids so overheated that their glow lit up the car body and the platform. This meant the motorman would have to cut out the motors on that car. So I got on the P.A. and told Mark.

Then I did my blasé act in front of the riders swarming on the platform. "Yeah, it's nothing. Ho-hum. *Yawn* How unutterably dull. The motorman will come back and fix it. How boring."

Mark appeared with his fuse puller. When I looked out of the cab, I saw the riders stuck like pigs in the closed doors, "Why didn't you tell us you were going to close them?" they reproached me.

"I didn't close them," I muttered, slipping back to my position. There was the Mad Motorman, enthusiastically ripping out fuses. To get into the panel, he'd had to hit the door control switch, which closed the doors.

We were moving again. However, the riders were still complaining about smoke. At 86th Street, I threw in the towel. I got on the P.A. and said, "Motorman, we still have twelve-two issuing from the sixth car!"

"Discharge!" cried the Great One.

"This train is going out of service due to a fire."

That got them off fast. After I cleared them out, I went up front to see my Great Motorman.

He was seething, "Never, never use that word with the riders. You don't want them to panic and get hurt. You're going to get your ass in a sling."

I said only, "I'm still pretty new. I still have a lot to learn." That mollified him.

"Utica fifty-five [our call letters], what's the number on that car with hot grids?" Command asked us.

We each took out our notepads. We had two different car numbers. I went back to check. "You were right," I told him on the P.A.

"I know that," came the amplified response, "I don't make mistakes." When I got back to the front, he lectured me, "That comes with experience. I once made a fool of myself. And I determined I would never do it again."

But I got the last laugh. We laid-up the train in the yard and cleared at Woodlawn. Then, on the train going home, Mark started cursing and growling.

"What's wrong?"

"I left my brake handle on the train when we laid it up." He got off at Moshulu, heading back to the yard.

Back in the winter of 1983, while I was working on "the Deuce," Mark had taken and passed the exam for dispatcher. He was going to go to supervision where, he frequently proclaimed, he was going to "run my stretch of railroad right."

I dreaded his departure from Woodlawn, but I had the sensation of sailing in a small boat headed inexorably toward Niagara Falls: there was nothing I could do to forestall the impending disaster. Each rumor about "moving the list," promoting more people, filled me with gloom and anxiety. Each hint that the list might be "killed," thus delaying further promotions, filled me with hope. Rumor and hint affected Mark in precisely the opposite fashion.

One Sunday, our last train was a real piece of garbage, an inferior variety of equipment known as "married pairs." Cab doors curled up like the top of a sardine can. Missing vision glass in my operating cab. And spotted wheels: wheels with flat spots that made the train thump along down the road.

When we got up to Woodlawn, the platform P.A. blared, "Goniea! Change ends and take it to the yard!"

"Get your stuff if you're coming with me," he barked in my direction, "I'm going home straight from the yard."

When I got to the south motor, Mark was trying to open his cab that had been wedged shut with a wad of postcards, which used to be attached to subway advertisements for trade schools and their ilk. Mark cursed and clawed at it with his keys, and went roaring off to tell the train dispatcher he needed an R.C.I., that is, a road car inspector, while I cowered in a corner. He returned and started swatting at the door with his brake handle. He had loosened it a bit by the time the R.C.I. arrived. The R.C.I. dislodged the wedge with his screwdriver. "It's a matter of the right tool," he said.

Goniea got into the cab. "The door lock is broken," he observed. "It was an employee who did it," to keep riders out while the train was being operated from the opposite end.

After we laid-up our train, Mark told me, "They're making people sign out now at the gate and I'd rather not. I know a different way out."

He led me through the shop. He was grumbling, "I don't know where they're going to put a wash here. It will tie up the lead. Unless they intend to wash them a car at a time."

"Maybe that's what they'll do."

"You really are a moron, aren't you?"

"Yes, I'm pretty stupid. Especially compared to you."

We were out of the shop and trudging along the narrow isthmus of track that connected the yard and the structure. Suddenly I lost my footing in the greasy ballast, the pebbles that cushion the tracks, and went down smack on my left side, landing against the panel protecting the third rail on my right.

"Are you okay?" exclaimed Goniea. He helped me up. We both looked at the insulating panel, without which I would have been cooked, literally.

"You're very lucky."

I was thoroughly shaken up, "Yeh, lucky."

"Sit down a minute. Take your time."

I sat.

"Are you hurt?"

"I don't think so."

"Do you want a cigarette?"

"You know I don't smoke."

"Maybe you should start."

"Maybe I should."

After a bit, we resumed our trek, out to the catwalk to the Bedford Park station, where we got the train.

"Everyone has these close calls," he assured me, "I've fallen on the structure, had a leg go through the structure. Once, I was running along the structure and fell, and my glasses dropped to the street and smashed." Aboard, he promised me he would not tease me about this for a couple of weeks, "Then, I'll be merciless."

One Saturday, at 167th Street, I couldn't open the storm door in my position. I tugged, tugged, and finally kicked. No use. A gallant male rider came to my assistance, and he had no luck either.

Over the P.A., I said, "Motorman, the storm door in my position is stuck shut."

"Uh-huh," T.G.O. responded over the P.A., in a tone that had the ridership in stitches, "Okay, I'm coming back there." And at length, he appeared, striding down the platform, a sight to remember. He was wearing a black tee shirt and jeans, and a blue baseball cap with an M.T.A. "M" on it. His shoe slipper was on his shoulder. To me, he looked like Paul Bunyan, my hero, come to save the day.

Coolly, he moved the door catch at the top of the door. What was high above my head was shoulder level for him. Soon he'd worked it loose. As I fastened it open, he growled, "If anyone says anything you don't like, get a cop and have 'em thrown off the train." The King of the Road. No one said anything.

We had plenty of time between our trips. One afternoon, Goniea took all the empty soda cans he had been storing out of his locker. He stacked them on the table, building three tall pillars. After he had used all of them, I tapped lightly on one and knocked them all over. The noise turned every head in the crew room, and all joined me in hearty laughter.

Mark's face looked as tense as a thunderhead. He picked up my grey bag and turned it upside down on the floor. Still laughing, I began to pick up my things.

He restacked his cans and picked them up to take them downstairs to get refunded. "If you had waited a minute," he growled at me, "I might have done it myself."

Another day, I had kids close to my operating position who were blowing dope. Mark got the cops for me and announced over the P.A., "Attention, riders: If we have problems, we are prepared to wait for a cop at every station. So, be cool." It was nice to know he would protect me.

Mark would drive fast, and then at the station say to me, "Stop a minute or two here." Crews didn't like to run ahead of schedule, for fear our running times would be cut, and we would have more work.

"Why can't you just go a bit more slowly?"

"The urge to wrap it around is just too great," he answered.

He developed the conceit that I resembled the moon as depicted in an animated cartoon, with a face that beams a big benign grin as it rises above the horizon. If I smiled, he would say, "Oh, the moon has come out." Then he would insult my (two-hundred-dollar-an-ounce Guerlain) perfume, "Skunk essence!"

He was proud of his ability to operate almost any piece of junk and get it out to Brooklyn or back. One day out in Brooklyn, the motorman who had just driven the train we were about to take told Mark, "I don't want you to start complaining how I brought you a bad train. This train's got bad brakes on the north end. Riggs brought it up. He called for an R.C.I. who rode him and told him it wasn't too bad, and to tell the dispatcher when he gets to the terminal. He told the dispatcher, but the dispatcher says I have to use it. I don't have another train. It's not so bad going south, just a little slow. You can take it out of service."

I said, "Don't take it out in Brooklyn. They'll send us to New Lots to lay it up."

At the mention of Riggs the Radical, Mark's lower lip had protruded just a fraction of an inch. After Lock was gone, I asked him what he planned to do.

"I'll see. Candy asses!"

We went all the way in service. At the terminal, Mark told me, "It's 40 percent skill, 50 percent concentration, and 10 percent luck."

Trains were not the only thing he could get to work. Once the crew room toilet was running without stopping. Mark opened the door of the shallow closet that housed the pipes. He took his brake handle and began hammering on one of them. The flushing subsided and eventually stopped.

One morning, we had starting lights, but our train was not charged. No Mark. And still no Mark. And still. At last, I saw him pop aboard. I asked him over the intercom, "What was wrong back at the terminal?"

"I was trying to get a radio key."

He had left his key home.

"Boy, if your head weren't attached to your body, you'd forget it, wouldn't you?"

Very upset, he cried, "I don't need annoying today!"

By the time we got to Atlantic, he was in high spirits. He brandished a piece of string that looked as if it had been used in a child's game of cat's cradle. He explained it was a device for getting a radio out of the R-62 bracket without using a key. "The Great Goniea strikes again!" he crowed.

I said, "I'm glad you're in better humor."

"Who says I am?" he thundered. But he was clearly very pleased with himself. He opened a package of coffin nails and dropped the cellophane pull tab into my lap as though it were a litter basket. In response, I unzipped his fly. If I'd intended to annoy him, I'd miscalculated. "Don't stop there! Keep going!" he growled. I had just finished eating a peach, so I slipped the pit into his open fly. "Oooh!" he bellowed, "you piece of shit!" He fished it out and dropped it down my shirt. The he wiped his hands on my shirt, making noises of disgust.

Yet in some ways, he was terribly soft. Once, while removing a piece of wood debris from the roadbed, he got a splinter in his finger. He was in too much pain to operate, and two motor instructors had to come, one to operate the train and the other to take him to a hospital emergency room.

One evening around eight, I got a phone call from T.G.O., "I want to read you something.

On Tuesday, July 24, I was working the 211 job at Pelham Bay. On my last trip, at approximately 4:30 p.m., at 125th Street, I was rerouted as a local and was ordered by Command Center and by the train dispatcher to make all stops to Pelham Bay. I arrived at Pelham Bay three minutes late.

At St. Lawrence Avenue, a male Hispanic opened my cab door, thrust a pass and badge in front of my face and said, "I am Superintendent Gutierrez. Why is this train going so slowly?" I replied that there were slow-speed orders, that we were going over switches, and the train was a bit slow. He said, "Well, I think you are dogging it and I am going to have you ridden and watched."

I said, "Do as you please. But now kindly close the door so that I can work. You are not a motor instructor, train dispatcher, assistant train dispatcher, so please close the door to four inches, or I will call Command Center." At this, he began to yell at me and told me I was out of service. I called Command Center twice to report this.

That was as far as he had gotten. The rest he told me. When he arrived at Pelham Bay, the train dispatcher took him out of service, and he was ordered to report to the Chief Trainmaster's Office at 9:00 A.M. the next morning.

I was very affected by the way he had taken a stand and refused to grovel. He's a real man, I thought, knows what he's doing, and stands his ground. That's part of what makes him great and why I love him. I felt I couldn't say that, though. I only said, "You're perfectly right, but you're in trouble anyway."

"Because I didn't kiss ass."

"Yeah, because you stood up for your rights."

"I'm thinking of finishing the G-2 like this: 'I charge Superintendent Gutierrez with violations of the following rules. . . .' I could go down swinging."

"Sure, you could. Or you could be apologetic and just lose a day's pay. If you stand up for your rights, you'll get deeper into trouble. If you act contrite, you'll add to your store of impotent rage. You're not going to get off scot-free, even if you are completely right, because this guy has it in for you and he's going to make sure you get into some kind of trouble for showing you know you're as good as he is. Trainmaster Booth doesn't care. You didn't delay service or make T.A. vulnerable to a lawsuit, which is all he really cares about. But he's got to give you something."

"I know everything you are saying," said Mark, "Still, it's reassuring to hear it."

The next day, he told me, "I got thirty days' suspension." He jerked me around a bit more, then admitted, "I'm joking."

What had really happened was that Booth had called it a "personality conflict" and decided that Mark had not in fact broken any rules. Nevertheless, Booth would have to give him a "rap on the knuckles," because Gutierrez was his superior. So he gave Mark a caution, ostensibly for "failure to report a slow train immediately."

"My first caution!" he wailed, then boasted that he'd made their day in the Crew Dispatcher's Office by reciting his saga.

Mark definitely had problems relating to women as human beings. He upset me one Sunday by commenting as he paged through the *Times* fashion section, "No tits. . . . Ah, this one has knockers. . . ."

I said at last, "You know what I should get you for your next birthday?"

"Fifteen minutes with a prostitute?"

"Yeah, that's all you'd need anyway. In fact, you wouldn't know what to do with the last twelve."

Lock and Dabney were listening, half-amused, half-shocked.

Goniea fired back, "That's right. Who needs more than three? I belong to the 4-F club. You know the 4-F club?" He turned to Lock and Dabney, "find 'em, feel 'em, fuck 'em, forget 'em. C'mon, all men belong to that club." Lock and Dabney were silent, their amusement giving way to embarrassment as Goniea implicated them.

I burst out, "They're embarrassed. I've never seen transit workers embarrassed before. No, they aren't embarrassed," I turned on Mark, "they're just more sensitive to the feelings of others than you are."

Dabney let out a gasp. Goniea only laughed.

Dabney decided it was time to tell a story. "There was this lady and she looked, you know, good. And she was passing by these dudes and they all say, 'looking good,' 'alright,' you know, that sort of stuff. And then she comes along to another bunch and they are all ready to—you know—the same thing. But then she starts saying, like to herself, 'Looking good, I'm looking alright.' Well, they stopped, you know?"

In the crew room at Utica, Mark was showing off his misery, complaining that all he ate for dinner was peanut butter and jelly sandwiches.

"That's how you get fat," Motorman Shaw reproached him.

"Any time you want a good meal, I'll take you out for one," I offered Mark.

"Yeah, and you'll pay for it," said Shaw to Goniea.

"No," I said, "I'll pay for it."

"You ought to get married," Shaw advised Mark. "Family is the essence of life."

Mark turned away, "It's hard to find one who isn't crazy who will have me."

One day we got such a wreck of a train that even Mark gave up and called an R.C.I., who found four dead motors and took the train out of passenger service. Without the weight of the riders and the necessity of stopping and starting at each station, we did okay, until they stopped us to switch us onto the middle track. Mark couldn't get it moving again. Mark had to go back and throw a reverser. Then, we were just able to inch along the middle track, until we turned a curve north of Fordham and saw a train standing on the middle track.

"If it's a lay-up, we'll be stuck here all night."

But it was no lay-up. Soon enough, we heard its motorman calling the 205th Street tower. "It's getting toward my clearing time," he said plaintively.

Mark chimed in, "Two-oh-fifth Street tower, this is your second in place. The sun is setting. Will I be here when it is rising?"

Over the radio came an anonymous transmission, "Cock-a-doodle-doo!"

A long wait ensued. We waved to passing trains. We talked about the trees in the park beneath us. Mark tried to teach me how to imitate the call of the mourning dove. He radioed the tower from time to time. They ignored him.

He got restless and decided to call the desk trainmaster at Command Center from the token booth at the Kingsbridge Road station. He descended. When he came back, he had three "Big Macs" and diet Cokes with him. "I found out what's holding us up. There's a problem in the yard. But we should be moving soon."

Two hours later, our leader did move. But we still had the signal against us. And the tower vouchsafed not a word. By 7:30 Mark had run out of cigarettes and resorted to his pipe. "They're punishing me because they think I take too many trains out of service," he fretted. He radioed a northbound motorman, "Tell Harry it's not my fault!" (Harry was the Woodlawn A.T.D., Harrison.) "The R.C.I. did it!"

"That's who usually does it," was the response.

The lights were going on in surrounding apartment buildings. Mark was calculating how much T.A. was wasting on overtime for the two of us. At last, he decided to take another hike to call the trainmaster. He came back to tell me the trainmaster had been surprised, "You're still at Kingsbridge!"

Around 7:45, the signal changed to green over green. Big "G" released the brake in an instant and wrapped it around. As we lurched forward, the tower broke three hours of silence, "Okay, you've been talking on the radio so much, you can move now."

"Look at your board," Mark snapped back, "I am moving."

We cleared two-and-a-half hours late. I calculated I had netted about twenty-five dollars. Uncle Sam made out the best.

Sunday, I was waiting for the train at Fordham. When my train came, Greatness was aboard, reading the Sunday *Times*. I smiled. He sneered. I extended my hand to touch him. He recoiled. All typical.

"How are you?"

"Crabby."

Oh, Lord, I thought, "how come?"

"I haven't had a cigarette in twenty-four hours. I've stopped smoking."

"Why are you doing that?"

"I just don't enjoy it anymore."

"Well, I hope you'll be civil to me."

"You're very supportive."

I saw the Woodlawn porter. He told me about a lovers' quarrel that he had just witnessed. The man had threatened the woman with a knife. Then, the woman had threatened the man with a knife. At the end, they went up to the platform hand-in-hand. "And they paid their fare!" he concluded incredulously, "she tries to kill him, and then they pay their fare!"

"She was only angry," I said, feeling I could identify with her.

"That's some way to be angry."

When we arrived in the crew room, I made coffee for Mark and tea for me. I brought the cups over to the table and was on my way to the fridge to get the milk when he griped, "Where's the milk?" Before I could respond, he said, "See this ad? They'll give me a car for free to drive to Florida for ten days, because they need people to deliver cars down there."

"But I asked if we could spend our vacation together—" I protested.

"All you need is a driver's license and a valid credit card, which I have. . . ."

"You're going to see that Cherry down there! The one who scammed you for five hundred dollars!"

Mark had a habit of falling in love during each vacation trip he took. On his previous holiday in Florida, he had been smitten with Cherry. She told him she lived with her mother and so he had to take her to a motel. In the morning, she claimed her five hundred dollar paycheck had been stolen, but she couldn't go to the police because her mother would find out where she'd been. So Mark gave her five hundred dollars.

"This means going down to Florida will only cost me two hundred dollars, as long as they have a car on the date I want!" He was delighted—and oblivious to my disappointment and jealousy.

"Give my regards to Cherry!" I snapped, and on the last word, I kicked him in the shin.

"You bitch! You can take your croissant and shove it up your ass! Get away from me!"

No matter how much I cried and apologized, he refused to speak to me. I went down to the mezzanine and brooded. I felt totally hopeless. I felt as if I had no goals, no connections, and no future. I couldn't bear the thought of getting through the rest of the day, let alone a future, this desolate.

I shuffled back to the crew room. Somehow, a bird had gotten inside. It was one of the multitude of starlings that made Woodlawn their home. I loved these birds for their whimsical speckles and their awkward, bobbing strut. They would hop in and out of the open train doors, like cheeky riders, and somehow never get stuck inside when the doors closed. Maybe they'd learned to understand the conductors', "Watch the closing doors." Maybe they'd learned to recognize the starting lights. But one had somehow blundered into the crew room. Now it was flying back and forth, over the last row of lockers near the washroom and the table with the hot plate.

"That starling can't get out," Mark said to me. I was surprised he was civil.

He opened up a window, but the bird was flying above the windows. No wonder. The crew room cat, its grey eyes wide, was carefully following its every move. First, Mark led the cat outside, but she followed him right back inside. So he put her in the washroom and closed the door. I suggested we put some bread by the open window. "Get me some bread," said Mark. I brought some, and Mark reached up and laid it on the window sill. A few moments later, without touching the bread, the bird took off through the window.

Mark didn't speak to me the rest of the day, and I did not try to apologize again. On my days off, I intensified my efforts. I gave him flowers. I felt neither loving nor apologetic as I trudged, thirsty and feet aching, to his building to leave the box of roses with his doorman.

That afternoon, my phone rang, "Why only six?" asked a Great voice. "I accept your apology. I *was* looking forward to never speaking to you again, but this was quite a clever move on your part. I had the cold shoulder ready for you, but now instead I've got a hot bod."

"Two-twenty-one? It's you and me today," the motorman said told as I walked into the dispatcher's shack.

"I guess my regular motorman's sick," I said, "he didn't feel well on Sunday."

The dispatcher, Stein, who didn't like Mark, said, "No, he's gone to train dispatcher. He had the physical Wednesday. This is my dream come true. I only hope he gets a motorman who's like him."

The radioman leaned toward me, "If you were mine, I'd put you in a glass cage."

"I wouldn't stay in a glass cage," I said, but my thoughts were elsewhere. Dazed, I staggered back to the crew room and telephoned him, "Congratulations," I said.

The quarter dropped. "Don't spend any more money," he said, "I'll try to catch your train when I come up to get my paycheck."

Up at Woodlawn, there was an immense figure in tan slacks and an orange parka on the platform. We sat down on a bench on the platform and talked a few minutes. I was growing maudlin, which increased his discomfort, "It's a big loss for me," I said, "I'll miss you so much."

"I enjoyed working with you. I enjoyed the feeling I was getting away with something, on the job and in the relationship."

"Will you still talk to me when you're a train dispatcher?'

"No. You know I told you that. Isn't that a woodpecker in that tree?"

"No, it's a blue jay. I mean, seriously, seriously."

"I have ethical problems about having a relationship with . . . ," he searched for the right word, "an underling."

"You're kidding! I mean, you're teasing, aren't you?"

"Look, forget I said anything."

"Forget it? How can I forget it?"

"Forget what I said. But you have to stop clawing at me all the time. We have to be more discreet."

"You're the one who's always starting with me!"

"That's true," he admitted.

Sunday morning, I didn't even have the heart to walk up to Jerome Avenue, as I usually did. All my Sunday routines reminded me too painfully of Mark. Sunday had been my favorite day at Woodlawn. A long w.a.a., having coffee and croissants with Mark over the Sunday *Times*. I didn't remember the days he wouldn't speak to me or was too sick to do anything but sleep, or the days he was fixing the lock on his locker or watching Lock and Dabney play chess.

I asked the dispatcher, "When train dispatchers first comes out, do they work extra-extra?"

"When we first come out, yes, we get sent anywhere and everywhere. Then, they usually give you an empty job as your regular job—a 'hold-down.'" He started telling me about his personal career, but after a polite interval, I interrupted.

"What's a low-seniority job for a train dispatcher?"

"The first job you're likely to get is a 'pull' job. You report somewhere and if they need you someplace they 'pull' you there."

"Like our board jobs. Which have more seniority, gap stations or terminals?"

"Oh, the gap stations. But that's changing. Some people always liked terminals—they're where the action is, gaps are pretty dull. But now they're trying to build the r.d.o.s into the jobs. They're going to make the big terminals like Woodlawn and White Plains Saturday–Sunday r.d.o.s, to attract the experienced people, the old-timers."

"Goniea thinks he'll be working up here at Woodlawn terminal soon."

Stein snorted, "Never get up here. Even I'm going to be picked out when they make it Saturday–Sunday R.D.O.S.

"What's bothering you?" Motorman Shaw asked me.

"Goniea seems to have gotten a swelled head," I said. "He says he can't go out with me now that he's a train dispatcher."

"You've got to be kidding! I guess he's going to dissociate himself from all of us common people."

Conductor Lowell Dabney was sympathetic, "Uh-uh, swelled head? Ah, he don't mean it. Women take stuff so serious! My wife, she's like that. He's puttin' in like 20 percent, and you're takin' it like 90 percent. He's gonna find it's a lonely life. In a couple of weeks, he'll be real glad to get a call from you."

HELL ON WHEELS

The leadership of the Transport Workers Union Local 100 treated its members with contempt. The big shots cast the workers' problems as gripes and whining. Even deaths on the job were regarded as annoyances, products of the members' stupidity that inconvenienced busy union officials.

Union meetings were an exercise in futility and masochism. If you asked the officers to back you up, which presumably was what they were being paid to do, they would suddenly decide that "you are the union."

After the accidental death of Conductor Rogers, some conductors were complaining about being ordered to work on unsafe trains. Union officials replied that they should certainly refuse such orders. Dave Stone asked that successful refusals be publicized in the union newspaper, so people would know about it.

This enraged the officers. Each told how he had stood up for himself, all alone, stuck his neck out totally as an individual, without any encouragement or solidarity from union or workmates, and advocated the same for us. Strange testimonials from trade unionists. "You are the union," one said, "you are out there by yourself. If you are right, the union will back you up. But no one's going to tell you what to do."

At last Dave got the floor again. "I don't think I've made myself clear. I'm not asking for the union to hold our hands. I'm just asking that the information get out there."

Another rank-and-file conductor supported Dave, pleading that the union give the members "communication." He also got the business.

Organizers would scold us, humiliate us, make fun of our ignorance, "You fellers screw yourselves because you don't know the rulebook." Of course, the information wasn't in the rulebook. It wasn't in the contract, and we didn't have copies of the contract, anyway.

I hated these meetings because they were so frustrating. I would sit and stew, literally grinding my teeth, as the other members and I were insulted. I believed the officers deliberately abused the members at meetings, so workers would not come to them. But in order to run for many union offices, you had to attend a certain number of these meetings. By discouraging people from attending, the officers were whittling down the number of potential candidates.

My role as union shop steward was extremely frustrating, too, because I simply had no idea of what the T.A. could and could not tell us to do. The contract said virtually nothing about our working conditions. It had little to offer about any limits on what management could do to us or about our rights. The rulebook was basically an operating manual.

Once Motorman Crosby came into the crew room, exclaiming, "Stein just took me out of service! It was an hour before my clear. Stein wanted to send me down the road. I booked sick. He took me out of service."

I said, "He should have given you the option of going to the clinic."

Crosby's face showed he didn't think much of that idea either. "Have you got the union's phone number?" he asked me, and got into the booth.

I turned to Mark, "Can Stein do that? I mean, doesn't he have to offer him the choice of going to the clinic or to a hospital? That's what happened to me."

Mark said, "A supervisor has the right to take you out of service for anything. Of course, it's his ass later."

Crosby came out of the phone booth. Organizer Washington had told him to call the crew dispatcher himself, book sick, and get doctor's lines.

Afterward, I wondered if, as shop steward, I should have gone up to Stein. And said—what? That was the problem. Nothing covered this in the rulebook. I had no idea of our rights, and no idea how to find out.

The little I knew was based on my personal experience. I felt I was a very inadequate steward. It seemed as if the T.A. had almost complete freedom to order us to do anything and to penalize us, in any manner, for anything it chose. The rules applied to us. Not to them.

At one union meeting, one of the organizers complained that I had told a member, who had been ordered to take a urine test, to call an organizer. "A shop steward should know how to handle that situation."

I asked, "How should a steward handle that situation?"

The organizer answered, with great amazement at my ignorance, "Why the man has to go for the test!"

My handling certainly hadn't hurt the member any. Only some organizer got disturbed at home!

"Ninety percent of the problem," he concluded, "is that the guys don't know their rights."

I was boiling. Blaming us again. Ninety percent of the problem is that the guys don't *have* any rights, I thought. What were my rights with the eye exam? Joyce's with the supplement? "The man's got to go."

"It's not written down anyplace. You just have to know the procedure."

Well, if the procedures aren't written down anywhere, how are the guys supposed to know their rights?

Organizers are appointed by the president of the local. The president is elected by the entire local, of which the subway workers make up only about a fifth. They don't have much to say about who chooses their organizers.

The subway workers choose their own divisional officers. "Turn Around" Torrelli was elected by the "A" Division conductors, so he had to be responsive to them. This forced him into a perpetual balancing act. He had to please the members enough to get reelected, yet like almost every divisional officer, he hoped to be "made" an organizer. So he tried not to ruffle the feathers of organizers or local officers. That made Vinnie Torrelli a little inconsistent in his views and actions, to say the least.

At election time, "Turn Around" Torrelli's leaflets were all over the crew room. They carried his picture and a fifteen-point program. Most of the "planks" were complete pie-in-the-sky things, like "air-conditioned crew rooms with showers," "cost of living clause in the union contract," and "elimination of the three-tier pension." The desirability of these things was beyond dispute. It was nice to know Vinnie thought these would be good to have, too. How voting for him would bring these things one iota closer to existing was the big imponderable.

Arnold Cherry had been the standard bearer for the most popular opposition slate in 1979. Three opposition candidates had run against Lawe in that election. Added together, they won 57 percent of the vote. Cherry alone won 26 percent. He believed the two other candidates had cheated him out of winning, and the fluke would not be repeated in 1981. His two rivals for the opposition vote were soon out of the way: MacDonald sold out to take a union staff job; Lewis was framed and fired. Cherry felt pretty confident about winning in 1981.

In 1981, however, the opposition vote shrank to 43 percent. And even that percentage was not for Cherry alone: a candidate from the buses took 17 percent. Cherry emerged with exactly the same share as in 1979, 26 percent. Demoralized by the strike defeat of 1980, fewer transit workers had voted. Even the number of votes Cherry received shrank from 6,019 to 5,439.

Cherry issued a statement, "Where I Stand," to explain why he was sitting out the 1983 race. He cited the large proportion of the rank and file who could not vote because they had lost "good standing" for failing to pay the full amount of union dues during the suspension of the dues checkoff. He also cited the "long five-year struggle against the Lawe bureaucracy, which has taken its toll on Local 100 activists."

All this was admirable in its realism. Less admirably and less realistically, however, he scapegoated the Spartacist League's Committee for a Fighting T.W.U. as "spoilers" for running in 1981 and for their intention to run again in 1983. This was unfounded red-baiting. In 1981, the Sparts had gotten 127 votes, less than 1 percent, hardly enough to qualify them as "spoilers." In addition, Cherry condemned the opposition slates that had run against him in the past for refusing to form a common slate with him this time.

Cherry called upon transit workers to denounce not only the Sparts but what he described as "*all 'outside' political groups*, whether on the left or far right. For attempting to use transit workers for their own political or ideological causes." (The emphasis and the grammar are in the original.)

Oddly enough, as long as it was the right, and not the "far" right, Cherry didn't seem to mind, while the left, even if it wasn't the "far" left, was denounced. This show of evenhandedness was quite empty, since no far-rightwing group showed the least interest in winning leadership of Local 100, and the right already had it.

On the other hand, regarding the union leadership, Cherry was careful to limit his fire to Lawe himself and "the same old candidate running with Lawe," the singular candidate probably being Recording Secretary Paul Caizzo. Cherry seemingly wanted to leave the door open for future alliances from within the Lawe slate by mentioning that "a substantial number of

Lawe's team privately" have doubts about his policies. "It's too bad they're not willing to stand up," was the closest Cherry came to criticizing Lawe's hypocritical cronies.

Cherry was thereby being much tougher on left dissidents than on ambivalent labor bureaucrats. My sense was that Cherry was trying to distance himself from the left. I thought he still had hopes of winning the presidency, but had decided that his left image was costing him the votes he needed to win.

The 1983 local elections finished off the "old opposition." Not that I'd cherished any hopes for them. I didn't even believe that those among them who held office were making any difference. Still, when the Lawe slate swept all the Executive Board positions, and all but two or three of the old dissidents bit the dust, I couldn't help feeling discouraged. The same old unreliable equipment and hostile riders ate into me a little more deeply. I felt angry at the incompetence of these self-styled leaders. They had completely failed to convince the rank and file that they were preferable to the bureaucrats.

Track and power was the only division of the union that had elected an opposition slate to its offices. There were a lot of problems in that division with the way overtime work was given out. The officers organized the track workers to boycott all overtime for one weekend in protest. They wrote and distributed a leaflet explaining the contract language on overtime and what the workers' rights were.

The boycott was a success.

The T.A. retaliated. It gave each of the divisional officers a thirty-day suspension, charging them with "distributing unauthorized literature." T.A. took away their released time for union duties and put them back in work gangs, pending their hearings on their suspensions. The union, rather than fighting the T.A.'s action, went along with it. It amounted to the employer ousting union officers. The union designated a group of Lawe supporters to take over the duties of the suspended officers.

I had come onto the job with the intention of working with the old opposition. I knew it had weaknesses, but I believed it could be reformed from within. My experiences on the job soon changed my mind about that. But I wasn't totally isolated: I had one person to work with, Dave Stone.

Dave and I had lunch together after union meetings, a custom we'd started when we first met. We shared many ideas and reactions, but I saw he had thought them through further, could express them better, and drew far more convincing and confident conclusions. His inexpressive demeanor, however, often inspired in me the fear that I was boring him.

When we discussed the upcoming 1983 union elections, I told him I didn't know whether I could avoid carrying nominating petitions for "Turn Around" Torrelli or the "Lawe slate." We agreed I'd be a lot better off in the eyes of our coworkers if I didn't identify myself with the union leadership.

I felt moved to tell him that I really valued our talks, that I got feedback and support from him I found no place else. He said, "After your probation is over, you'll probably be working more closely with the u.m.c.t.," the United Motorman Conductor Tower, the opposition group in the subways formed before the strike, "if your probation is the reason you haven't done so up to now."

"I don't think that would help me much. I mean, u.m.c.t. is better than John Lawe. But only a bit more benevolently paternalistic. They either won't or can't envision a really open, democratic, militant union. It's not just a question of putting good people in office. Vinnie's been saying to me that he'll put me on a slate in the election in two years. But if he and Lawe put me on a ticket, and I win office, how will I be in any better position to change the union than I am now?"

Dave said, "I think you're absolutely right," and he seemed hugely pleased.

I was delighted he agreed, for I had grown to respect his judgment. His thinking was free of the ideological "should-bes" and "have-to-bes" that interfered with the ability of most leftists I'd known to see reality. He apparently wanted to strengthen and mobilize the rank and file. My ambitions were replaced by an intuitive trust in Dave's vision, a vision I was still far from seeing fully or understanding, of a different kind of union organizing.

"What keeps you going?" I asked Dave at one of our lunches. He smiled and shook his head. The question made no sense to him. "It doesn't even seem as if there's anything to do. I keep feeling there's something I should be doing."

"I don't think there's anything you can do. Activists rarely make the issues. You have to wait . . . until something flares up. Of course, it dies down again. But the next time, things are easier. Some activists have gotten to know each other, contacts are made, lessons are learned. Some kind of ongoing organization is left behind. Some people go into motion sooner than others do. You can't suck a movement out of your thumb, but you can work with people who are earlier in moving."

So when the red-tag zone crisis flared, we organized with the petition for a special union meeting. And it did die down again. But Dave did not merely wait until things "flared up." Ultimately, as he had told me the first time we'd met, he dreamed of issuing a newsletter. Meanwhile, he constantly tried to find a project that would bring together a core of activists, the people who are earlier in moving, as he would define them.

One project was to get some of our coworkers, particularly his contacts in the track department, to do something together about the health and safety issue of noise. When this did not pan out, he thought of setting up a committee against the fare hike. We called together a meeting of the old opposition and our own contacts. Around ten people showed. After some discussion, we agreed to form an ad hoc committee to issue a leaflet signed by as many activists as possible. But this foundered on the shoals of one statement it contained: "We cannot rely on politicians to substitute for our organized strength." The old opposition found that veiled criticism of the Democratic Party objectionable.

My activities led "Turn Around" Torrelli to seek me out, "Marian, you know you aren't going to be a steward much longer. You've been the cause of a lot of aggravation."

I laughed, "You flatter me."

"Marian, do you want to stay a steward?"

"Not if it means being a flunky, but if it gives me a chance to serve the membership, I very much want to be a steward."

I told the folks in the crew room what Vinnie had told me. About a dozen wrote G-2's supporting me as their shop steward.

I told Dave about Vinnie's warning. He shrugged, "There's not much you can do."

"I could show I have some support."

"Just how much support do you think you really have?"

I was stung by this. "I seem to have some."

"With the small amount of support you have, I don't see the point."

I was terribly hurt, but kept trying to argue my view rationally, "Sometimes people do become interested in an abstract issue through a concrete case."

"It would be a very small circle of people."

This pushed me close to tears, "If I have so little support, why should I speak to Lawson," the union vice president, "at all?!"

Perhaps it dawned on him he was hurting my feelings. Dave was not unkind, only insensitive. "It's not a reflection on you, Marian."

It was too late. "I'm not stupid, you don't have to tell me that!" I sniveled. I felt very let down by his lack of support. His objectivity contributed to the political acuity I so admired in him, yet it was a different matter altogether when he directed that detachment toward things I felt personally.

At the next union meeting, I spoke. "I've been hearing a rumor that I'm not going to be reappointed as shop steward. People have been coming up to me and saying that and they're very upset and concerned and they've been talking about getting a petition together and writing letters. I want to be able to tell them that it's just another stupid crew room rumor, that they can stop worrying. So I'd like to ask Mr. Lawson," I looked directly at him, and he looked down, "whether I'm getting my credentials renewed, and if not, why not? I've been given all these letters from people who think I've done a fine job." Then I read part of Mark's letter, saying that I had "elevated the image of the union." When I finished, there was silence.

At last, Lawson said they hadn't decided yet about my credentials and that they were reviewing the credentials of all the stewards, not only mine. He promised that anyone denied renewal would be invited down and given an explanation.

About a month after that, I got my renewed credentials in the mail.

After our anti–fare hike initiative faltered, Dave and I met to discuss our next move. He proposed some sort of series of classes on occupational safety and health. I saw this initiative as a way to reach out to new conductors and motormen we'd met who could become the activists of the future. Dave's conception was different. He wanted to draw in people who were already activists, like his pet track workers and assorted "generic Trots." I agreed to try it his way.

In the meantime, I started going to classes held by NYCOSH, the New York Committee on Occupational Safety and Health. Each class was taught by a different specialist. The first one I attended was about noise. I had assumed that noise caused hearing loss and that was all. I learned noise also caused muscle constriction, resulting in tension, irritability, headache, and digestive problems. It also made blood vessels constrict, thus contributing to hypertension and heart attacks.

Another class session dealt with dust. I learned that, despite the fact that steel dust is merely a "nuisance dust," prolonged exposure can still damage the lungs and reduce their capacity. Reduced lung capacity, in turn, forces the heart to work harder to deliver the same amount of oxygen to the cells of the body. The instructor said he believed that all subway workers should have periodic lung-function tests. It was now becoming much clearer to me why so many guys on the job had suffered heart attacks.

When the instructor said the next class would discuss radiation, I commented, "I guess I won't need that one until they get nuclear-powered trains."

She asked, "What voltage do you work with?" When I told her, she mentioned electromagnetic fields and nonionizing radiation. "But it's hard to find anyone who knows much about that yet."

But the health and safety course Dave and I put together did not achieve our goals for it. Dave and I began to discuss our next foray into rank-and-file organizing. Perhaps something about the referendum on binding arbitration planned by the union.

The union leadership was planning to hold a membership referendum, to get the members' approval for the union's support of a state law that would give the union the power to seek binding arbitration of the union contract. Union leaders wanted binding arbitration because, in 1984, the union was still quite weak after the debacle of the 1980 strike. The leadership was afraid the next contract was going to be terrible. If it was too bad, they didn't want responsibility for it. Even more, they wanted to avoid the members voting on it—and voting it down—because the union policy of "no contract, no work," still in effect, had contributed to the 1980 walkout.

A few days later, I woke up to find this recorded message from Dave: "We're in trouble. The referendum is going to be held next month. The choice will be whether we will seek binding arbitration or leave ourselves at the mercy of the Taylor Law." We got together to discuss our prospects and decided to draft a leaflet and organize a meeting of the "usual suspects" of our contacts and the old opposition.

By the time the meeting took place, it was actually too late to do much about the binding arbitration referendum, "which just points up the need for the opposition to get organized," said Dave as he opened the meeting. He raised his proposal for a newsletter. Everyone liked it, and a committee was set up to work on it.

The union leaders were clever in writing the ballot on binding arbitration. The choice was:

_____ I favor legislation similar to the 1982 law, which gave the
Union the right to require arbitration

or

_____ I oppose arbitration and choose to remain under the Taylor
Law.

The last two words, "Taylor Law," were anathema to transit workers. For them the Taylor Law was synonymous with its provision for a "two-for-one penalty," under which they were individually fined two days pay for each of the eleven days of the 1980 strike. Would they "choose to remain under the Taylor Law"? Hell, no!

The outcome was that 80 percent of the members who voted favored the legislation.

Riggs the Radical asked me how the vote on binding arbitration had gone. "Four to one for binding arbitration. It's a real defeat," I said. He was silent. His group had called for burning the ballots. So I guessed he didn't see it as a defeat.

By summer, there was a small group of us still meeting on the newsletter project, Dave's pet track workers, a couple of people from cars and shops, and a new conductor named Ron. Other folks from various divisions of the union floated in and out. The old oppositionists had long since disappeared from our meetings.

We considered holding a forum on the presidential election and a proposal to march as a contingent in the Labor Day Parade, but we didn't have enough agreement among ourselves to pursue either. In the end, the only thing we could agree upon was the newsletter. We were even divided on a name for it. The two from cars and shops wanted *Transit Worker Solidarity Committee*; other suggestions were *The Rising Tide* and *Hell on Wheels*.

The last was favored, although someone cautioned, "Some of our religious members might not like it."

"How 'bout *Purgatory on Wheels*?" quipped Dave.

"*Limbo on Wheels*," said someone.

"I've never met transit workers so religious they never said 'hell,' even the 'reverends,'" I said.

Hell on Wheels was chosen as the best of the offerings.

REJECTION

Ivan was a track worker and the only person involved in *Hell on Wheels*
who was actually an elected officer of the union. We were holding most
of our meetings at the Village apartment of Ivan's father, where Ivan had
been living since he split with his wife.

Ivan found it easier to give a speech than to speak. He would rise to his
feet, pace the floor, wave his arms and declaim. He had especially beautiful
eyes, greyish blue, although they were open just a bit too wide. Because of his
Irish ancestry, he fancied himself a new incarnation of Mike Quill, the
union's first, militant, president. Somewhere along the line, I began to find
him attractive.

Ivan mentioned to me that he would like to see an opera. He knew I liked
opera. I assumed it was a self-improvement project. I got tickets to Mozart's
The Magic Flute. I can't quite reconstruct my reasoning. Something about
the universal appeal of Mozart, probably. To my chagrin, the performance
seemed endless. Ivan was obviously sleeping for stretches. He did rouse
himself for Sarastro's address to the assembly of priests announcing his
abdication. First, the chorus of priests protests vehemently, but after a few
bars, they all raise their torches in unison to signify agreement. "Just like a
union meeting!" observed Ivan.

I was certain I had alienated him from opera forever. On the way out of
the hall, descending the endless red steps, I was sunk in remorse. Then Ivan
said enthusiastically, "I think I'd like to try another opera, maybe something
by Verdi. How about *La Traviata*?"

He also invited me to his father's for Thanksgiving dinner. It turned out
to be a big informal buffet, not at all the family-gathering-round-the-table that
I had envisioned. His father's girlfriend, his mother, his own former wife,
their kids, his siblings—all were there. Lots of folks introduced themselves to
me and I was too dazed with social anxiety to introduce myself. I was cajoled

into getting a plate of food, and I found a couch to occupy. Ivan joined me. We chatted about our families and our union. He commenced speechifying about the unique nature of the transit industry in New York. He rose to his feet, proclaiming that the stakes were so high that for starting a newsletter, one might easily be targeted for death! He turned and strode off across his stage, leaving me sitting alone, wondering whether he was coming back.

Our new newsletter, *Hell on Wheels*, was well received at the Woodlawn terminal. Only Riggs the Radical disliked it, and he confronted me in the crew room: "It's procapitalist, liberal garbage. It's written by a lot of people who just want to get elected. That's all you want, Marian. You just want to run for office."

One motorman was busy eating scrambled eggs on a roll. His conductor was staring off into space. Another conductor, Dabney, was playing chess with a switchman. My motorman was reading about the sales. Another one was watching the cartoons. No one was paying any attention to my slugfest with "Red Riggs."

I said, "You're the one who's actually run for union office, not me." I appealed to my coworkers: "Has anyone here ever heard me say anything about running for office?"

Someone asked, "Why shouldn't you run for office? What's wrong with it?"

My motorman said, "I'd vote for you."

Things were certainly not going Riggs' way.

My motorman said to Riggs, "You'd like that paper if they'd let you be on it."

"If I was on it, it'd call for a workers' government and a workers' state!"

I rolled my eyes at that one.

"Marian," Riggs addressed me, "There's nothing wrong with running for union office, but you just want to be a union bureaucrat, like Vinnie Torrelli. I'm just worried because you're going to fool people."

After he was gone, Dabney said to me, "Don't pay him no mind."

His motorman grumbled, "He never lets up."

Dabney agreed, "Uggah muggah! Yeah."

On Saturday, I gave copies of *Hell on Wheels* to a couple of old-timers at Pelham Bay. One of them gave me a handful of religious tracts. (It didn't dawn on me for a couple of days why he lectured me on "taking the name of the Lord in vain," although it still wasn't clear to me what "hell" had to do with the "Lord's name.")

Another one looked it over, by no means disapprovingly. He said, "You know, you could get into trouble with this if they know who you are. Other people have tried to change the union and ended up in a lot of trouble. Because if you're in trouble with the union, you're in trouble with the T.A. You know how they do it? They slowly build up a case against you. They write you up over and over again. Then, they can just get rid of you."

I asked Ivan out to dinner. I felt awkward to the point of numbness. He seemed delighted to accept. He drank more than he ate. He told me about his life. His parents separated when he was six. His mother, brother, sister, and he were poor, although his father gave them money when he could. He became politically active in high school and dropped out of City College "for the revolution. . . . I think someday I'd like to be a professor, because I like to talk and I like to write," he said.

He considered the union work we were doing to be "narrow economism," secondary to the need for a political party. "This stuff's boring," he said, "I want to win workers to socialism."

"Like the Spartacist League?"

As his alcohol content rose, he turned to his marriage. "What made it break up, after nine years?" I asked.

"I came to my senses."

"What's coming out of your marriage counseling?"

"That I was an idiot to have taken all that shit so long."

"Do you want to reconcile?"

"Not unless she really changes radically, like a bolt of lightning. I've read about such things—"

"Yeah, in the Bible. . . ."

"To be frank, I really ought to warn you. I am attracted to you, but I'm still a married man. I won't be making any long-term commitments in the short run. Do you want to be . . . boyfriend and girlfriend?"

The next morning, he warned me, "Don't fall in love with me. I'll never be able to love you." After that, I tried to reach him by phone for two days. When I finally did, he said he was "very depressed" over a long talk he'd had with his wife. Talking to him felt like hitting him on the head. Still, we made a dinner date for the coming week.

Ivan canceled our date for dinner by leaving a message on my answering machine. That day "turned out to be" his mother's birthday. "So I'm requesting a rescheduling. . . ."

I was a bit early to Ivan's for the meeting the next night. I was the first person there, so we were alone together, but he was formal and distant. Finally, I said, "How about a kiss or something?" He gave me a cold, light nothing.

"Look," I said, "are you angry at me, or something?"

"We're looking for two different things," he said, "I don't want to hurt anybody. . . ."

Monday, the temperature dropped below zero. The Woodlawn crew room was a cozy haven. People were even friendlier than usual, as if human warmth could overcome physical cold. It was so cold that they laid-up trains underground during the day between the rush hours.

Tuesday, the temperature rose into the twenties. It felt like spring compared to what we were used to, and folks were exuberant.

The topic in the crew room was the firefighters' tentative contract. One motorman described it to me, "6 percent a year for three years. But it'll take the new people longer to get to full salary."

"Then that's what will happen to us."

Everyone was saying, "Binding arbitration! We're going to get screwed!"

A very senior platform conductor said, "I don't like to strike. But if they don't even think we could strike, what kind of deal can we get?"

"We got to get back to the January first date," said someone, "No one cares about a strike in April."

Ivan and I agreed to have dinner and then see a movie. He was waiting at the bar with a scotch on the rocks.

I enjoyed listening to him. Not the way I enjoyed listening to Dave Stone, for precision and insight, but for his fervor and the way everything seemed to come out from the bottom of his heart. Maybe it was just sex. I found myself feeling attracted to him again.

We lost track of the time and hours passed. When we looked at our watches, it was eight-thirty. All the tables around us had been filled. We'd missed the movie.

We walked out, still talking. At the subway, he offered to wait with me for my train. As it came into the station, he asked, "So you're going to go home to sleep by yourself?"

"What choice do I have? You're not willing to sleep with me."

"I don't want to sleep alone," he said. "Can I sleep with you?"

I looked at him. Why was I amazed that he was like any other man? I said, "If you change your mind again, I'll break your nose."

And we ran for the train.

It was a snowy evening. As usual, I got to the *Hell on Wheels* meeting early. Ivan let me in. He looked grim. I sat down to take off my boots.

"Jack Shea got suspended," he practically spit the words out. Jack was the other track worker, a big red-head, who helped with *Hell on Wheels*. "In fact, I should call him now." Whereupon he got on the phone.

He was still on the phone when Dave arrived fifteen minutes later.

The meeting was long and rambling. We had a lot of ground to cover. By a quarter to ten, everyone had left, except me and Ron, the new conductor. And Ivan of course, but he lived there.

The snow was getting deeper. I didn't know if Ivan even wanted me to stay the night.

Around ten-thirty, Ivan marched to the window, "Gee, it's really coming down. If you want to crash here, you can."

"Sure," I said.

"Nah," said Ron, "I think I'll head home." And he put on his jacket.

The next morning, Ivan made us coffee, "You know," he said, "this is quite a good committee we have here. Really good people. We attract some real gems. I think this committee is the bright spot of my life right now, which shows what my life is like."

"What about our relationship? Is that a bright spot?"

"I don't want to say that, because I don't want you to get too involved in this. I'm an unstable force in your life right now."

When I got to Ivan's for the next meeting, he asked, "Have you seen the list of management demands?" Our contract was due to expire in April. As I read them, he howled, "This is war! It's war!"

Dave Stone read them, grinning with amazement, muttering, "Oh, shit! Oh, shit!"

It was eight pages long. Something for everyone. Unlimited unpaid swings in all titles. No sick leave pay for the first two days out. Half-pay for training. Picks at management discretion, with assignment by management in between. I was calm until I got to the abolition of A.V.A.S.

"What's scary about it is how weak we are," said Dave.

"And to think we would go to binding arbitration with this!" I said.

We agreed to organize an open meeting in March, in the name of *Hell on Wheels*, to discuss how to organize for a good contract. I posted a copy of the demands at Woodlawn. A lot of folks were upset by what they read.

A young motorman started talking about putting on his old army gear and getting a gun to "go jump in their trunk, when they stop the car. . . ." I wasn't too clear on his plan, but his rage was unmistakable.

A senior conductor talked about his experience in demolition—and putting it to use. A very senior white motorman, Judson, who had been coming on to me since the beginning of the pick, said to me, "I want to talk to you about these demands. Most of them don't affect us. They only affect people who haven't been hired yet."

"But we can't neglect the new people," I said.

"I'm not talking about the new people," he said, "I'm talking about the people who haven't come yet. We have to take care of ourselves. We can't worry about them."

"We do have to worry about them. Because you weren't thinking of me before I got here, now I have to wait for two-and-a-half years for full salary."

"I've been thinking about you *since* you got here!" he said. The others laughed and this made me angrier.

"We can't let the job go downhill. We do owe something to the people who aren't here yet, just like we owe something to the ones who built this union before us."

Judson said, "If the job gets worse, they don't have to take it. Let them take a different one."

"That's the boss's line. 'If you don't like it, go someplace else.' These are the people we'll be working alongside!"

"How can we work alongside of them if they don't take the job?" he snickered. "Let them do what I did. I waited until the job was good before I took it. I waited until they got the twenty-year plan."

"So! You took advantage of what the people before you fought for! You took advantage of what they risked their jobs for, what they struck for. But you don't want to fight for those who come after you. You wanted to take, but now you don't want to give."

He retreated, sullen, "I'll never argue with you again."

"Suits me," I said.

The senior conductor said, "I wish I'd had a tape recorder to record that whole thing! Then, anytime I wanted to hear a good argument, I could play it back."

But there was one thing we all agreed on. We should have the right to vote on our contract.

Ivan was very excited about his new idea, "We have to do something that will get the attention of the media. So we explain to the public why there's been a slowdown."

"A slowdown? There's no slowdown!"

"Sure, there is. Service was messed up for hours this morning on the B.M.T."

"Ivan, that was a water-main break!"

"No, no. It was a slowdown."

"Ivan, I was working the past five days. Things were running okay."

"Sometimes people don't recognize what's going on right in front of them. The riders think there's a slowdown."

On his third shot of vodka in thirty minutes, Ivan suggested that if no one else were willing to do it, he would run for president of the local. He'd been reading Shirley Quill's biography of Mike Quill and saw all sorts of similarities in background and character between Quill and himself. "Quill was no typical union leader. He was really extraordinary. Much better than Reuther. When he purged the left from the union, he didn't do it for the same reasons other leaders did. Maybe he was right to trade the five-cent fare for a wage increase."

Dave Stone made a proposal that at our open meeting in March, we call for a picket line at the site of contract negotiations.

"What do we do if all we get is seven Sparts?" asked Cesar.

"Adjourn," said Dave.

"Go out and have a drink," I said.

"A lot of drinks," amended Ivan.

Ivan walked me to the subway, "Are we crazy, trying to do this?" he asked.

"No, I don't think so. There's brains, and some experience, among us," I said.

Thursday was our long-awaited open meeting. I popped out of the elevator and there was Ivan. "'This looks like a T.A. person!" he cried.

The Spartacist League was giving out their literature and getting people to sign their mailing list by acting as if it were their meeting.

Dave was in the hallway, waiting for Ron, who was supposed to make the opening presentation.

"What time did he say he'd be here?"

"A quarter to six."

It was six-fifteen. By six-thirty, we really had to start without Ron. About thirty-five people had shown up.

Dave gave the introductory rap. He started off a bit nervously, but soon became very calm and effective. "We're facing a tough fight. And we don't think our union leadership is doing the job that needs to be done. What we believe is that the union has to renounce binding arbitration. It has to put out information, keep the membership informed. The union has to organize demonstrations. We have to be prepared for a strike. . . . What we want to discuss here tonight is what can we do to pressure the union to do these things?" He laid out our proposal: a demonstration at the negotiations site, with a focus on no givebacks, no binding arbitration, and a membership vote on any settlement.

Most of the folks from *Hell on Wheels* and some of the rank-and-file members who showed said that we had to get ourselves organized and also work at getting support from the public. But most of the workers who came said nothing.

Also present was a layer of union officers who did not align themselves with Lawe, but who didn't want to commit themselves to outright opposition either. They generally urged that we ask the leadership to organize a public relations campaign, or that we adopt other issues. One warned, "We have not exhausted all petition to the union leadership. Everyone here is open to charges of antiunion activity."

Dave called for a vote on the proposals. Our demonstration proposal, a resolution at division meetings to fire M.T.A. President Robert Kiley, testifying at hearings on March 21, and an informational picket line at Governor Mario Cuomo's office all passed. A motion for a petition campaign directing union leaders to call for a demonstration failed.

The attendance had realized our most optimistic projections. The folks voted, gave money, and took hundreds of copies of *Hell on Wheels* with them. But what did they think of the meeting? To us, it was a success. But to them, it was "too few, forget it." We saw how many *were* there. They saw how many were *not*.

The next evening at Ivan's, we planned the demonstration. We set it for Friday, March 29, since the contract was set to expire two days later.

At nine o'clock, Ivan's wife appeared. She was dressed in a pink leather jacket, a sequined scarf, and very tight pants. Her hair was very short. I thought she looked like a Times Square hooker.

I went home very depressed and had a hard time falling asleep. When I did, I dreamed of Ivan and his wife, of coming across them together, of calling him and getting her on the phone. These were interspersed with images of violence and horror. A car with a headless driver, forcing other cars off the road and over cliffs. People with their faces and eyes slashed apart by flying glass.

The next morning, I headed down to Jay Street to get my paycheck. I had to show my pass downstairs to get in. When I got to payroll, I reached to show it again, and my wallet was gone. I searched through my pockets. Then something in me shut down. I sat down and started to cry and couldn't stop. "Get a cop," I heard a man's voice, "Get her out of here."

But someone else got me up, went back downstairs with me and spoke to the receptionist in the lobby. "You can get another pass," she reassured me. She phoned the lost and found and then the pass unit. "Go to room 618," she said, "I told them your pass was stolen in the elevator. They're waiting for you."

I had to fill out a million forms and soon I was crying again. I went to a pay phone and called Joyce but she wasn't home. Neither was Mark. I was desperate enough to call Dave. He was much more supportive than I had ever known him to be before. Maybe he realized what it was really all about.

I cleaned myself up in the ladies' room. On my way out, I stopped to thank the receptionist. She was delighted to see me, "We have it! We found your wallet!" And we gave each other a big hug.

That evening, I called Ivan. "I guess you've gone back to your wife."

"We're trying to reconcile."

"Well, I wish you'd told me, instead of leaving me hanging and giving me the runaround."

"I guess I'm a coward."

"I know my feelings were not a priority for you."

The unstable influence was out of my life.

By the third week in March, there was strike talk all around the system. I heard that Vinnie Torrelli had come to Woodlawn, telling everyone there's going to be a strike. Someone told me that "downtown" had called the Woodlawn train dispatcher to ask him whether the train dispatcher's office could be locked in case of a strike. Many people asked me what was going on with negotiations. I had no idea. As always, the crew rooms were full of rumors.

"It will be binding arbitration or a strike," said one.

A popular view was that we gave up the right to strike by voting to seek the right to binding arbitration, and "we lost everything when we gave up the right to strike."

By March 28, three days before our contract expired, President Lawe was threatening to strike if the state didn't pass legislation giving us the right to seek binding arbitration. The arbitration in 1982 had been a particularly pernicious sort called "last best offer arbitration," which amounts to a game of chicken between union and employer. Each submits its "last best offer" for a settlement, and the arbitrator chooses one which, to the complete exclusion of the other, becomes the new contract.

Lawe wanted the T.W.U. to have the right to arbitration in which the arbitrator put together a settlement by considering both sides. In this process, the settlement would most likely be somewhere in the middle, between the two sides.

To me, it was wryly funny to threaten to strike in order to get a process aimed at avoiding strikes. It's got to be just saber rattling, I reasoned. The union leadership has spent five years breaking down morale, scaring the members, and disorganizing the union. We don't have what it takes to strike. We're too weak.

But the subject dominated the crew room.

"They can go. I'm coming in," said a fiery young motorman. "They don't pay my rent or pay my food bills. They've never done anything for me."

A senior motorman said, "If we all stick together, you have to look at the long run. But all the guys look at the short run. The kids in college, or the payments due on the house. We could lose a lot with binding arbitration."

Another said, "This is the wrong time of the year to strike. When we gave up the January expiration date, we gave up the real power."

A young conductor said, "Lawe's not serious about striking. If he were, he would send the Exec Board members out here, getting people's names, giving assignments. . . ."

The rank-and-file sentiment about the union leadership was so negative that Dave told me, "We would get the biggest crowd if we had our demonstration in front of the union hall. But it wouldn't be correct politically."

Our picket line at the negotiations site was scheduled for 5 P.M. I left work early, but by the time I arrived at 6:40, I found nothing but a few cops, a few police barriers, and the remains of the sunset.

When I got home, I called Dave. He told me it had been small, perhaps twenty folks, counting the people from the "Committee for a Fighting T.W.U.."

"We had media there," Dave continued, "Channel 5 was very hostile. They interviewed one of the people from the Spartacist League. WBAI interviewed Ron. The *Times* guy was very friendly. He seemed to want to make the contacts, a rising reporter, rising young activists—"

"I hope we're rising young activists."

"It seems the union called the media to tell them about the rally so they'd have something to frighten the legislators with. Ivan almost hit Red Riggs. Ron had to hold him back. I think he's still angry about Monday night."

Monday night had been the March meeting of the Joint Executive Board. President Lawe had opened the floor for discussion by calling on one of the Spartacist League members, who introduced a resolution calling for a demonstration against police brutality. Lawe ruled it out of order and used the ensuing hubbub as a pretext to adjourn the meeting, precluding any discussion of the contract negotiations.

Ivan had been furious at the "Sparts" for becoming Lawe's dupes.

"The time and place may not have been ideal," Dave concluded about *Hell on Wheels'* first demonstration, "but the main thing is a demobilized, discouraged, and cynical membership. And the thing we have to decide is what to do now."

The *Times* reported that Lawe said there would be no strike, definitely not, when the contract expired on Monday. I had my own interpretation of what he was doing. I saw him trying to pressure the Albany politicians into passing the binding arbitration legislation he wanted. I figured the fact that he was backing down showed that he had gotten the legislation he wanted.

On Sunday, the day our contract expired, the news came that Governor Mario Cuomo had agreed to back the new binding arbitration legislation.

The mood among the crews shifted. Up to that point the mood had been unsettled, tense. With the announcement that binding arbitration was a done deal, the mood shifted to passive hopefulness.

At the April conductors union meeting, Vice President Lawson tried to convince us that the union was between a rock and a hard place and that we should not expect a very good contract.

A rank-and-file member tried to make a motion for a general membership meeting, "to discuss our situation of working without a contract."

First, he was ignored, so he raised it again. Vinnie Torrelli, who was chairing, told him that his motion was dead because it was not seconded.

"Seconded!" I said.

"Would you formulate the motion?"

The member tried.

"Slow down!" yelped the recording secretary, "I'm not a speed writer!"

But Vice President Lawson whispered something to Vinnie, and Vinnie ruled the motion out of order. "We don't have the authority to call such a meeting," Lawson suavely explained, "I suggest you write a letter to Lawe."

A construction flagman said, "The city money comes from the federal government. If all the city workers went on strike together, we would have a national emergency and we would get federal aid. And if we all got together like that, maybe we could beat the Taylor Law."

A very apolitical Long Island white guy from my training class liked what the construction flagman said. "We should look into the possibility of discussing the idea of us all striking together, since we are all without a contract. We should ask for voluntary contributions from all of our members, just to put together a war chest for public relations and not depend on the *Daily News* or the *Post*. I would give a hundred dollars, myself."

Out on the Woodlawn veranda, the fellers were talking about the contract. I told them that the union had given up the overtime for the construction flagmen.

"Well," said Motorman Reggio, "I don't care about that. That doesn't affect me."

Someone said, "That's a shitty attitude."

"Yeah," chimed in the rest, "that's the wrong attitude to take."

"Yeah," Reggio admitted, "that's the wrong attitude."

"I don't think we should give up anything," I said.

A senior white conductor said, "I agree, and we shouldn't accept lower pay for the ones who haven't come in yet, either. If you'll pardon the expression, this union leadership sucks. We almost took over the union in 1980. I don't regret going out on strike. We weren't getting raises at all. If we hadn't gone out then, every increase we've gotten since then would have been smaller."

Reggio said, "That's our only power, the power to strike. The union leaders are afraid to strike. They're afraid to go to jail."

Angelo Gonzalez said, "The people around here don't want to strike. They're living from paycheck to paycheck."

The car cleaner supervisor agreed with him, "I've never seen guys like this who cry over losing a day's pay."

I suggested that the union should have a strike fund, and determine to strike until the Taylor Law fines were amnestied.

Motorman Lee wandered over, "Stop talking shit, Swerdlow. The union is beautiful. The problem is they're on T.A. payroll."

"Who exactly is on the T.A. payroll?"

Gonzalez and Reggio both said, "You don't know which ones."

"Is that what you're saying, that they're secretly on the take?" I asked Lee.

Lee said, "It's the guys right here, they won't take a stand."

Gonzalez nodded, "See, it's what I was saying before," and he stuck his head into the crew room to do a little reality testing, "How many of you guys would go on strike?"

Everyone inside turned and stared at Gonzalez, trying to figure out what the hell he was about. Gonzalez turned back to the assemblage on the veranda, "See?"

"No!" I said, "You have to be concrete. People aren't going to strike just for a strike." I stuck my head into the crew room, "How many of you would strike if the T.A. offered us no wage increases for three years?"

Most put their hands up.

Later, Gonzalez commented, "It's a shame not everyone did."

On June 27, the union announced that it had a "tentative accord." In it, the conductors working as construction flagmen lost their hour-and-a-half bonus, night differential was frozen, and new people would start at only 70 percent of full pay, instead of 75 percent, and it would take three years, up from two and a half, to achieve full pay.

We found this out in the newspapers. My motorman mentioned at Atlantic, "The flagman told me we got 5, 6, and 6," that is, a 5 percent raise the first year and 6 percent raises each of the last two years. Because the new contract was retroactive to April 1, we would be owed money. This back pay is called "a retroactive."

I thought it was just another rumor. But when we got up to Woodlawn, one of the car cleaners asked me, "What have you heard about the new contract?" and he showed me the article in the *Daily News*.

I rushed down to the newsstand to get the *Times*. I quickly wrote the highlights on a piece of paper and taped it to the crew room door.

People were pissed off about the cut in the construction flagmen's pay and the night differential. "That's a giveback, isn't it?"

I kept saying, "It's a take-away," but then I thought that in a way they were right, the union was giving these things back.

The next day, a motorman who was riding my No. 6 train told me he was going to vote no. "What this union needs is some radicalism," he explained, "I don't want to say anything bad about anyone, but what we need is more white workers. The black workers are too happy with what they're getting. White people coming in have more education and they expect to make more money."

However, plenty of black workers were against the proposed contract. While most people weren't talking about it, those who did were saying, "We should not accept it," "You should vote no," and "I'm voting no."

The freeze on shift differential created a lot of confusion. "Frozen at current levels," the press reported it. A lot of folks, indulging in wishful thinking, assumed that meant it would remain 10 percent of the hourly pay. What it actually meant, however, was that the differential was frozen at the current *cash amount*. For instance, a conductor at top pay, making $10 an hour, got a dollar an hour shift differential added to his pay at night and on weekends. The freeze meant that even when his pay rose 5 percent, to $10.50 an hour, his shift differential would remain a dollar an hour, dropping it below 10 percent.

What was not clear was how it would affect people not yet at full pay and the new hires. There were rumors that new people who might be getting a $.70 hourly shift differential would never make any more, even as they progressed to full pay, and even if they got promoted.

A lot of people, after criticizing the contract, would also say, "It will be approved, anyhow." One guy I spoke with didn't even realize we would vote on it. Others weren't sure.

It still angered me when people condoned the stretch-out to full pay for new people, saying, "No one has to take the job if they don't like it." I would try to explain this was akin to saying that if we didn't like the job, we could always quit.

This deeply upset one very senior black motorman. "I know you're only joking, but it's a heck of a thing to say to a man seventeen years on the job, and you just here, how long is it?"

Another said, "We, who are working here, have something to lose. Someone coming in here has nothing to lose."

Dave brought a draft of a leaflet on the contract to the *Hell on Wheels* meeting. Its subheading, "Increases Paid for with Givebacks," was its thrust. It concluded:

> We feel the contract should be rejected. We don't have to make any givebacks. Our union officers should be sent back to the bargaining table with clear instructions to do two things: first, to negotiate a contract without givebacks, and, second, to prepare the union for a strike in the winter, in case such a contract can't be negotiated.

By Saturday morning, Dave had it ready to distribute. It was the only thing that had come out in the week since the tentative settlement was announced—even union officialdom had nothing in print. People were eager to read it, and it was passed from hand to hand. By Monday, a senior motorman told me, "Everyone's talking about how *Hell on Wheels* says we should reject the contract."

The following Sunday, Riggs the Red and "Turn Around" Torrelli were in the Woodlawn crew room at the same time. Vinnie Torrelli was saying the contract wasn't so bad. "You sound like you're trying to sell it," said Riggs.

"I may vote for it," said Torrelli.

I had been wondering about the bus drivers. Since the tentative accord had been announced, none of the bus drivers with whom I'd ridden had said anything about it. A few MABSTOA drivers ate their lunches in the Pelham Bay crew room, so I asked them.

"Well, we don't know yet. Union Vice President Hall came to our last union meeting. He said we'd be getting something in the mail with the ballot that would explain it to us."

I asked what people in the garage were saying about the settlement.

"They're not saying much." He said he had asked Hall about shift differential for people not yet at full pay, and Hall had answered that it would be frozen for the life of the contract.

On my way to work Sunday, I talked to another bus driver about how Rapid Transit felt about the contract, telling him, "For one thing, we don't like the cut in the differential."

"*Our* differential hasn't been cut," he said, "we had no givebacks at all."

"It's not obvious that it's been cut," I explained, "because it's frozen. But as the pay goes up, the differential will stay the same. So the 10 percent rate is what's being cut."

"No, that doesn't apply to us," he said.

I knew that he was wrong. However, if his view was common among the MABSTOA drivers, it would help explain why they backed the contract so strongly.

In some ways, MABSTOA drivers had it better than we did. If they worked their lunch, for example, they'd get twenty minutes to eat as well as the thirty minutes pay that we got, while we could be sent right back out on the road. It was also fairly easy for them to swap R.D.O.'s with another driver for a week.

I was telling this to the crowd out on the Woodlawn veranda. One of the old-timers observed, "MABSTOA only came into T.W.U. twenty years ago, so they made a lot of progress only recently."

At our *Hell on Wheels* meeting, we discussed Arnold Cherry, the old opposition leader, taking the union to court. He claimed that MABSTOA should not be voting on our contract. The basis for this claim was that the contract put an end to our use of the civil service trial board and MABSTOA, because they were not civil service, was not affected by this.

Ivan thought the claim had merit, "Why should they vote on something that doesn't affect them?"

I said, "If you stick with that logic, track and power division shouldn't vote on it either, because it contains clauses that affect only the construction flagmen."

Dave said, "What it comes down to is: are we one union? I guess it would be better if somebody wrote the article and we talked about it. I guess that somebody is going to be me."

At the end of the meeting, Ivan announced, "We can't meet here anymore, because I'm going to be living someplace else."

The guys didn't get it and asked, "Where?"

But I had been expecting it. He was moving back in with his wife.

Over the radio, motormen were saying, "The word is 'reject.'"

Everyone at Woodlawn was saying they were going to vote, or had already voted, against it: McCray, Gonzalez, Delgado, Nelson, Fernandez, Joyce. One motorman said, "This is the first time I have ever voted down a contract." Joyce said even Vinnie Torrelli told her, albeit furtively, "Vote no!" Only the Spartacist League was silent.

Still no one expected it to be defeated. Switchman "Brandy" Brandfield, the cynic, predicted, "Eight to one." There were several rumors circulating: Anyone who doesn't return a ballot is counted as a "yes" vote. That the union was going to say the contract was accepted unanimously. And that the new contract would allow unpaid swings.

We had very little idea of how they would conduct the count of the contract referendum ballots. We didn't know if there would be discrete department tallies, who would be counting, how long it would take, and whether observers would be allowed.

I got to the union hall around 4 P.M. The ballots were being counted by the clerical staff of the union and the Health Benefit Trust. Each division used a different colored envelope and had been mailed to a different post office box. The ballots were arranged by pass number and checked against the list of members in good standing.

The ballot counters worked in groups of about seven. First, they would take the ballots out of the inner, anonymous envelopes and place them all face down. Then, they divided them into "yes" and "no." Next, they were counted into piles of twenty-five. A second person checked the count, bound the pile, and labeled it.

As the grand finale, Kevin McGarvey, head of the Health Benefit Trust, counted the piles and produced the final tally.

While I was there they finished three of the smaller divisions, signal, track, and transit authority surface maintenance. Each ran about four to one for acceptance. However, as we watched the motormen ballots being counted, it looked to me like it was running about three to one to reject.

The next day, I called the union hall from work to get the tally for motormen. After several attempts, I got Vice President Lawson. He said the motormen vote was about 1,100 to 480 to reject. Conductors hadn't been counted yet.

At Brooklyn Bridge Saturday morning, a conductor told me, "They accepted it. It was in the news."

I went right to the newsstand and bought the paper. In a small item were these figures: 13,343 to 4,800. About three to one. I learned later, however, that both motormen and conductors had rejected the contract by a margin of about three to two.

By the end of the day, everyone was wondering when we would get the retroactive.

LACKLUSTER

Even before the 1985 contract was approved, the people putting out *Hell on Wheels* had started to consider the possibility of running a slate for our union's international convention.

"Would you be willing to run in the conductors' division?" Dave Stone asked me.

"I don't want to," I laughed, "because we'd lose!"

"It's a statement to the members that this stuff is important enough to stick out your neck for."

Ron said, "We have to look at victory in a different sense. If we get more people involved in *Hell on Wheels* through it, we'll have won."

We had heard that one of the old opposition conductors, Henry Tinker, was fielding a slate for convention delegates in the conductors' division. He said he'd be interested in talking with us. He certainly had a lot of questions for me. Tinker wanted to know how I had decided to approach him as a running mate, whether I was one of the founders of *Hell on Wheels*, what jobs I had had previously, and what else I had done politically.

"This job is first and foremost a livelihood for me," he stated. He said he considered himself a black nationalist. As far as the job was concerned, however, all workers were treated equally: badly. So, he felt, as far as reforming the union was concerned, race was irrelevant. "The main thing is to oppose Lawe, because since Lawe came in, we've never had a good contract."

He was apparently satisfied with my answers, because he agreed to meet with Dave and me. When we did sit down together, he still seemed quite cautious about us. "What do you hope to get out of this?" he asked.

Dave answered that we wanted to get our ideas out to the rank and file and begin to get them mobilized again. Then he turned the question around, directing it at Tinker, who said he was in it to get "a decent salary and benefits and to be able to afford to buy more. And I want to be proud of my job in my community." He also warned me, "Woodlawn is my territory, so don't go messing up there."

I was annoyed with him for being suspicious, and Dave was annoyed with me for being annoyed with Tinker.

"He's disingenuous!" I said to Dave afterward.

"He's an honest reformer," Dave corrected me.

"Why is he so suspicious of us? Why is he afraid of me 'messing up'?"

"He's suspicious because we're radicals. The 'messing up' you might do is acting like the Sparts."

Tinker was out of town on vacation on the day of the union's nominations meeting. He had given me some signed papers, confident these would get him ballot status without the inconvenience of actually having to attend the meeting. When I tried to submit the papers Tinker had given me, I was told they were not acceptable. Then they asked anyone who wanted to run as a slate to fill out and submit their slate forms.

"I don't know if I'm going to be on a slate anymore," I said.

"If you want to be on a slate, you have to sign this. If Tinker comes down here, he can sign it, too."

That was logical, so I signed.

I called Tinker long-distance and I told him that if he didn't come to the city within two days and sign the papers, he wouldn't be on the ballot. He said he would have to talk to his wife before he could decide what to do. I said I wouldn't be home that night (it was a Great night).

When I came home the next evening, there were messages from Tinker who had arrived in New York. He said I had to come to the union hall immediately to sign a new slate sheet, because I had signed the first one on the first line, making my name first on the ballot. Tinker wanted his own name to run first.

There was also a message from union Vice President Lawson, "You have to come to the union and sign a new nomination sheet. The wrong sheets were signed last night. You were given the sheets for nominees for alternates."

Of course, the union office was already closed.

I was pissed off. Those incompetent staffers gave me the sheet for alternates to sign and I get the extra work of going down and signing a new sheet.

I decided I would go down the next morning, before my late A.M. report, to take care of it.

Tinker's line was busy until eight o'clock. When I finally reached him, he wanted me to drop everything and come out to his house in the far part of Brooklyn to sign a new slate sheet. I explained it was too late for me to make that trek. I had to get up early the next morning and go down and sign a new nominating form.

"Don't worry about that," he told me.

This exasperated me. "But if I don't sign a new nominations form, I won't be on the ballot." But he only cared about the slate sheet and making sure his name came ahead of mine on the ballot. I offered to meet him the next morning down at the union hall, but he wanted to be out of town by then. Finally he said, "I can get somebody else to meet you."

He called me back a little later, "My brother-in-law can meet you at nine-thirty at West Fourth Street."

"Fine," I said, "I'll go to the union hall from there." Feeling resentful, but glad it was resolved, I went to sleep. The next morning, there were four messages on my machine.

From Dave: "Sounds like everything is alright."

From Tinker: "My brother-in-law wasn't able to find you at 9:30."

From Tinker again: "I think what the union means by the wrong form was that you checked 'independent' instead of 'running with a slate.'"

From Vice President Lawson: "If you do not come to the union hall by 5:00 P.M. tomorrow to sign a form for regular delegate, your candidacy will be invalidated."

I tried reaching Tinker, but he had left town. When I called Dave, his wife answered the phone. "You screwed up," was her unsolicited observation, "Tinker's brother drove all the way to your house, but your line was busy."

Now I was totally baffled—and very frustrated.

I went down to the union hall and signed the proper form. It turned out Tinker had meant I should meet his brother-in-law that evening, while I had assumed he meant the next morning. No one "drove all the way" to my house. I didn't particularly want to hear again that I had "screwed up," so I put off calling Dave for three days. When I finally did, he was less reproachful than his wife had been. "The only bad part is that Tinker might suspect we are using him."

I suspected the opposite. He had used us.

Dave and Ron had met with a few old oppositionalists in motors and they'd agreed to run together.

It was May 22. The ballots were being mailed out the next day. Neither Dave and Ron's slate nor Tinker's and mine had any literature yet. On Friday after work, I went to the home of another old oppositionalists, Roger Marcus, to pick up the literature. I noticed that the only other woman on the slate, Mary Hansen, was not included in the campaign literature. Why?

Roger said, "We never asked her to be on our slate. She's unpopular and she's always boasting about all the men she sleeps with. The organizer talked her into signing the slate sheet. I'm sending a letter of protest to her."

I began to campaign in earnest.

At Woodlawn, one conductor told me, "I couldn't figure out the ballot, so I just checked one of the big boxes."

But Conductor Milton told me, as though speaking for the whole P.M. crowd, "So you're running to go to California. Well, the terminal is going to vote for you. The terminal is going to send you to California."

I said, "Only as far as Nevada. Thank you all. I'll bring you all back souvenirs."

Later the A.M. R.C.I. told me he thought I was going to win. "I hear all the guys campaigning for you. They say 'she really works.'"

One conductor told me he would vote for every A Division candidate, regardless of slate, "What do I want with B Division? I left eight years ago."

A conductor from my training class told me, "I'll vote for you because you give people information." Another said our platform sounded good.

I visited the crew room at the 207th Street terminal of the "A" line. There was one woman there. She asked me how they could get separate women's facilities.

Another day after work, I visited Van Cortlandt. A woman there asked me, "How can the women get their own facility?"

Another conductor started telling everyone, "Vote for her. She's one of the most militant union members I know."

Tinker and I also gave out literature to conductors at Times Square. Tinker seemed to know most of the conductors on the Nos. 2 and 3 lines, and we received many promises of votes. On the No. 1, only a couple of guys said that they voted for Torrelli's slate. Another guy said, "I have a criticism of your literature. The International's issues should have come after the union issues in your leaflet, but I voted for you, anyway."

At West 4th Street, we split up. I didn't have the heart to hand the leaflet to the conductors on the "CC" line, who had to operate the doors standing between the cars and using controls outside the doors called "caps and triggers." The very senior conductors on the "E" line were friendly. A couple who had holding lights chatted with me. One asked, "Do you think you'll stay a conductor?" Another asked, "Do you think any good will actually come of this?"

I tried not to expect to win. I even dreamed about losing. But when a conductor shouted to me, across the platform, "You've got my vote!" or another told me, "Everyone voted for you," it was hard not to hope we would give the Torrelli slate a run for their money.

I had asked a new conductor who was coming to *Hell on Wheels* meetings, Melvin Stockman, to be my poll watcher. Subsequently, he related to me how he had returned his ballot the wrong way, invalidating it. After that, I was not thrilled with my choice of poll watchers. However, I was sure he'd try his best. I consoled myself with the thought that winning wasn't the only thing, anyhow.

The ballot count for the convention delegate election was June 12.

Melvin, my poll watcher, called me with the results. The Torrelli slate swept it with 457 slate votes. The membership slate—Tinker and me—got 43 slate votes. We did better among the 254 members who voted split tickets. Among them, Tinker got 140 votes, and I got 115. In comparison, Torrelli, the highest vote-winner, received 163 and the lowest guy on his slate got 126.

Tinker was even more surprised than I was. He had been saying for weeks, "No one ever votes slates." Even Dave was surprised at how poorly we'd done.

The Torrelli slate got most of its slate votes from B Division. They had no reason to split their tickets, except to vote for the two independents. Most A Division voters split their tickets so they could vote for us. But we just couldn't pull anything from B division, because we had no one on our ticket from that division. In retrospect, I think 158 votes was good for a rookie on a two-person slate, but at the time I was devastated.

I returned to work feeling pretty sorry for myself. As I prepared for my first trip, who should appear but "Turn Around" Torrelli, who was now the chairman of the conductor's division after the former chairman had been "made" an organizer. He told me how surprised he was at how well he'd done. He even did well, he told me, the first time he ran, finishing just behind Henry Lewis, a prominent dissident. "That's when I decided to really get involved in union politics, when I saw how well I did." He even talked about how well the two independents, who finished behind even me and Tinker, did. Why did I think that he would be a graceful winner?

I gave him my analysis.

Torrelli had nothing to say to that, and I went into the train dispatcher's shack after my motorman. I told him, "Vinnie asked me to run on his slate, but I wouldn't."

"You should have," said Hodges, "you ran with a bunch of losers. Lackluster personalities."

"To me, it's more important to run on a program than to run on personalities."

"You take this very seriously."

"Sure I do."

"Are you embarrassed?"

"I was. But now that I've heard the stupid things Vinnie had to say. . . ."

"He takes all the credit, doesn't he?"

Other people were supportive and sympathetic. Rivera assured me, "This doesn't affect your credibility." Conductor Smith encouraged me with, "You should try again."

One of my former motorman at Van Cortlandt told me, "Vinnie Torrelli told me he asked you to run with him. You should have done it. Then, eventually you could have become an officer and changed some things."

"No," I said, "to become an officer, I would have to have changed."

"That's right," said another motorman. "You get in there and soon you are looking down on the same people you are working with now. You just stick to that."

I said, "Institutions are stronger than individuals."

He agreed, "Yes. Everything will have to change all at once."

Tinker and I had a lengthier discussion of the election results. He rationalized the defeat, claiming that all the slate votes were from new conductors. "The organizers talked to them in the training classes," he explained.

Local union elections were coming up in the fall. That was what we discussed at our *Hell on Wheels* meeting.

"I don't think we have to worry about winning. We have to decide what kind of impact a campaign could have."

We all agreed that anything we could accomplish through the campaign—raising issues, meeting people from other worksites—could be accomplished nearly as well by other means.

"But," I said, "there's something else to consider. It will be a real defeat if there's no opposition slate."

Ivan said, "I think Ron would make a great candidate for president."

I said, "The problem is these local officers are not elected by their divisions. They're elected at-large from the local as a whole."

Dave made some humorous mention of "the first woman to run for vice president." I was not amused.

"What about conductors? Aren't we running anyone?"

I said, "There really isn't anyone to run with me. And it's pretty much impossible if you run alone."

"You run to win, eh?" asked Ron sarcastically, and his tone rubbed me the wrong way.

Ivan said, "By not running, you're depriving the members of any way to express their opposition—"

"—and you're such an *attractive* candidate," added Ron.

That did it for me. "Well, I'm certainly not going to run if that's the kind of support I get from my own circle!"

"I don't think that was meant to be sarcastic," said Dave.

John Shea said, "But we're all sarcastic to each other. You're sarcastic to Ivan."

"To Ivan, yes! But not to anyone else. But Ivan and I . . . have a history. I've paid for the right to be sarcastic to Ivan."

"But Marian," said Ivan, "you are an *attractive* candidate."

I grabbed the plastic bowl of popcorn that lay between us, and swung it back, as if to throw it at Ivan. He cowered. I laughed and put it down. This broke the tension and everyone laughed, ha ha ha, and we went on to the next subject.

Turn Around Torrelli rode downtown with me. "If I were president of this union," he babbled, "I would be dictatorial. That's what makes a union strong: one man gives the orders and the others all back him up. The first thing I would do is turn around and abolish the dues checkoff. But the guys would all pay because they knew if they didn't, they've have their legs broken. And the first time the contract came around, I'd turn around and tell them, we don't want anything, not a change in benefits, not a raise, only that the expiration date is December thirty-first again."

"What have you been eating for breakfast?" I inquired genially.

"I know the union isn't going to change for a few years," he went on, "until the composition of the membership changes. I ain't prejudiced, but the black workers have no union consciousness."

I disputed this, so he started in with one of his favorite subjects, how no one ever "made" him, how every office he ever held was elected.

"Except, of course, the one you're holding now," I pointed out in a mild tone. He had been "promoted" from vice chairman to chairman by the Local's Executive Board.

"I made you!" He pointed to my steward's pin, "Who got you that button?"

"Not you," I said, "When I asked you, you said you couldn't get me one. Another vice chairman gave me this." Ivan had gotten it for me.

"When Lawson wasn't sure whether to renew your credentials—" Vinnie launched into the same old story: he was always in there pitching for me.

I said to him, "I guess that's what's missing from my life: fantasies like these."

"Why is it a fantasy? I might run for president someday. If they make me an organizer—"

"If they make you an organizer, you'll do what they say, and if you run against them, you'll be back on the road."

In the motorman's division, an old opposition motorman, Frank Haines, had agreed to run with Dave and Ron on a slate for Executive Board. On Monday, on his way to the union hall, Ivan saw Roger Marcus, of the old opposition. Marcus told Ivan, "We have to stop Haines, before he hooks up with these *Hell on Wheels* people."

"Why would he say that to *Ivan*?" I asked Dave.

"He doesn't associate Ivan with us," Dave replied, "Remember Ivan's not an open member of *Hell on Wheels*."

Tuesday, Haines called Dave to tell hem that the old opposition was forming an Executive Board slate and had asked him to be part of it. Haines claimed he'd turned them down.

Thursday, I was collecting signatures for the *Hell on Wheels* slate (Dave, Ron, Haines) at Woodlawn, when a guy from my training class came in. When he saw my petition, he asked me, "Are you sure Haines is running on it?"

"Sure, I'm sure."

"Because," he continued, "I was at the union hall Tuesday, and Haines was there with a couple of guys from the opposition, and it looked like they were trying to get Haines' name off that slate."

By Sunday, I had thirty-three signatures for the *Hell on Wheels* slate. Dave called me in the evening, "Time to start worrying. I was down at the union hall and I saw that you, Ron and me are the only ones who have petitions out. Haines hasn't picked up any yet. I called him and he told me he's been out with a toothache. But he's confident he can get all we need."

Haines picked up his petitions the following Wednesday. According to Dave, he was still confident he could get all we needed, although that Friday was the deadline.

Dave, Ron, and I agreed to meet outside the union hall that day at four, and turn in our signatures together. Dave and I got there first, then Ron appeared. The three of us together had 134 signatures. We needed 225 to get on the ballot.

We went upstairs. "If Haines didn't get a hundred, we're sunk," said Dave.

As the woman took our petitions, we could read the ledger.

Haines had handed in thirty-four signatures.

I was so furious that I felt paralyzed. Dave spoke first, "I don't know what I'm angrier about: all my wasted time or that we didn't get on the ballot."

I was outraged at Haines. Did he really misjudge, despite all his years of experience, how long it would take to gather all those signatures? Or did he simply give in to pressure from his longtime pals in the old opposition and double-cross us?

GREATER GREATNESS

When Mark went to dispatcher, he made a big point about breaking off our relationship. Almost immediately, he remembered that he needed someone to take care of his cat while he went on vacation, so he softened his stand just enough to secure me as a cat-sitter, but not so much that it would bother his conscience if he subsequently gave me the old heave-ho.

Mark was never definite about when he would return from a vacation. Maybe it was because he didn't like to contemplate the ending. Or maybe he just felt it was nobody else's business. I knew he would be back any day. I just wasn't sure which day.

Sunday night, as I trudged up the hill to my apartment, I saw a large figure perched on my steps. Even in the deep twilight, I recognized him immediately. It was Mark, come to get his cat.

"What if I'd been turned at Mott?" I asked as he hugged me.

"In another half-hour, I would have called the Woodlawn dispatcher."

We went upstairs, with him complaining that he had pulled an Achilles tendon. "It's always something with you."

"I guess it is."

Madeline wasn't at the door to meet me as she usually was. He strode into my living room and picked her up, hugged her, and showered her with cat endearments. As soon as he put her down, she ran straight to me.

He said he was apprehensive about his new job as a supervisor.

"If you don't like it, you can always come back."

"I don't intend to come back. People who intend to come back don't make it. I'm worried about dealing with those assholes at Jay Street," he said, referring to management. "The crews I'm less worried about. I know how to call them assholes without saying it. I know how to make them feel stupid."

I told him Riggs the Radical was back at work, after being out sick with pneumonia for weeks.

"Does he still smell?"

"I hadn't noticed that he smells, but it struck me that he resembles Gordon Liddy."

"If he's ever in my terminal, I'm going to take him out of service."

"For smelling? Is there a rule about how you have to smell?"

"Sure. Personal presentation."

I laughed, "And you're afraid I'd pick into your terminal! You'd take me out of service if you didn't like my perfume. 'Conductor Swerdlow, your perfume smells like skunk essence. You are out of service!'"

He had to smile.

I told the weekend dispatcher at Woodlawn that Goniea had gone to dispatcher "He says it's not as easy as it looks."

Both the dispatcher and the assistant dispatcher laughed heartily at that. "He says he's going to take any motorman who smells bad out of service."

The dispatcher: "You can't. Unless he smells like alcohol."

The assistant: "If he can walk straight, put him on a train."

I: "If he doesn't fall in the pocket on his way to sign in, he goes down the road."

Up at Woodlawn, everyone asked about Goniea. The carder, who puts the advertisements up on the trains, hollered to me, "Where's the Frenchie?"

One motorman told me, "Your friend's a traitor."

Another reported, "I saw Goniea in the back. He's hard up for money. He says after he pays the rent, he's got fifteen dollars left."

"Maybe his cat will lend him money," I said.

On my last trip down, there was the usual crowd at 86th Street. You deserve a medal for merely getting the doors closed. As I was patting myself on the back for my accomplishment, I heard a deep voice from the platform, "Marian!" Not "Conductor," not even "Miss Swerdlow," but "Marian." And it was the former Great Goniea. What a shame. As my train pulled out, we both shook our heads.

I was first stunned and bitter. Then I told myself, "It's for the best. He would only hurt and insult me. If he wants to speak to me, let him call me."

At Brooklyn Bridge, after announcing that it was the last stop, I slipped out of the cab to make sure my train—or at least my two operating cars—had no riders. Who do I see but a Great Dispatcher.

"Close down the train!" he bellowed. A direct order! I complied. I went toward him where he sat alone on the grey plastic seat. "Keep your distance!" he remonstrated, "We're coming up to the dispatcher!"

"Where are you headed?" I asked after some affectionate banter.

"I'm selling my target pistol. I never use it anyway. I picked up my check and I now get for two weeks what I used to get for one."

"How are you feeling?"

"You mean emotionally? I still haven't really got my bearings. You know how I'll know when I'm alright? When I come home and my apartment is clean."

"Then you'll know the cat has learned how to clean."

I didn't hear from him for about a month. Then, one Saturday evening, my phone rang just before ten, waking me from my first sleep.

"I thought you would be out whoring," said Goniea.

"No. I was out snoozing."

"Ohhh, did I wake you up? I was thinking of coming over tonight."

"Well, you'd better hurry up before tonight is over."

Once arrived, he took me on his lap and told me about his experiences as a new train dispatcher. "The people who were most arrogant before are now the most helpful. One has been almost like a mentor." He dreaded the day when he would be up there alone. "I don't know how to run a terminal. It'd take me months to catch on." But he was still rigid and resentful, especially— it seemed to me—toward women. He mentioned an assistant train dispatcher who got annoyed with him for reading her some car numbers inaccurately, and a motorman who had complained because she did not have a working windshield wiper. He said he intended to "teach" such folks "they can't get away with this with me."

The drop in pay had finally forced him to file for bankruptcy. He asked to borrow money from me, with his IBM Selectric typewriter and his Rolex Oyster watch as collateral. He had gained about twenty pounds, a result—he claimed—of quitting smoking. He had lost his vacation. "The first May vacation I'd gotten!"

He called me again a week later, sounding very down. He hated his training class. He was afraid his bankruptcy would lose him his Amex card. He had accidentally thrown away his silver flask of Lagerfeld cologne.

"Maybe someone nice will get you a new one for Christmas."

"It's the last thing I need!"

"I know. Actually, I see Grand Union supermarket has gift certificates."

"I don't want groceries for Christmas! Don't get me anything, because I can't give back anything in return, and it will just make me feel bad. I'm not doing very well. . . ."

I got into the dispatcher's shack at Woodlawn and caught a glimpse of Goniea's (by now rather broad) back. I signed in and turned to leave. I felt someone seize my arm. It was the old radioman, "Hey, didn't you see him?"

"Sure," I said, and sailed out the door to the platform. I heard a Great bellow behind me, "Marian!" I turned to see someone Great, wearing a grey tie, waving to me. I waved back, and continued on my way. "Marian!" I heard again, and I turned. He motioned for me to come. I sighed and went; it was, after all, a direct order.

He handed me a set of keys for the new R-62 trains, "Put them away. Don't let anyone see 'em. Just a little perk of the job, to express my appreciation for the loan."

My motorman was in the crew room. "This is gonna be a bad day for us," I warned him, "Goniea's up there."

I walked out on the platform. The "Next Train" sign was pointing to an "old rat" in the west, but Conductor Dabney was waving people off it, "Other side, other side. . . ."

Over the platform P.A., "That's a lay-up in the east. The train in the west is next to go. Flag, clear out the east."

"Oh, no," said the flagman, "and I already kicked riders off that train!"

My motorman and I went into the dispatcher's shack. The dispatcher said, "The federal inspectors are here today to begin investigating the track fires."

"It's the largest group of agents ever sent in an investigation," added Goniea, "so, if you see a pretty girl, just give a quick look and get your eyes back to the road—"

"Because she might be an inspector!" I interrupted.

Out at the Atlantic Avenue station, we heard that, because of a fire on the west side, they were running everything on the east side.

"You hear about the fire they have especially for the federal inspectors?" I asked my motorman.

"You mean the 'Welcome to New York' fire?" he replied.

On our second trip, they sent us out to New Lots, local all the way. My motorman, who was ever the optimist, kept saying we might get a drop, since we would return after our next interval.

I kept answering, "Forget it. They'll send us out three behind."

Back at Woodlawn, they told us we'd be going out twenty-five minutes late. I went to the shack to put in my "no lunch" slip. Goniea was processing overtime slips, so I handed mine to him. Ever the wit, he exclaimed, "What's this 'no lunch' shit?"

"Yeah!" I shouted, "what *is* this 'no lunch' shit? How come I don't get to have my lunch? How come I get in fifteen minutes after my lunch is over and I'm sent out nine minutes later?"

The assistant dispatcher turned around, "Oh, for a second I thought she'd gone nuts."

Goniea said, "It so happens, Miss Swerdlow, that there was a fire on the west side."

"Let her go, Goniea!" the dispatcher interrupted. "She's got the lights."

My motorman put in our overtime slips when we cleared. I asked him how much we'd gotten. "Forty-seven and twenty-seven," he answered, "and thirty for the 'no lunch.' So we got some money."

"We earned it," I said.

"We earned more than it," he answered.

Before the federal inspectors arrived, if a motorman reported smoke, Command Center said, "Can you see the signals, motorman? Alright, then, take a deep breath and drive through it." The federal agents' presence was being felt. Console operators were using "please" and "thank you" to motormen on the radio. And now any hint of smoke meant reroutes and "stop and stand."

Sunday, at Boro Hall, uh oh! I smelled twelve-two! I got on the intercom, "Motorman, guess what I smell."

"I reported it already."

"I hope we get out of Brooklyn!"

"It was only a small fire," said my motorman.

"There's no such thing these days as a small fire," I answered glumly.

All I got for Christmas from Mark was a message on my machine, wishing me "Merry Christmas," then adding, "Oh, I forgot. You're a kike." The night of New Year's Day, I was awakened by the phone ringing. I turned on the light and saw it was ten minutes before three. I figured it was a wrong number, but it was Greatness. "I thought you'd have your machine on. Well, anyway, Happy New Year. I would have called you last night, but it was my first night on my own and things kind of fell apart."

For almost a month I didn't hear from him. I started my disastrous relationship with the Unstable One. Then, as that was on the decline, I awoke one morning to a Great message, a welcome distraction from Instability. A Bronx cheer, then, "Remember that? What are you doing after work Friday, dummy? Let me know if it's okay. Leave a message."

Mark was more affectionate than usual, though of course, in his own Great way: gently slapping me, laughing, pushing his hand into my face, growling such endearments as, "I'd like to rip your nose off."

I told him about my general sense of discouragement. I couldn't get my sociological articles published. I couldn't find an academic job. "I just don't know what I'm going to do with the rest of my life."

He retorted sharply, "You're going to live out your life as a good, warm, giving person. That's the main thing, isn't it? That matters more than this 'historical graffiti,' as I call it."

On Valentine's Day, he left a message on my answering machine, "Maybe I don't want to leave my name. Maybe I have no message. Ever think of that?" The name was not necessary. The message was pure Greatness. It ended with "Happy Valentine's *DAY*."

I returned his call.

"I just took my bread out of the oven! That's all I can afford for dinner! I'm broke!" Nevertheless, he was planning a week or two in the Caribbean. He grumbled about his new bargaining unit, the Subway and Surface Supervisors Association. "I went to their meeting to vote on that sell-out contract that took seven hundred positions out of the union and I thought everyone would be like me! They were slobs, badly dressed, poor grammar, stupid."

On the next Great visit, he was his usual self, slapping me playfully and teasing, "Here's the rest of the money I owe you. Now I never have to see you again! Whaa-ha-ha-ha! I love to tease you about that! Whaa-ha-ha!" Snooping around, he noticed my American Express bill, "Marvin Gardens, twenty-four dollars. Donaghy's Steakhouse, twenty-three dollars. You've been taking all these men out to dinner!"

"It's only one. That guy from track and power. And I don't take him out. We get separate checks. We go out together and occasionally we sleep together."

"Oh, ho! So the cat's out of the bag!" He teased me, called me a liar and a cheat. Then he'd moan that he was "number-two now, old meat." "You don't need me anymore. Good-bye and good luck."

In the morning, he actually came into the kitchen to have breakfast with me, "You moved my post cards!" he charged.

"I did not!"

"Yes, you did. You moved them from up here, to this low place on the wall. And what did you think of my birthday card?" The card referred to had a drawing of an ostrich with its head in the sand and lauded the recipient's "clear vision and keen insight."

"It was funny. I was insulted, but I think you meant it to be affectionate."

He laughed heartily. "It wasn't meant to be affectionate. If it were, I would have written 'love, Mark,' and I didn't." Then he relented, "I'm sorry I didn't write 'love.' Right after I got promoted I was," and he raised his hand over his head, "way up there."

"Welcome back," I said.

After that, we began to see each other regularly again. But he was usually in an awful mood, because he was being bounced around from one job location to another. "There's only two of us left from my class. We should go back, too! I come home from work, put on the television, watch *Naked City* until two A.M. Then I watch a movie. I usually fall asleep about halfway through the movie and wake up with the set blaring. I get up around noon and go to work. I'm sort of straddling two worlds. On one hand, to remain as I am, a recluse. Or to start pounding the square peg into the round hole."

"What does that mean?"

His responses were elliptical, and I never found out what he meant.

Maybe he meant settle down, get married, to me even. Maybe he didn't know, either.

We went out for dinner at Marvin Gardens. I thought how, even with the massive belly he'd acquired, he was still a striking figure. As we parted, he said, "I'm not going to kiss you in public."

"No one cares. People do it all the time."

"I'm not people," he said, but he kissed me.

I called Mark to remind him that his birthday was approaching and offered to take him out.

"Well, I don't know. Have you shaved your underarms?"

"Have you gotten me that shaver? I'll send you the ad."

"From the back pages of the *Enquirer*?"

"No, from *Glamour*."

"Glamour, my ass."

"Your ass has no glamour."

"Neither does yours, if you want to get into it."

"I don't. But you always seem to."

"Good-*bye*, Marian."

"Good-bye, Mark."

By the middle of August, it turned torrid for the first time that summer. I woke up to find a Great message on my machine, "Call me back. As soon as possible is not soon enough. Call me in the morning. I'll be crabby, but call me anyway."

"It hurts me to tell you this," he began when I complied. "Are you sitting down? Darlene is all in a huff, because I'm seeing you and not her for dinner."

For some reason, I suspected this was a reversal of the facts, that it was Mark who was huffed, because Darlene had other plans for dinner. So I said, "If it means that much to her, see her for dinner. It doesn't mean enough to me to be worth making her unhappy."

"You don't mean that!" he exclaimed.

"Sure I do."

He just laughed and asked me where I wanted to meet.

We met at Marvin Gardens and after dinner we took a cab home, and he told me about the train dispatchers he had been working with, capsule descriptions of their competence or incompetence, their "shuck and jive." Then, he said, "I think it's only fair that I be as objective about myself as I am about the others. I'm competent, but I tend, under pressure, to lose sight of the big picture, and concentrate on only one thing. I don't have enough self-confidence."

Later, at my place, he said, "I want to stay, and I want to go. I'm not used to being with people. It makes me nervous. I'm used to being alone. I'm not used to talking this much, or being this intimate."

I said, "I'm getting that way myself, withdrawn. I'm afraid my ability to be close to anybody is atrophying."

He was amused. "Intimacy isn't something you serve an apprenticeship in, Marian. It's not a skill. You don't take courses or get degrees in intimacy. You know what it's like? It's like a rain barrel that's full of water. Whether you dump it all out or let it keep accumulating so it sloshes out of the barrel, it's always going to be full, because it always keeps on raining. What I miss in my life isn't intimacy. I used to have something in my life that I really enjoyed. I used to love to sail. I loved to carry as much canvas as possible. I used to love to wait until the last possible minute to reef. There's nothing like that in my life now."

Saturday morning, there was a message on my answering machine. It was Mark. He asked me to call him and left a phone number that was unfamiliar to me. Frightened, I dialed as fast as I could. Where was I calling? A bar? Work? Some woman's apartment?

Mark answered.

"What's up?" I asked.

"Would you take care of Madeline—" the cat— "while I'm in the hospital?"

"What happened?" I whispered. What came into my mind was that he must have had an accident.

"I have a blood clot in my leg."

He'd had increasing discomfort for some weeks, until he had trouble walking. At that point, he'd called the HIP (Health Insurance Plan, his HMO) emergency number. He was admitted to Beekman Downtown Hospital.

"They think the clot might be traveling . . . ," he said. I knew that could mean a stroke or a heart attack. He wanted me to take care of the cat because Debbie, his former girlfriend and customary cat-sitter, was heading for Europe.

"I'd like to come see you," I said.

"I'll bet." he answered, "Well, you can't. I'm all wired up and I don't want you *leering* at me."

That evening, I went to see Mark. I was all prepared to be gentle and solicitous toward the helpless invalid. The moment I came in, he began trying to undress me. Only a curtain separated us from the other patient in the room. Annoyed by my resistance, he said, "If I die tonight, you'll be sorry you didn't."

"I'll take my chances."

The following week, Mark asked me to pick up his paycheck, since he was still in the hospital. Thursday evening, he called me again. After initial pleasantries, he asked if I'd picked up his check. I said I had.

"Where is it?"

"Just where you'd like to be: in my pants."

"You're not going to bring it to me?"

"Did you want me to? You didn't say anything."

"I assumed you would. This is what they meant in dispatcher training classes when they told us never to assume the employee knows. You have to spell it out. . . . I'm just joking."

"I'll come after work tomorrow. But you'd better be very nice to me." When I got there, he had no roommate. So he was very nice to me, indeed.

Mark came home from the hospital but was soon readmitted. "I've got another blood clot in my right leg, and I may have an embolism in my lung. They'll give me a test tomorrow to see if it's a big clot or a little clot, though the doctor said a little clot is like a little pregnancy. Afraid if I do have an embolism, my lung is permanently damaged."

They had released him before he was stabilized on the blood thinner. He was already planning his malpractice suit. To amuse himself, he made a special antenna out of tape and soda cans that enabled his little hospital television set to bring in Home Box Office.

Mark and I were fighting. He wanted me to bring him cigarettes, and I wouldn't.

"Next time I'm working at your terminal, I'll turn you on your last one!" he threatened.

"You'll never get away with it! I'll write the G-2 of the century!"

He told me there'd been a consultation with the floor resident and the vascular surgeon. Two of his former girlfriends had been there.

"Is there any reason why I wasn't there?" I blurted out.

"I didn't think you'd be interested. You don't ask much about my condition, or you ask in a casual way. Besides, you're so busy with your politics and your union meetings that you don't really have time for this kind of thing."

"If you aren't more important in my life, it's your choice, not mine."

For weeks, he had episodes of excruciating pain, and his clotting time swung from one extreme to another. Now his blood was clotting too slowly and he was in danger of hemorrhaging. The pain was from the breakup of the second clot. Blood was pooling and pressing against his large nerve.

The doctors were trying to figure out why his response to the blood thinner, Coumadin, was so erratic. Finally, he was transferred to a different hospital, to be under the care of a hematologist.

When I visited him there, he was in excellent spirits. The hematologist had appeared in the morning and talked to him an entire half-hour, "like an equal." The hematologist also brought him thirty pages of medical journal articles about genetic causes of resistance to Coumadin.

The hematologist believed the problem was genetic, but the residents had another theory. They told Mark to stop the nicorette chewing gum he'd been using to quit smoking. But the hematologist, eager for data useful for journal publication, had told Mark not to change anything he was taking. Mark, eager to get his name in the medical books, was cooperating with the hematologist and fighting off the residents.

I was convinced the residents were right and Mark should give up the gum. But with Mark on the far side of crazy already, I wasn't going to speak up. I told myself it was what he deserved for preferring a place in medical history to getting well.

Finally, Mark called me, "The experiment is over." He had stopped the nicorette gum. After that, he responded normally to the Coumadin.

In another week, Mark was released from the hospital. He was laid up at home for a long time. He had exhausted his sick leave. He made a pilgrimage to T.A. Headquarters at Jay Street to beg for alms, but he got nothing. So the next morning, he set out for the welfare office, wearing his two-hundred-dollar sunglasses and his Rolex Oyster watch.

MISCELLANEOUS

Twice a year, a subway worker "picked" a job on the work schedule. If there was any change in the work schedule, the union would hold a schedule meeting for both the motormen and conductors of that division. There was nothing in the contract or the union bylaws that said this meeting had to be held. It seemed to be a tradition, or a routine. Its most interesting feature is that it was the only time motormen and conductors, who worked together daily, attended a union meeting together.

Not long after the 1985 contract was ratified, there was an I.R.T. schedule meeting. As the officers reported on the new "pick," I felt they were trying to make the changes seem unimportant. They dismissed the new category of jobs, "utility," as an extension of an existing category, the extra list. They then dismissed the important fact that board jobs were cut, by saying "utility" would replace board jobs. A board job entailed a worker's reporting to a specific terminal at a specific time to be used if and when needed. If the worker waited eight hours without "picking up a job," the worker was paid straight time. If, however, the worker did pick up a job, he or she was paid straight time for the eight hours of the job, and time-and-a-half for the time "waiting on the board," that is, time in excess of eight hours.

Board jobs were seniority jobs, because they were coveted by people who wanted lots of overtime pay. This was especially common among guys about to retire, who wanted their final annual income to be as high as possible, because their pensions were based on it.

I got the floor. I pointed out in strong language that replacing board jobs with utility jobs was a concession. A board man picks his hours and his terminal. A utility man does not. People picked board jobs to make overtime on the board. A utility person may, or may not, make overtime, because he can be assigned a job before the working day begins. "So this is a loss in our control over our jobs. It's a loss in our power. It's not a neutral name change."

I heard someone say, "Good point," and another, "Well said!"

I concluded, "I point this out because we'll be voting on this. I think we should not accept this."

Will Washington, an organizer, responded, "We are not delighted with this schedule. But we believe that it is the best we could get." He listed changes they'd already gotten from management. "The name of the game is 'budget.' The goal is to cut out overtime." He read us the management prerogative clause out of God-knows-where. "That's what we're up against," he announced.

After that, the questions became more angry. Finally, a conductor demanded, "Just tell us how many jobs have been cut!"

Finally, an officer from motors did. "Sixty-three A.M. jobs, sixty-five P.M. jobs. All of them were yard jobs." Yard jobs were the best jobs, the easiest jobs, the jobs people waited years for, while pounding the road.

You could hear the meeting hold its collective breath for a second after that. In the quiet, Washington said, "They're planning to use the utility men to cover these jobs."

People began to mutter that they would vote "no" on it. All around the room, there was whispering and head-shaking. A conductor got up and angrily asserted that the vote meant nothing, that the union had lost all power over scheduling.

Washington claimed that the schedule meeting was required by the union bylaws regardless (although I've never found such meetings mentioned in them). It was as if he were rubbing our faces in our impotence. "Even if you vote 'no,'" he said, "we're not going to boycott this pick. We've gotten all the changes we can get out of them without drastic action."

The same conductor jumped up, "You've got to tell them we voted it down!"

"That is not required!" Washington shouted back.

Quiet was restored and Turn Around Vinnie Torrelli called for "all in favor."

Not a single hand went up.

"Opposed?"

Every hand in the place, a sea of hands. An organizer counted. Thirty-six.

"Abstentions?"

There were four. The officers had not voted.

Sure, it was a formality. Yet I was proud we had not been bamboozled into accepting it.

In the crew rooms, the turbulence increased. At Utica Avenue, the election leaflet had been defaced. Someone had written on it, "The T.W.U. is dead." Below that, in a different handwriting, "The T.W.U. died a long time ago."

Motorman Reggio was on the veranda, haranguing Motorman Colon and another motorman about a petition regarding the new pick. "We should pick, but sign this petition saying we will not work the pick."

"Ah, that won't faze them."

"We'll say we'll strike."

"But they know we can't."

"What about the union?" asked another train operator.

"Fuck the union," said Reggio. "We'll do it without the union."

Then, an important bulletin came out. It said that no motorman with less than two years' seniority would be allowed to pick "miscellaneous."

"Miscellaneous" jobs were jobs on the work trains. They were sort of like foie gras, a matter of taste, but for those who loved them, something nonpareil. Like the board jobs, they had lots of overtime practically guaranteed. Plus, they were not road jobs. No pesky riders or radio chats with Command Center.

But not everyone wanted the long hours of "miscellaneous" jobs. Not everyone wanted to work with the heavy construction equipment and the diesel engines.

We picked our jobs in order of seniority; that is, the most senior people picked first, getting first shot at the best jobs. So this bulletin was a clear violation of the principle of choice of jobs according to seniority. What if not all the "miscellaneous" jobs were picked by motorman with more than two years' seniority? What if there were still "miscellaneous" jobs open when the pick got down to the motormen with less than two years on the job? As it turned out, that was exactly what happened.

Management's answer was that, in that situation, they would count the number of open "miscellaneous" jobs, and motormen who were just above the two-year cutoff would be *assigned* to those miscellaneous jobs.

The process of picking began, with the real old-timers in the lead. Some folks were pooh-poohing this bulletin. But when I got into the Woodlawn crew room, Reggio and McAllister grabbed me. McAllister said, "We're going to get a court injunction to stop the pick, because it's violating the contract."

"The pick by seniority isn't even in the contract!" I said.

The moment I said this, silence fell over the crew room. Everyone was listening.

"We have nothing," I went on, "Nothing in writing that gives us the right to pick by seniority."

Then the storm broke.

"You mean, they're right?"

"What do we do?"

"We got to strike!"

"We got to get the vice president and them—"

I said, "That's what we got to do. Go down to the union and tell them."

Everyone was talking at once. Calling the union officers jerks. Threatening mayhem at the union hall. Finally, they got down to the practical means of reaching people at other terminals, to get them, also, to come to the union hall with us.

As we went down the road, my motorman, Colon, was running off the train at what seemed like every single gap station, to buttonhole somebody. He gave this long rap to a guy from his training class, whom he came across at Utica, "We got to do this, because if we don't soon they could be taking anyone, right? Or anything, right?"

To me, he said, "This is supposed to be a progressive society. Things are supposed to get better, our jobs, our benefits. They want to put us back to the thirties or forties."

That evening, I called Dave. He cautioned me not to imply to people that going down to the union hall was going to get us anyplace.

"Well, I wouldn't have wanted to say to them, 'Don't bother, the union put this in the contract.' Let the union officers tell them that."

On Tuesday morning, about ten of us went to the union hall. We let ourselves into the vice president's office. It wasn't Lawson anymore. He had been promoted to local secretary-treasurer. It was now Fred Lang, a white man in his sixties. I stated why we were there, our concerns. "We want to know what the union is going to do about it."

Lang began by giving a little spiel, which embodied the line of the new local president, Sonny Hall. "Management thinks we are afraid of the Taylor Law. We have to show that we are not."

Everyone agreed, fervently.

Lang confided in us that Sonny had a plan, yet undisclosed, which would demonstrate this lack of fear on our part.

We were gratified by this.

Then he showed us the notice he'd received from management, and the response he'd had hand-delivered to the head of T.A. Labor Relations.

Riggs the Radical asked where in our contract were our seniority pick rights given.

Lang said they were not, they were just "past practice."

In the response to the head of Labor Relations, Lang had written that the union considered assigning motormen to miscellaneous to be a violation of seniority. Lang assured us he was "pursuing it through channels. The head of labor relations on the sixth floor has referred us to his assistant on the third floor."

I asked, "What will the union do if management refuses to change its mind?"

Lang said, "When it gets to the point that motormen are being assigned to miscellaneous jobs, the pick will stop."

"What will make it stop?" I asked.

"You're all union men and women," he said, "if your seniority is violated, you refuse to pick."

People were silent, unconvinced that this would happen. Riggs came up with the suggestion that we destroy the pick books.

Lang was scandalized, "They're not our property!"

Several of us asked what would happen if motormen who didn't pick were assigned jobs?

Lang said, "Then, we won't work the pick." Pressed for details as to how this coup could be pulled off, he was vague: it was up to Sonny. There was plenty of time until the pick began. We could hope it would all be settled by then. Through channels.

But a week of going through "channels" produced no change in management's intentions. Motormen were still picking. It was quickly approaching the turn of the people who had two years on the job, and there were still "miscellaneous" jobs empty.

Lawson told me, "Management wouldn't budge. So we'll just have to go ahead and tell people not to pick."

"Who will tell people?" I pressed him.

"The pick men."

"How will they be informed?"

"We'll call them," said Lawson.

"Who will call them?"

"The people at Jay Street are calling them right now," Lawson assured me.

However, the forced pick had already begun. An hour earlier, while Lang had still been meeting with the head of labor relations and a dozen or so of us waited outside the union office at Jay Street, management called the pick men, who were all train dispatchers, and told them to stop allowing people to choose their jobs freely and to make the train operators choose miscellaneous. They were told that if a train operator refused to pick a miscellaneous job, one was to be assigned to him.

When a worker chooses a job, the supervisor "pick man" officially records it. There is also a union representative at each pick location who is, confusingly, also called the "pick man." His role is to fill in each person's choice on big work schedules mounted on boards. In this way, anyone, at any terminal, knows exactly what job each person in the division is working. During the picking process, this also allows workers to know which jobs are gone and which are still available.

A union pick-posting man phoned Lang to tell him that motormen were being assigned jobs.

"They gave us their word!" Lang exclaimed. "They pulled a fast one!" He told the man, "You can't tell them not to pick, and don't promise them anything." But this guy was conscientious. He did tell them not to pick, and he printed a "model grievance" and gave it to each one to copy.

One motorman got up to Woodlawn to pick that afternoon and was told he had to pick miscellaneous. It was the supervisor doing the pick, the assistant train dispatcher, not the union pick-posting man, who told him he could fill out a grievance. The union man was busy playing checkers.

By the next morning, we all knew that the union officers had betrayed us again. The guys were just picking, and all that most of the union pick men were doing was asking them if they wanted grievance forms.

The next morning, the pick was canceled.

I was jubilant. It felt so good to win!

The conscientious union pick man said, "I told the fellers, 'See, in unity there is strength.'"

I put a sign on the door of the crew room:

> We won!
> T/O Pick Canceled
> As of Tuesday A.M.
> In Unity We Are Strong!
> United — Invincible!

The last line was a T.W.U. motto. When I came back from my first trip, someone had written another of our union's mottoes underneath it:

> The best is yet to come.

It was, but not in the sense our union's leaders meant.

Although a few people were enthusiastic about the stopping of the pick, "Moneybags" O'Cauthen, a white motorman whose middle initials were "O.T.," for all the overtime he worked, was complaining, "The union claims two victories, and we're back where we started!"

"How are we back where we started?" I asked. "We've preserved seniority!"

O'Cauthen clarified the origins of the problem. "The senior men used to pick the work trains to make the O.T. Then the T.A. started sending in new men to relieve them after eight hours." The senior men apparently figured the two-year floor would rule out the use of very new motormen who were still on the extra-extra list for this purpose.

"But that's backwards!" I said. "If the motormen want the overtime, let them get something in the contract guaranteeing them their O.T., not limiting how other people can pick." But, for the first time, I understood why members had made the demand, and why the union had supported it.

When we got down to Utica Avenue, I saw McAllister. "Bad news, Marian. I was just talking to the pick man here and he says that they're just going to do the same thing to the motormen with *one* year!"

So the best had been yet to come.

In the end, about thirty people were forced to pick miscellaneous jobs. The union did nothing for them at all.

Throughout this whole struggle, as at other times, I was struck by a paradox. Transit workers felt themselves to be powerless, yet they generally believed they had legal and contractual rights that they actually did not have. For example, they were sure that, written down somewhere, they had a formal right to pick by seniority. They believed the T.A. was obligated to tell them the composition of steel dust, as if it were an industrial commodity. They believed restricted duty for workers with non-job-related disabilities was a contractual right, and when T.A. stopped supplying it, they believed the contract must have been changed. They believed we were eligible for disability payments if we ran out of sick leave. They believed T.A. was required to give us a lunch break, that there were legal limits on cab time. They believed that they couldn't be assigned work during their W.A.A. ("work as assigned") periods that had not been allowed under the earlier form of these periods, "T.C." (transferring cars).

Then, they blamed the dispatchers, they blamed the T.A., they blamed the union for letting the T.A. get away with these violations. And although they constantly rejected the legitimacy of the orders they were given, they nearly always complied with them.

COWORKERS

Subway operatives work as a two-person "crew": one train operator and one conductor. The other crew person had a tremendous impact on your job, and vice versa. This interdependency created a real incentive to get along well with all other workers, because you never knew whom you'd be working with, if not tomorrow, then sometime during your career.

As a conductor, my train operator could make my work easier or make my life a living hell. Probably the worst motorman I ever had, from the point of view of poor operation, was a new man named Toomey. I was first paired with him at Pelham Bay. My regular Saturday motorman had been promoted before the pick even started, and I was doomed to work with this fledgling almost every week.

Toomey often failed to stop the train in time. I would be doing my job, watching to make sure that when the train stopped, I was stopped in front of the zebra-striped conductors' board. But with Toomey, when I reached the board, the train would keep moving. He took me way past the board! More than half a car-length! This meant the front part of the train was probably out of the station. The door controls at a conductors' position only allowed a conductor to open all five front cars of the train at once, so you couldn't pick and choose which cars to open. If I opened the doors, riders would step out and drop down into the tunnel.

I would get on the P.A. "Motorman, are we alright in front?"

Typically, there would be no answer.

I would repeat my question.

Still no answer.

So I would have to open the rear, push my way out to the platform and, dodging riders like obstacles in an obstacle course, make my way to the front of the train to take a look for myself. Then, if the first door panel of the train was just barely inside the station, I could go back and open.

This might happen once, twice, even three times on a single trip. Once, they gave us an old train, a "jalopy." This was more than Toomey could handle: he put me past the board four times on that trip.

Another superstar was "Fast Eddie" Edwards, who— as you can tell from his nickname—was unutterably slow. On one trip, "Fast Eddie" was even slower than usual. As we schlepped along, I wondered, "What does he think? That if we're late enough we'll get a drop?" A drop was cancellation of your trip, or another crew's making your trip for you because you weren't in the terminal when it was scheduled to begin.

Two stops before we got to the terminal, "Fast Eddie" asked his favorite question, "Conductor, what time is it?" It was eight minutes past our "interval," the time of our next scheduled trip. Feeling he had already achieved a "drop," Edwards put on a tiny little bit of speed.

At the terminal, I dashed back to the crew room to fix a quick cup of tea. I expected we'd be sent out again immediately. But no word was said.

"Did the dispatcher say anything to you about when we go out?" I asked "Fast Eddie."

"Do not think the thought," murmured my motorman.

I had not been dropped once in the whole pick. Ironic that Edwards' recalcitrance should be so rewarded, but I, in any case, deserved the break. Edwards went downstairs to buy potato chips, and a motorman asked me, "What'd he pick?"

"Vacation relief."

"Thank God," said the motorman. He didn't want to be stuck behind a slow-mover like Edwards, who would make him miss lunch and finish work late.

"What are you complaining about?" I asked, "I'm the one that's got to work with him."

"She's right, you know," he said to the others.

At Van Cortlandt, I had another motorman who was slow. He was my Sunday motorman, and I called him "Molasses" Mulligan. I complained about him to another motorman.

"Mulligan's just always been slow," said the motorman.

I said, "And he always calls for an R.C.I.," the repairman you call when there is a problem with your train that might mean you have to take it out of service. "They should just assign an R.C.I. to whatever job he picks."

"He's a moody guy, too," said the motorman.

"I thought only intellectuals were moody," I said.

"He's no intellectual," said the motorman.

However, I found out something new about Molasses near the end of the pick. Around the fifth month of the pick, supervisory policy flip-flopped, as it so often did. All of a sudden, slow was out and fast was in. The mantra over the radio became, "Motorman, where did you lose your time?"

Mulligan, the coward, blamed it on me, and when we got back to Van Cortlandt, I had to call Command. I was pretty sore, and argued that they should just take a look at their sheets to see that all my trips during the rest of the week were on time, while Mulligan was late no matter whom he worked with.

The next time I worked with him, it was as if Mulligan had for the first time discovered "multiple," the highest speed on the motorman's controller. For the first time we got our breaks and our lunch. So long as Molasses thought the boss wanted slow speeds, he crept along at a pace that would make a snail restless. As soon as he realized the slow speed era had ended, he wrapped it around!

Thus, I lost all my respect for Mulligan. He wasn't a principled crawler, he was a company man! And after all those miserable Sundays without any lunch or any breaks.

My Monday motorman was a different kind of problem. "Hot-Rod" Reed was fast and aggressively cheerful. He was a maniac with a bellow for a voice. He consistently goaded me to shorten my station stops. We argued constantly about my practice of clearing out the rear of the train before we got to South Ferry.

The southernmost stop on the No. 1 line is South Ferry, one of the oldest stations on the line. It was built around a very sharp curve, and it is now a scant half a train-length long. Because only the front half of the train can fit along it, the conductor must keep the rear of the train closed and just open the front. Thus, woe betide the ignorant riders in the rear car. The train stops at Rector Street, the station before South Ferry, then stops again in the tunnel while, unbeknownst to them, the front half of the train is opening at South Ferry. Then the riders see South Ferry station whizzing (and squealing—that sharp curve is terribly noisy) by. Before they can make sense of the experience, they'll be back at Rector Street again.

Now, to prevent this nuisance, the conductor is supposed to walk through the rear cars at Rector Street and persuade all the riders to move to the first five cars, so they can exit at South Ferry. And that's pretty much what I used to do. To make it a little easier on myself, I didn't walk through the cars, I went out on the platform to go from car to car. Of course, not all the riders could be moved, but it was a pretty successful tactic. Reed didn't like me to do it. It took too long. "Just make your announcement at Rector Street, and close down."

"The riders don't understand the announcement. They don't know which car they are riding in."

"You know, the train could malfunction and close down and you could be left on the platform," he warned me.

"I could pull the conductor's cord before I go," I offered, "and reset it when I get back to my position."

Of course, we both knew that activating the emergency brakes would make our sojourn at Rector Street conform better to the rulebook, but also interminably long. Reed gave up, muttering under his breath, and I continued my mission to the rear cars.

I wasn't the only conductor who had problems with a motorman. I once heard two conductors discussing the trouble one of them was having with his Monday motorman. The conductor would close down the train, but his motorman would not move the train. The people would start accumulating on the platform, and shouting at the conductor to reopen the doors. "I dread Mondays," he said. He said he was sure the cause of the problem was that his motorman was getting into conversations with women on the train during the stops and didn't notice the indication light that would tell him the doors were closed.

Other conductors offered him advice.

"With someone like that, write him up."

"Say on the P.A., 'Motorman what's the problem?' Say, 'If there's no problem, motorman, let's go.' Then the riders will start getting on him."

"Nah, they won't," replied the victim. "They can't even see him. And if we get one of those new air-conditioned trains, they don't care if we sit there forever."

"You have to talk to him. Tell him, 'Listen, when we work together, when I close down, you got to go.' Because you can't reopen. Because someday someone's going to get hurt and you will 'go downtown.'"

I had another motorman, Hodges, who also blamed our lateness, which was merely a matter of a few minutes, on me. He would poke along, barely fast enough to keep on schedule. He'd hold thirty-five pounds of air until indication came in, which meant it took him a long time to release the brakes and start the train after our doors closed. At gap stations, he held seventy pounds of air, and on the new trains, that could take as long to release as the rest of the station stop. If we encountered a work crew on the tracks, he never drove faster afterward to make up the time. He also would shut off the intercom, so I could not reach him—until he had something to say to me. One day at Grand Central, he told me over the intercom, "Conductor, you're going to have to work faster! We're late!"

I was furious. I was getting the doors closed as fast as I could without killing or being killed. "You'd better work faster!" I answered. I was outraged. At the next stop, I deliberately held the doors open. He thought I was slow? I'd show him slow!

He called me again, "Conductor! Why can't you close those doors?"

"To show you that I do my job, you do yours. I don't tell you how to drive, you don't tell me how to operate my doors."

"I'm tired of them calling me on the radio, asking where'd I lose my time."

"We lost it in the tube! We crept through the tube!"

"I told them that I have a slow conductor."

Once, I made the mistake of yielding to this pressure and trying to work faster. By the end of the trip, I had a transit policeman threaten to write me up for closing the doors on him. I couldn't win.

When we got to the terminal, I reported the incident to the dispatcher. "It was a mistake to try to do that," he advised me. "They can't say a conductor is working too slowly."

After I called the trainmaster to report the incident, the transit patrolman saw me on the platform. "Get a job you can handle!" he shouted at me.

Everyone in the crew room took my side against Hodges, even the other motormen.

"He's a little . . . ," one of my other motormen said, turning his palm over and back twice, to finish the sentence. "You're not a slow conductor."

"He's moody, very moody," said a conductor.

Another motorman said, "I'd trade most of my conductors to work with you any day."

A third motorman said, "The doors are the conductor's responsibility."

And still another motorman, "He's wrong. The motorman doesn't know what's going on back there."

Conductors could likewise plague motormen. Once, in the crew room, everyone was talking about this one female conductor.

"Man, she's really crazy."

"She used to drive me crazy."

"She almost got me killed construction flagging."

"I worked with a lot of females, and they were all good. But I hear so much about Mendez. . . ."

A conductor patted me on the shoulder, "Poor Swerdlow. Here we are all talking about another woman conductor like this. I'm sorry."

Crew members depended on each other, and traditionally, cooperation was expected to go above and beyond merely performing their respective jobs harmoniously.

There was one very senior motorman, Crosby, who liked to play chess. In fact, in general he liked the crew room very much. He made a point of never leaving it until the starting lights for his interval were turned on. One Saturday when I worked with him, he missed the first trip entirely because he came late. For the second one, he stayed in the crew room until the starting lights went on, as was his custom. No sense closing the doors before he had the train charged up. When I finally closed the doors, my front section indication doesn't come in. I snapped the doors a few times, and when that accomplished nothing, I put it on the P.A. The R.C.I. came bouncing out on the platform. He pushed the doors around a bit, and, voila, the indication came in. So, by the time we left, we were ten minutes late, and I was already a nervous wreck, knowing I had doors that stuck, as well as a side window that showed a reluctance to open.

At Hunt's Point, as I was closing up, I saw someone holding the doors in the front car. Of course, I tried valiantly to close 'em. I heard Crosby announce, "Hold your doors, conductor." So I did.

I heard the horn signal for assistance. I stood my ground.

About a minute later, riders started streaming out of the first car. My stomach started to hurt. Something dreadful seemed to be happening. A variety of code twelves—twelve-two, twelve-nine, twelve-eight—rushed through my head.

People began to get back on. Crosby gave me two and we proceeded. As we returned to Pelham Bay, I heard on the platform P.A., "Conductor Swerdlow, call Command Center." My heart went to my throat and I felt the familiar panic. I marched into the train dispatcher's office and asked him, "Do you know what it's about?"

"About the armed passenger."

"Armed passenger!"

"Yeah, about the woman who was pistol-whipped."

I got the story from Crosby. Going into Hunt's Point, a woman approached him, saying she was being pursued by a man with a gun. Crosby put it on six-wire, the emergency transmission system. She couldn't decide whether or not to get off the train and make a run for it. The guy came into the front car, hit her, and took her pocketbook, saying, "I ought to kill you, bitch." Then he walked off the train, right into the arms of the cops.

Crosby complained to me, "You stay in the middle too much. What if I'd been in trouble?"

"You don't seem like the kind of guy who would need help," I replied.

At its best, the crew relationship could be a deep and appreciative one. When his conductor's wife died, one motorman collected money for him. He told me he had picked a later job, just so he could work with this conductor. "He can put up with me, so I figure I might as well stick with him."

At worst, a crew member could stab the other one in the back—and even cost him his job. The worst incident I ever heard along such lines took place between Spruce and his conductor O'Rourke. One day the road was so bad, we had a full cast of characters in the crew room. The main topics of conversation were a motorman who had split a switch at 138th Street and a conductor who had been taken out of service.

"Which conductor?"

"Spruce's Sunday conductor."

I had argued with Spruce a year earlier about refusing a dangerous order. "I put the bread in my family's mouths," he had said. Since then I had found he was disliked because, in order to put a little extra bread in those mouths, he habitually operated very slowly, tying up all the trains behind him, making the crews lose breaks and lunch. "Spruce goes down the road at switching speed," they grumbled.

Someone checked the pick board. "O'Rourke works with him Sundays." According to Spruce, he was pulling out of 125th Street, when the dispatcher told him over the radio to "hold up." So he stopped and the doors of the train opened. He looked out of his cab and saw the doors were open, the first two cars were out of the station, and there was a motor instructor right there. So, to cover himself, he called Command and reported that his doors had opened. They asked, 'Were you standing or moving when it happened?' He said he was standing. When supervision came to get the conductor, he beat it. Disappeared. Now he was AWOL.

Soon I heard other versions of the story. A conductor told me that the motor instructor who had been there reported only one door panel out of the station. "Well, this is a whole different ballgame," I said, "Spruce is claiming O'Rourke had opened up with two cars out. That would have been gross negligence. If he only had one door panel out, he was probably close enough to the board to have assumed the whole train was still in the station."

Another motorman added, "Not only that, but the motorman told Command that he smelled alcohol on his conductor's breath!"

If that were true, Spruce was trying to get O'Rourke fired. He couldn't possibly justify it by saying he was covering himself. A conductor's sobriety is not his motorman's responsibility.

These stories all traveled back to the crew room. The next time Spruce entered, Riggs the Radical, scourge of scabs, descended upon him, "What's this I hear about you reporting your conductor?"

"I had to do it to cover myself, protect myself."

"But it was wrong. Now the man's in hot water. If you'd kept quiet, neither one of you would be in trouble."

"He's in trouble because he split."

I could well understand why he split. Most of the workers believed that alcohol would show up in your B.A.T., blood alcohol test, for a full twenty-four hours. They were afraid of losing their jobs from drinking the previous evening, even though they were completely sober the next day.

Finally, I myself spoke to the motor instructor who had been on O'Rourke's train. He confirmed the story that there had been only one door panel out and that O'Rourke had radioed Command with a false report that there were two cars out. The motor instructor told me he had immediately called Command on his own radio with the correct story. "The whole thing could have been handled differently," he said. "It should have ended right there. Except the motorman put the whole thing on the air, and that not even the true situation."

O'Rourke was busted down to token clerk, "the booth." Years later, I was going through the Fordham Road station on my way home and whom do I see in the booth but O'Rourke. He invited me inside and we talked of this and that. He was in good humor. But his days as a conductor were all behind him.

Sabotage by one worker against another was unusual, but I did come across one instance. "How do you spell 'sabotage,' like when you sabotage a train?" Angelo Gonzalez asked me when I came in the crew room one day. He was busy writing something. "That relay man at Utica Avenue is an idiot," he continued, "I won't leave him my handles. I got burned a couple of times, so I won't do it." Gonzalez meant that he was removing his brake handle from the train before the switchman relayed it to the uptown track for the return trip. This meant the switchman had to lose time charging up the train before moving it.

"So he's started sabotaging my train," Gonzalez went on. "In the summer, he put my heaters and my cab heater on. He took out my sealed beams [the train's 'headlights']. I didn't want to do nothing. I didn't want to report him. But this week I got to Franklin Avenue Station, and I didn't have no brake. You ain't got no brake, you go out of the station."

Although fuses on trains have been replaced with circuit breakers, it doesn't prevent this sort of sabotage. And riders are put at risk, although there are some fail-safe features to ensure safe operations. Motormen are supposed to do a "rolling test" at the terminal when they first get their train. After they allow the train to roll a few feet, they apply the brake to make sure the train stops. It's not clear why this didn't bring the problem to Gonzalez' attention.

After that, Gonzalez found that switches were "cut out," that is, turned off, on his train when it was relayed at Utica. He was forced to do a pretty thorough check whenever he got his train back at Utica to make sure he didn't have any dangerous conditions like cut-out brakes.

Gonzalez was mystified when he was notified that he was to start working

Broadway. In turned out someone had submitted a bid in his name to change to a job on the Broadway line. He had his hands full convincing downtown that he hadn't put in the bid and should keep the job he was working.

For me personally, relations with my coworkers were shaped by the fact that I was a woman, and there were still only a few of us in a sea of men. I have already described the way men reacted to me when I first came on the job. We were a tremendous novelty and were regarded with more curiosity than hostility. Dave Stone once predicted relations would get worse when there were more of us, but that hasn't been my experience.

We women were propositioned endlessly. For me, it tapered off after the guys in a terminal got to know me, and especially insofar as I was associated with Mark Goniea. For the most part, Mark didn't have to do anything to protect me.   He just had to stand there, well over six feet tall, weighing nearly three hundred pounds, carrying a pistol and, above all, well-liked by his coworkers. Still, occasionally, I was approached. On at least one occasion, he actively defended me, despite my begging him not to.

This was the pick that Mark and I worked together on Sundays. We made the 4:27 out of Utica. On this particular day at Utica, I had been talking to Mark at the front of the train for most of my break. I got to my position about three minutes before my interval was scheduled to leave, a minute earlier than I was required to.

My follower, Conductor Ambrose, was already standing there. He started in with me, "You're lucky there isn't a motor instructor here. You'd be in lots of trouble. And the train is dark. The riders were asking if this train is in service. You'd better cut this out, or you'll be in trouble."

Since I hadn't broken any rules, it annoyed me to be lectured, and I told him so. He maintained his stance that he was trying to keep me out of trouble. Finally, I said, "I know what's really going on. You told me the other day on the platform that you had your eye on me—"

"I was never interested in you. I don't get particularly interested in white girls—"

"—and now you see me with someone else—"

"Anyone can say anything they want. Now, if you are prejudiced—"

"Me? You're the one who just said you don't get interested in white women."

He shook his finger at me, "You're going to get yourself in trouble. And your color isn't going to protect you!"

"What the hell has my color got to do with this?" I got the lights, and I started "closing down," shutting my train's doors.

"You're nasty!" he said.

"You're a liar!" I shot back and, even as I spoke, I realized that Ambrose wouldn't consider lying to a woman to be really lying. I was so upset that I told Mark the whole story over the intercom.

"I'll have to take care of him," said Greatness, "I hate it when I have to play the role of protector."

"So don't."

"There's no other language he'll understand," said Mark lugubriously.

"Listen," I said, growing concerned, "if you don't want to do it, and I don't want you to do it, why do it?"

"Because you told me, and so I have to. Let this be a lesson to you. If you don't want me to do anything, don't tell me anything."

Nothing I said could shake his logic, or lack of it. When we got back to Woodlawn, I went up to the dispatcher's shack, where Mark was returning his radio, and continued to plead with him. "A man's got to do what a man's got to do," he told me.

"Jesus Christ," I muttered.

Our follower was coming into the terminal. Mark walked down the steps of the shack to the conductor's position. The train stopped. Mark leaned into the window of Ambrose's cab, lowering his huge bulk. I couldn't see Ambrose, but I could picture him. He was a slight man, about a foot shorter than Mark. Mark was smiling and rotating his right hand. I felt faint with mortification.

For about a month after that, Ambrose treated me as if I were invisible. After that, we both acted as though nothing had ever happened. As subway workers often repeated, you got to work with people.

In another incident, my motorman had a student along. At Atlantic Avenue, the student laced into me, "You hold the doors too long! Let me give you some advice—"

"I don't need your advice," I interrupted, "I work the way I please. You're the student. Learn your job and don't criticize mine."

"You know something? I'm going to call you Carol, because you look like Carol Bellamy." Bellamy was a fairly high-profile municipal official at that time, who was not considered to be good-looking. "I guess all us white girls look the same. Let me ask you, what stop are you complaining about?"

"All of them."

"Because at three of the stops, I had little children with their teachers getting on and off the train. Do you think I should have closed the doors on them?"

"Listen," he said, "now don't be offended, but I wouldn't care if all those kids fell between the platform and the train. Being a conductor really has changed the way I look at life."

Abruptly, I felt my anger dissipate. "Now I understand why you said that. Now I see where you're coming from." What I saw was that he was totally crazy.

He said to me, "You're very forthcoming. So I figured I had to go after you before you went after me. A woman can always outargue a man." He offered his hand, "Do you like me?"

"Sure."

"Wanna make a date?"

"You're kidding!" I cried. "You just said this morning that your wife just had a baby! I know you're only kidding."

"Is that all you can say?" he asked, "'You've got to be kidding?'"

I took my things and walked to the door, smiling, "I know you're kidding. Your wife just had a baby."

"Yeah," he said, "I was kidding."

When we got up to Woodlawn, I met my motorman. "What a messed-up motorman!" he said of his student. "I hope I never see that dude again! He's got a personality like a cactus!"

One day when I was very new, still extra-extra on the P.M.s, I worked with a motorman named Krieger. He was a middle-aged white guy with a craggy face, warm grey eyes, and a wiry body that looked like he worked out often. He was taciturn and gruff, but good-natured. He asked me if I wanted to go out for a beer after we cleared. He took me to a red neck bar in Throgs Neck. The beers made him slightly more expansive, which isn't saying much. "Ever been married?" I asked him.

"Yeah."

"What happened?"

"A disaster." He practically spit out the words, "I wasn't made to be married. And you, are you divorced, too?"

He said he had two kids, and smiled with sudden warmth. "They're great." At one point, he told me, "You think too much," but added quickly, "but I like that, I like that. I like being alone," he said, and added quickly, "or out with a pretty girl."

He drove me home and kissed me. "Say I can come upstairs," he urged.

I was distrustful. "I'm going to give you my phone number," I said. "If this means something, you'll call me."

He did call me the next morning, but only to say he did not know when he could see me. He finally called me again weeks later on my R.D.O.S. He said he was in the city and wanted to see me. I explained that I had resumed my relationship with Goniea and didn't want to see anyone else just then.

"Marian, don't do this to me! I drove fifty miles to see you!"

But I was adamant.

I ran into him just a few days later when I got on the lead car of his train. He leaned out of the cab and beckoned to me. "You don't have to avoid looking at me," he said, "I'm not angry at you or anything."

"I wasn't aware I was doing it."

"I have something to tell you. I hope you won't be angry at me. Maybe you will be. I'm married."

I was more surprised than angry. "But didn't you tell me—?"

"That I was divorced?" he grinned. "I told you my marriage was a disaster, and then I asked, 'How about you? Are you divorced, too?' So I implied. . . ."

I shook my head, like someone who's just had a close call with a truck.

"Are you angry? It is a disaster," he reiterated, "but I can't leave. Because of the kids. It's not fair to them. They didn't ask to be born."

I learned from this encounter to assume guys on the job were married until proven single. Almost all of these guys were already spoken for. And there was evidence all around me. At the panic control refresher class, where the motor instructor was supposed to be reinforcing the procedures to follow in case of emergencies like fires or derailments, he saw fit to announce something like, "Women always have the advantage in dealing with men."

Then, evidently remembering the solitary female present, he turned to me, "Isn't that right?"

In total honesty, I told him, "I haven't the faintest idea what you are talking about." I plunged on, "All I know is you guys will tell any lie and, if we believe it, it's our responsibility. Every man in this T.A. says he's not married. But, somehow, they all have wives!"

There was silence in response, until the instructor, who had repeatedly referred to his own wife, said, "Only the wives are married!"

My favorite example was Antonio Gustavo.

Gustavo was a radioman up at Woodlawn. He worked the radio job, keeping track of the radios, because he was "restricted" due to high blood pressure. After a certain number of years on the job, if you had some kind of physical problem, even one unrelated to the job, rather than go on a disability pension, you might get a "restricted duty" job, but there was nothing in the contract or the rulebook about this. The T.A. could just as easily choose to give you N.W.A. status— "no work available." meaning they had no work for someone with your restriction. Then you were thrown back on your sick leave. After that ran out, there was any vacation time you might have coming to you, then sick leave at 60 percent of pay, the duration of which was based on your length of service and set out in the rulebook. After that, you could try going out on a disability pension, but that would mean a sharp drop in income.

Of course, if your problem was caused by the job, T.A. would move heaven and earth to find a restricted job for you, even in the booth. Since T.A. would be paying your compensation and differential if you didn't work, it wanted to get some productivity out of you. Then you'd have to prove you couldn't do the job they wanted you to do: work a "plat" with a torn ligament in your leg, for example.

Gustavo was in the first category. Anyone who looked at him could make an educated guess about what caused his high blood pressure. He was what Jasmin Joyce uncharitably referred to as "a tub of lard." Since noting radio numbers was not the most demanding job, Gustavo had plenty of time on his hands. One of the things he did with this time was talk to me. Since I had considerably less time on my hands, our conversations occurred in snatches, but, over the months, he told me this story about himself.

He was a single fellow, he claimed, who used to hang around with the fellows with whom he had grown up. But now, somehow, they seemed shallow to him. He was searching for a deeper meaning to things.

It was hard for me to imagine that anything could have less depth than Gustavo and exist in three dimensions at all. Nevertheless, when he suggested we go to a museum together so that I could introduce him to art, I figured, why not? In any case, it would force me to do something recreational, which I rarely did. As we were making the appointment, I asked him for his phone number, just in case I had to change my plans.

He told me he had no phone.

"Then I can't do it," I said, "I never do anything with someone who has no phone."

"You're being materialistic!" he accused.

"Yep, you've discovered my true nature." Actually, I had discovered his. My rule of thumb was that you could tell whether a transit worker was married by the ring—the one you couldn't give him on the phone.

A short time after that, Motorman McAllister asked me, "Did you hear about Motorman Gustavo? The T.A. gave him a permanent restriction and then told him they wouldn't give him restricted work anymore. And now the other departments won't take restricted people either. He went down to the union and they told him to apply for welfare!"

"Does Gustavo have a family to support?" I asked, pretending deep sympathy.

"Oh, sure he does! A wife and at least two kids! Maybe three!"

My friend Jasmin Joyce had an admirer who was much more persistent, although he made no bones about being married. He was a white guy from the T.A., but not the subways, with ties to the "old opposition." They met when she came to a meeting about a fare increase—or maybe a contract or a union election—and he was smitten. He appeared on her train within a week to invite her to another meeting. When he was getting off, he had apologized for "being a pest," but then added, "I'm not really worried about being a pest. Actually, I've become quite fond of you."

Because he had described himself as "the glue between the old opposition" and the newer people gathering around Dave Stone, we started to call him "the glue." The name—er—stuck.

He started writing her poetry:

Let's meet
Let's fete
'Nuff said!
Let's wed!
Jasmin Joyce,
You're my choice!
Fourteen daughters
All good lawyers
Fourteen sons
With East Side runs
Father writes books
As well as she cooks
Or shares his stories
With crew room cronies
Please note that this letter is written
As a proposal
Not a proposition

The next time the Glue saw her he piped up, "I know why you didn't answer it."

"I didn't understand it."

"No. You were scared. I've never been unfaithful to my wife. I was just irritated with the job. I thought you'd understand."

On New Year's Day, the Glue got on her train again and renewed his suit. "I've decided that my wife is not the right person for me to have children with," he informed her, "but I've been watching you for several months now, and I've decided that the right person is you."

"This is all so sudden," she answered, between P.A. announcements.

"Give me one reason why it wouldn't work."

"Well, ahem, I am involved with someone else right now."

A month or so later, Joyce called me, "I'm pretty upset. I just opened the mailbox, and this letter stuck to my hand. He's been sending me a poem every week. I sent him a note asking him not to send me any more stuff. Now he's sent me this button that says, 'Jackson in '84—Transit Workers' Coalition,' and this leaflet, 'Why Transit Workers Should Vote for Jackson.' On the back of it, there's this letter. It doesn't make a whole lot of sense, but it's very insulting." She read it to me:

Dear Esquire (Since this is how all but incautious lawyers style themselves):

I hope you aren't *intimidated* by a little—well—POLITICS. Not that you would be by my prose on the reverse side, any more than by my verse—the lawyerly, low-key animals' darling intimidated by moles? by sparrows? As well cats by mice—as I rhymed, I recall, and as you doubtless understood. You are a treacherous liar, once you fall to writing, Madam Attorney—you will tell any lie, no matter how outrageous, to seem shy, bland, and charming—such as the obvious falsehood, your standby, of puzzling over the mere meaning of my verse scribblings. You are no more an interpreter, even of these, than a mole is a sparrow—you like or dislike, enjoy or discard—but fear if you display your taste, I'll differ, and the game end.

Not at all—you forget my emotions precede me—as yours trail you.

Which suggests, by the by, that even the button may "intimidate" you—wear it—if you can sleep with one, you can vote for one—horrors!

You don't know how lucky loveliness makes you—the mole portion of humanity, self-denied it, bristles at the mirror, which plays political tricks, like a fairy tale, so that only communists and madmen see people other than as contributions to census data on the races. This leaflet born at a meeting—two caucasians there—one of those a Jew—only one a representative of such as we—and he is thoroughly ashamed—and now, it seems, at his wits' end . . . .

It was, of course, unspeakably racist, elitist and vile. I told Dave Stone about it. He was appropriately shocked and disgusted. A letter like that, written by an activist, had no place in his tidy and rational world.

It was less foreign to the dark, brooding universe of Riggs the Radical. "I think he is dangerous," he said. "His letter is like Hinckley's writings to Jodie Foster. She ought to watch herself."

Even before women came into the job, married male subway operatives regarded their jobs as happy hunting grounds, with female riders as the prey. Conductors had the easier pickings. In spiffy uniforms, with plenty of time between stops, and a mandate to keep an eye on the riders in their cars, they were great flirts. Motormen kept the tradition, too, during station stops and even while driving. Although they didn't have uniforms back then, and they often dressed in what amounted to dusty rags, savvy ladies knew that they were better-paid than conductors.

The pay phone in the crew room had a very important function in these workers' social lives. Since most of them, and even many of their lady friends, were attached, they would give their love interests the telephone number of the crew room pay phone and the scheduled time of their lunch or break. Thus all through the day and night, the phone would ring, until someone obligingly answered it. Even I did sometimes. "Woodlawn crew room."

I would hear something along these lines, "Is Conductor Thompson there?"

I would open the door of the booth and roar at the top of my lungs, "THOMPSON! THOMPSON HERE?"

And usually someone would shout back, "HE'S DOWN THE ROAD!"

"He's down the road, miss," I would relay.

"Oh. Well, could you tell him Dorabella," or some similar lovely appellation, "called."

"Sure. If I see him."

But I never heard of a single case of unwanted touching, or of any woman's being insulted in specifically sexual terms, as distinct from more generally sexist terms, whether in spoken words, writing, or pictures. On rare occasions, there were "pinups" in the crew room or in men's lockers. It seemed to me clear, however, that these were survivals from the all-male days rather than malicious affronts to us, the female pioneers.

The single case of harassment in sexual form (as distinct from other forms of harassment because of our sex) I heard of came from a woman who complained that a guy at the Lenox terminal continually undressed in front of her in what she described as a "hostile and provocative way."

The main feature of male chauvinism on the job was the myth among crews that women conductors and train operators had it easy, because T.A. gave them special privileges and extra breaks. (I have written about this elsewhere, in the journal *Gender and Society*, September 1989.) For instance, after a motorman was killed trying to fasten down a signal stop arm, the signals were redesigned so that they could be easily disabled, by the use of a key. However, one motorman voiced the belief that this improvement was made "because of the women on the job. The women get privileges."

Another myth was that "they put all the women in Jay Street," the Transit Authority Headquarters, where a handful of conductors have desk jobs. But there were plenty of men in those jobs, and the vast majority of women conductors were working the road. Mark Goniea, for example, had worked at Jay Street after nine months on the road. Conductor Richmond, who was in my training class, was there in less than a year.

Despite the fact that I, and many other women, had been assigned to work midnights, many men believed that "they never put a woman on the midnights."

One day I heard the old-timers at 137th Street passing around a story about how some woman had a pick job, a very easy job that kept you off the road, because of her relationship with someone.

I asked her name. They didn't know.

I asked where she worked. No knowledge, either.

I asked with whom she had the relationship.

They said they knew, but would not tell.

Despite the lack of detail, this story was vivid to them and confirmed their perception: women on the job had it easy. We got a lot of breaks, and that was the only reason we were able to do the same job as the men. This enabled them to hang on to their feeling of superiority even as women increasingly worked the same jobs they did.

To say that we were not harassed doesn't mean these men weren't sexist. One day I was waiting in the dispatcher's shack before starting when this young white motorman walked in, looked at me and said, "Just what I need."

"What is it you need?" I asked coldly.

"A vacation! I'm starting vacation tomorrow!" he said, hurriedly.

"I don't think that's what you meant," I sneered.

"I shudda kept my mouth shut. Look, we're gonna do just fine together."

"Yeah, and if we don't, I'll know the problem is your attitude."

"No, no. Women are the fastest—"

I don't know how many complained behind my back, because it obviously was a bad idea to alienate one's conductor.

And there were comments about our operation. Once during a very crowded trip, when I found it hard to close the doors because too many people were getting on and off, my motorman kept urging me over the intercom to close the doors.

When we got to the terminal, he said to me, "I didn't mean anything by what I said to you on the I.C. It's just that a lot of the lady conductors like to wait for people coming up the stairs."

There was also plenty of unconscious, gratuitous sexism in the way men discussed women in general—but no different from men in other work settings in which I've found myself. No surprises there.

A fair amount of friction between men and women was caused by the toilet situation. Our toilets were unisex. More accurately, they were for men. There were urinals out in the open, and no doors on the cubicles. The effect of this plumbing was that the presence of even one member of one sex made the whole bathroom off limits to the opposite sex.

As a woman, I had to wait until all the men were out of the washroom, then go in and latch the door of the washroom; no man could use it, even just to wash his hands, until I came out. Why couldn't they come in to wash their hands? Because I was sitting there in a cubicle without a door. Why couldn't T.A. put doors on the cubicles? Because to do that, the entire washroom would have to be rebuilt, which would take two years (at least), during which time the entire terminal would have to use the dispatcher's single toilet at the opposite end of the station.

One day, we had a only a short break and I needed to use the toilet. Three guys were already inside. Two came out but the third showed no sign of doing so. After a while I thought maybe I had been wrong in the count, and the room was now empty. "Is anyone in there?" I called out.

Then I heard singing coming from inside.

There were guys waiting behind me. They understood my situation and were waiting patiently, since I'd been there first, for me to go in and then leave. But they were getting restless. After all, by the time the crooner had finished, they could be in and out. So first my motorman, Angelo Gonzalez, went in. "Just to wash my hands," he said apologetically. He came right out. Then a conductor went in to piss. He, too, came right out. Then another motorman went in. This was a guy who had been teasing me with mock salutes and calling me "the future trainmaster" just because I'd taken the test for train operator. And as he went in, he was laughing.

The laughing did it for me. I started kicking the washroom door and cursing the occupants.

The singing halted, abruptly.

The guys outside looked at me soberly. I heard the nightingale flush and leave.

When I came out, a conductor asked me, "Are you okay?"

A motorman asked the same thing and added, "I spoke to the guy in there and I explained it to him."

On another occasion, one of the female conductors was in the bathroom. A motorman tried the door and found it locked. "Someone in there?" he called.

A motorman I hadn't seen before was there. "I think it is a motor-PUSS-on," he snickered. I could tell he was proud of what he considered a witty remark.

I said, "I think it's a conductor."

"And I think it is a motor-PUSS-on," he repeated.

"Why are you giving her a promotion?"

"Well, you ladies don't want to be called motormen."

"Especially when we're conductors. Even male conductors don't want to be called motormen."

He didn't respond.

During my first pick at Woodlawn, I circulated a grievance, in actuality, a petition, asking for a separate women's toilet in the terminal.

Not a single person, male or female, refused to sign. However, a few of the guys, including Mark, made cracks. "I don't mind." "I think we ought to do what the Japanese do." A few pointed out to me that the men's facilities were awful and that the men needed a new toilet as well. I said I was keeping a record of their conditions and I'd circulate a "grievance" for that, too.

At length, the dispatcher told me that T.A. had responded to our grievance. Women would be allowed to share the toilet that belonged to the supervision. It was being painted, and a lock would be installed.

This discouraged me. The supervisor's toilet was at the opposite end of the terminal from the crew room, a five-minute walk there and back, if your pace is brisk. Since there was rarely toilet paper or soap in T.A. toilets, many of us kept these supplies in our lockers. This meant after leaving our trains, we had to go to the crew room first, get our supplies, and then go to the ladies' toilet. The walk was out-of-doors, too, making it extra taxing in wet or cold weather. And, if the guys were going to use its availability to deny us the use of the crew room toilet, we would actually be losing ground with this change.

I adjusted by carrying a bar of soap and tissues with me. However, women who wanted to continue to use the toilets in the crew room were not bothered. It took about ten years for T.A. to put separate women's facilities in all the crew rooms in the "A" Division.

CHARACTERS
AND CRONIES

S ome of the people I worked with were "characters" who, far from trying to fit in, enlivened things with their strong personalities and made the job more interesting.

My best friend, Jasmin Joyce, was a real character. On Halloween, she picked me up at Van Cortlandt after work. In the back seat and the trunk of her car were approximately three hundred orange and black frosted cupcakes, which she had baked and decorated with candy corn, plastic spiders, and witches' faces.

We parked, appropriately, by Woodlawn Cemetery. "You have to help me on with my costume," she said. She had a sheet with holes cut for the eyes. Over her eyeholes, she wore shades. She'd even cut holes in the sheets to slip the temples of the glasses through, so she could rest them over her ears. Completing this effective disguise was a muffler to hold the sheet in place, mittens to cover her hands, and a derby. She said these were to rule out any resemblance to the Ku Klux Klan. The impression was certainly bizarre, more like Frosty the Snowman than a ghost.

"You'll have to show my pass for me when we go through the slam gate," she said to me.

Loaded down with boxes of cupcakes, we passed the token booth, where I flashed both our passes, and through the slam gate.

"Hey, Casper! Where's your pass?" a voice rang out. The plainclothes cop had stepped out of his hiding place in the men's room. I put down my boxes and dug out the passes again. The cop was terribly flustered and apologetic. Joyce sympathetically offered him a cupcake.

The denizens of the Woodlawn crew room were amazed and delighted, eagerly scarfing down the sweets while trying to guess the ghost's identity.

When we finally left, Joyce declared herself satisfied. "This will get talked about," she said.

On Saint Patrick's Day, the day "Lucky" Lewis derailed in the underriver tube, Joyce brought two giant bags of shamrock-shaped cookies tinted green up to Woodlawn.

Joyce persistently worked to make social animals out of the recalcitrant subway operatives. In addition to providing crew room refreshments on holidays, she also repeatedly invited her friends to her home, a house in Brooklyn that she shared with her parents, for Christmas parties, dinners, barbecues, and other social events. These events drew a diverse mix of races, ethnic groups, and political viewpoints. They were wholesome family events, with Joyce's mother and father passing the beverages and leading the singing.

When Joyce had to work on New Year's Eve, she took along several miniature bottles of champagne. She was hoping to get her last trip dropped, so she could spend midnight in the company of her true love, the motorman we called "the Normal One."

Alas, midnight found her on the road, southbound at 135th Street and Lenox, no less. Only her faithful friend, Conductor Marvin, was with her (not counting the riders, of course). Making the best of the situation, she gave a bottle to her motorman and another to Marvin. She poured her own portion into a juice can and quaffed it.

As she was making the station stop at Wall Street, Marvin barged into her cab, stuffed a handful of breath mints into her mouth and cried, "Here comes a motor instructor!" It was a timely warning, for after the next stop, the motor instructor came up to Joyce, "Where's your safety glasses?" he wanted to know. After he had given her the third degree, he went up front to harass her motorman.

New Year's Eve is a difficult night to work. All the riders are stoned out of their gourds. This motor instructor was being unnecessarily stringent. He opened up the motorman's cab and began to interrogate him. Suddenly, the motor instructor felt a heavy hand on his shoulder. He turned to see one of the riders, as bulky as he was pickled. He stuck his fist in the supervisor's face. "Hey! Stop bothering the guy while he's trying to drive. Now close the door and leave him alone!" He yanked the motor instructor away and slammed the cab door. The supervisor scurried out of the car. At the next stop, Joyce saw him shoot off the train and run off the platform. "Now I wonder what that was about," she mused.

Another character was McAllister, a.k.a. "Stream of Consciousness Mac." I worked with him one day a week for one pick. His specialty was nonstop discourse over the intercom. He talked about his daughter, his landlord, his dental problems, whatever came to mind. Once he told me over the intercom that he had paid six hundred dollars for a pair of sneakers. A very confused conversation took place before I realized he was talking about *speakers*, as for a stereo, not *sneakers*.

McAllister was a white guy who had done time in Vietnam. He once observed that working the midnights when he first went out as a motorman had been worse than Vietnam. He was very militant and radical and good friends with Riggs the Radical, though eschewing the full Spartacist League political ideology.

One Saturday late in December, the dispatcher at Utica was jumping all crews one ahead, that is, sending them out on the interval ahead of their scheduled one. McAllister, as usual, raced upstairs for coffee as soon as he came in. When he got back, he was being called on the platform P.A. The dispatcher told him to "jump ahead."

Afterward, McAllister claimed he merely asked, "Why?" and the dispatcher told him to never mind why and do what he was told. Whatever transpired, it ended with the dispatcher taking McAllister out of service. Then he tried to send McAllister's follower instead. But McAllister's follower was Riggs the Radical. Naturally, Riggs refused to go. As a sympathetic motorman commented later, "Riggs should have said he needed a comfort relief. But that's Riggs. He has to take a principled stand." So Riggs and McAllister were both taken out of service.

There were some calls to the desk trainmaster, and both motormen ended up back in service, going down the road. But they were told to write G-2s. At Riggs' instigation, they wrote a five-page denunciation of the dispatcher. McAllister was mighty proud of this. As the weeks went by, he became convinced that he and Riggs had gotten the dispatcher into trouble and not the other way around.

Then, about three weeks later, McAllister received his summons to the Chief Trainmaster's Office. When McAllister returned to Woodlawn, he was moaning and carrying on. He had seen the Chief, and he had been given a reprimand. He wasn't going to be paid for the time.

"I said to the Chief Trainmaster, 'All my life I was taught, if you don't understand something, ask. I guess that's my problem.' And the Chief said, 'Yeah, I guess that is your problem.'"

I said, "Sarcasm won't work with these people."

Some subway operatives were much further gone than McAllister, who was really merely idiosyncratic. When the dispatcher wanted to let Conductor Quigley know he was due on his train, he would announce on the crew room P.A., "Conductor Quigley, that's your spaceship on the stand." And there was Conductor Reyes, who was perfectly ordinary until one day he popped his cork and started explaining delays by announcing Command Center's telephone number and urging riders to phone for themselves. We saw the last of him soon after that.

But the craziest T.A. worker I ever came across was a car cleaner. He was a skinny middle-aged guy with bulging eyes and large, bad teeth. My first meeting with him took place when he plopped down beside me on the Woodlawn veranda and said in confiding tones, "You know, there was platties in the park before you was born." He was given to such utterances.

The other car cleaners didn't like him. On his first day, they reported with disgust, he had asked each of them for a gift of money, "Christmas is coming." They also felt he didn't do his share of the work when they "doubled up," that is, when they paired off and took turns doing four cars and resting, rather than each one doing two cars each time. And they claimed he was abusive.

It wasn't surprising that he got fired. I couldn't help pitying him. What would become of him? Where would he go, a lunatic like that?

Later, I saw him occasionally on the platforms. I couldn't tell if he was doing okay or had joined the ranks of the homeless. The last time I saw him was on the platform at 161st Street. He recognized me. I suppose we had always hit it off well, because I listened sympathetically to his ramblings. He greeted me with a wide-mouthed piercing shriek, between terror and glee, like a child's on the scariest ride in the amusement park.

Supervisors had less leeway to be characters than "hourly" employees, because they were just more visible to "downtown." Some stood out because they were abusive and tended to rant, rave, yell, scream. There were a few who were really "for the books."

Jimmy Fairfax was the supervisor you love to hate. People generally referred to him as "a nut," or "a screwball." The deed commonly used to characterize him was that "he wrote up his own brother," a reasonable and well-liked motor instructor. Writing up one's own brother was not considered evidence of incorruptible fairness, but a sign of inhumanity. Writing up anyone was unfair and inhumane. But your own brother?!

He was viewed as a deviant who got where he was through connections, through belonging to the same religious sect as the general superintendent. Then he was busted from line superintendent of the No. 4 line to an ordinary train dispatcher. Everyone talked about it. As they often said, "What goes around, comes around." There was much speculation as to what finally brought him down. One legend had it that he rented a hall at Hunter College to hold an "Awards Night" for the dispatchers under his supervision, invited the mayor and the heads of the M.T.A. and the T.A., and paid for it out of the operating budget for the No. 4 line. Another story claimed that it had been a lawsuit, brought by the relatives of a dispatcher who had died of a heart attack immediately after a dressing down by Fairfax.

We'll never know.

A more benign weirdo was Trainmaster Bobick.

One day, I was about to close the doors at 86th Street, when this unkempt, skinny man came bounding down the steps. Without knowing why, I held open my doors. When I related this story to Joyce, and later to Mark, at this point each groaned, "Ronnie Bobick." And so it was: the most unconventional trainmaster in the railroad.

"It's very disillusioning, going to trainmaster. But why retire on a train dispatcher's salary? With inflation, you could starve to death. I should have stayed a train dispatcher, but it's an extra; let's see, it's an extra two thousand dollars a year on my take-home, I don't have any dependents. And you get addicted! You get addicted to that money! They know you won't go back.

"There was a desk in a train dispatcher's office that the superintendent told me had to be moved. So I got a couple of porters and we moved it into the crew room. Then, on my R.D.O.—on my R.D.O.!—the superintendent calls me up and says, 'That desk has got to come out of the crew room today.'

"I said, 'I'm sorry, this is my R.D.O.,' and he replied, 'That's an order.'

"So I couldn't find anyone to help me carry that desk, so I had to take that desk apart, hack it apart, to get it out of that crew room. That's what they've got the trainmaster doing! Taking apart a desk on his day off! So y'know, they're supposed to give you a meal voucher when you work on your day off, so I put in for one, and the superintendent told me, if you don't withdraw this, I'll write you up for refusing a direct order. So I didn't. What the hell! It's not worth it.

"Do you know what it means to have 'full service'? When a terminal has 'full service,' it means that it has a sufficient number of trains to make all of its intervals. Well, the superintendent calls me up and tells me, 'Get down to the yard and make them get full service!' Make them! That's how he put it!

"So I went down to the yard, and I was very apologetic about it. I don't like to tell people they have to do something they just can't do. Really, they did their best. They fixed up everything they could. But you know, that is how some trains go out on the road, although they aren't really fit for service."

While some of my coworkers were real characters, others were just ordinary folks whose treatment by T.A. makes their stories arresting case studies.

In my training class was a lovely young man named Laurence Brown. He had been working as an orderly in a psychiatric center and was thrilled to be called by transit. At first, he seemed to love the job. I met him in the Times Square tower at the end of our first week on the road. He was eager to share his experiences.

"You know, Marian, I had this little old lady who got off my train the other day, because she wanted to get into an air-conditioned car. And, you know, she was scared to walk between the cars. But I had closed the doors, because I thought, you know, that she was getting off the train. She cried, 'Oh, oh, please let me in! I only wanted to change cars!'

"So I said, 'Sure, sweetheart,' and I passed a long buzz to my motorman and reopened.

"She hopped into my car and she came up to me, 'Oh, bless you, bless you.'

"'I have a grandmother, too,' I told her, 'and I'm going to treat you just like I'd like people to treat her.'

"And I like to make the announcements, add a special touch to them, point out the attractions, and say, 'Have a pleasant day.' The other fellers say to me, 'It's because of people like you that we have to make announcements.' And I try not to pay them any mind. They treat me like that because I'm new. When they've been here awhile, they get an attitude.

"You know, Marian, I think that most conductors feel the way I do, but are kind of ashamed to admit it. We all want to be the good guy, but a lot of times we can't be. So we make out to be real tough. Then we don't feel so unappreciated."

When our training class passed its probation, a year after our appointment, it was Laurence who got in touch with each of the twelve of us, to invite us to a celebration at his home. He and his wife had just had their first child, and as soon as I walked in, his wife gave me the baby to hold. The others arrived, and Laurence took a big ice-cream cake out of the freezer. On the top was inscribed, "Congratulations, Conductors."

Such a sweet guy, but he had so many problems on the job. An argument with a motor instructor about his not wearing his hat had brought him a reprimand. Then he had a fight with a rider. About a year after we passed probation, I got a call from him one evening, "Marian! I got arrested!"

He was calling from Transit Police Headquarters at Jay Street. A rider had been fooling around with his P.A. An altercation ensued. The rider ended up with a cut over his eye, and he charged Laurence with assault. The charges had been dropped. "But, Marian, they're taking me for blood alcohol and urine tests."

"Well, that should be alright. You haven't got anything in your system, do you?"

"Well, yes, I do."

"When was it?"

"Yesterday."

"It should be gone by now. The liver and kidneys clear an ounce of alcohol from the blood an hour."

"It's not that," he said.

Then I understood it wasn't his blood alcohol level that worried him: "But that's tough for them to prove. Say there were kids smoking in your car. Try not to worry."

The next day, Laurence reported to work, but supervision wouldn't let him sign on and told him he was on suspension until he saw the superintendent. At his hearing, Laurence was fired. He appealed, taking it through the steps of the grievance procedure. It was a slow process. By Christmas, T.A. was still postponing his case, and Laurence was driving a livery cab to make ends meet.

In February, he got a notice from T.A. setting a date in March for his next hearing. He got in touch with his lawyer, who told him the date wasn't possible for him. So Laurence went down to Jay Street to get a postponement. As soon as he made his request at labor relations, he was ordered to take a urine test immediately. He said that he wanted to speak to his attorney before submitting to the test. He was told that if he did so, it would be considered insubordination. Despite the fact that T.A. had fired him, despite the fact that he was not on the T.A. payroll, that his pass had been taken from him, that he, in short, was not a T.A. employee, he still had to obey this T.A. order, or be "insubordinate."

When the hearing finally took place, his termination was upheld by T.A. He and his lawyer could choose to go to an arbitrator or to the Civil Service Trial Board. Either one would be the last resort. They chose the Trial Board because it had a more favorable record toward employees. (Ironically, the employees' right to appeal to this board was abolished in the 1985 contract.)

The Trial Board judge threw out the T.A.'s case, because T.A. produced no witnesses and no evidence. The judge ordered Laurence to be reinstated.

Laurence reported to labor relations at Jay Street to be reinstated. They told him he was still suspended because he had refused the urine test in February! When his second suspension came before the Civil Service Trial Board a year later, the judge ordered him reinstated with merely a reprimand.

When he went to Jay Street afterward, the head of labor relations said to him, "I bet you're glad to be back." He wanted to shake Laurence's hand.

Laurence said, "Uh-uh. I quit." He had been working for the New York City Department of Social Services for four months.

"It shows you can fight the T.A. and win," he told me. "They told me I couldn't win, but I did. T.A. takes good employees and makes them into people who only care about the paycheck."

I was reminded of a saying that had been tacked up in the Van Cortlandt crew room: "Doing a good job here is like wetting yourself while wearing dark pants. You get a warm feeling. But no one notices."

Another employee who got messed over by T.A. was Eddie Perez. One Sunday morning in the crowded Woodlawn crew room, everyone was talking about him. People were saying, "He looks sick" and "He's going to go home."

"What's wrong?" I asked.

"It's Eddie Perez. He went to the yard to get a train, and when he came back he didn't feel well."

Eddie was on the system phone, calling the Crew Dispatcher's Office, booking sick.

"He says his lungs hurt," a conductor told me.

"He looks grey," I said.

"He took off his jacket, and he's still sweating."

The crew dispatcher apparently had asked to speak to the dispatcher at the terminal, because Eddie was shouting, "I'm in the back, in the crew room. He's not here! If you want to speak to him, you call him!" Cursing, Eddie hung up. He got his things and was walking out.

I walked along with him. "Did anything happen in the yard?" I asked him.

"I didn't get to the yard," he answered, and added, "It's hurting me to talk."

We got to the street. I walked him to the taxi stand.

"Maybe I should go right to the Emergency Room," he said.

"I think so," I said.

I called his family to tell them to meet him there. Then I went back upstairs to the crew room.

"Maybe it's flu," someone was saying, "that's how my case started.

"Maybe it's something he ate," said someone else.

No one wanted to believe that it could be serious.

We learned afterward that what Eddie had suffered on his way to the yard that Sunday morning had been a heart attack. They said he would be bedridden for six weeks. For his five years with T.A., he was eligible for three weeks at 60 percent of full pay.

Eddie returned to work in a few months. He wasn't really ready to come back, but the clinic had certified him "fit for duty," and, besides, he had long since run out of paid sick leave. Everyone shook his hand and slapped him on the back. "How are you, man?" Perez wore his customary look of cheer about to give way to dismay. Everyone asked him the same thing, how did he feel? "Are you still smoking?" "On a diet?"

His color was good, but when he came close, he looked like he'd aged. I asked him about filing for Workmen's Compensation. He said his doctor told him he couldn't make a comp case, because "it isn't likely I got it just from stress."

I said, "It's not just the stress. It's the steel dust, the vibration, the noise. I'll try to find you a doctor who will support your claim." I found him the name of a doctor who might help him get his heart attack established as job related. Eddie spoke to him, and the doctor told him it would be "difficult to prove in a court of law." But he referred him to a law clinic that might be able to help him.

Eddie kept procrastinating. Finally, I called the clinic for him.

Next time I saw Eddie, I told him, "You should call them, Eddie. They give you an appointment in a day or two and then they evaluate your case and let you know in a week or two whether they will take you."

"I'll tell you, Marian, I'm just lazy. I get home from work and all I want to do is drink beer and forget about everything."

But of all the people I knew, the person who was treated the most unfairly and cruelly by T.A. was the only other woman in my training class, Leah Goss. She was a young, intelligent, and ambitious young woman who would have made a good supervisor. But during her first month on the job, Leah had an accident.

On the northernmost stretch of the No. 5 line, way up in the Bronx, until recently, they closed the token booths and opened the gates late at night. People entered the stations without paying. Their fares were collected by the conductor, who had to carry a fifty-pound farebox for this purpose. (In fall 1996, this quaint custom ended, and this stretch of railroad was given over to one-person train operation during the late hours.) The conductor signed out the farebox from the token booth and carried it up the steps to the platform.

Both Leah and I had been forced to pick these jobs on Monday nights. Leah, although strong for her size, was very small. The porter usually helped her by lifting the farebox from the platform and putting it on the train for her.

On this particular night, however, the crews were going out "one be-hind," that is, on the train after the one they were scheduled to work on. So Leah and the box she had signed for had to get off the train. The porter took the box off the train for her, and put it into her arms. As she described it to me, "I have a special way of picking the box up and that's how I can manage it. But when I took it from him, I didn't handle it that way and I got this twinge. Then it went away. But the next day I felt really bad."

She had gotten herself a hernia.

She went out sick and filed for Workmen's Compensation. Then she was notified that the T.A. was contesting her claim. She was examined by a T.A. doctor who prodded her painfully and when she protested, told her, "It's not hurting you that much." She had surgery to repair the hernia, but since she was such a new employee, she had very little sick leave. It soon ran out and she was forced to go back to work on "light duty," that is, working on platforms.

After months, she finally was given a hearing on her claim. She got on my train one day at 14th Street, on her way up to report at Dyre, and she told me about it. "Even the T.A. lawyer couldn't figure out the reason they were contesting it. The hearing officer said, 'Anyone who would contest this has got to be sick in the head.'

"Finally, the T.A. lawyer said, 'It says here that she had the condition prior to hiring.'

"The hearing officer said, 'That's ridiculous. No one walks around with their stomach hanging open!'"

Leah won her case, but it was a Pyrrhic victory. She called me about eighteen months after her accident. She hadn't been well enough to work for several months, not even to do plats. "I went back to work too soon the first time," she explained to me. "It was because I wasn't getting any money, because T.A. was contesting my claim. I went back because I needed the money, but it was too soon. So it never healed up right."

Now she was filing again for Workmen's Comp for her present inability to work, and T.A. was once more denying it. She was ordered to report to the T.A. clinic. The doctor there gave her two sets of papers. One set said her condition was not job related and gave her "no work." This, in effect, admitted that her physical condition made even light duty impossible, but also precluded her getting any compensation from the T.A. The other set of papers said her condition was job related but gave her "full work," in other words, determined that she was capable of performing full conductor's duties and must report to work. He told her to choose.

Leah had originally wanted to get off the road by becoming a dispatcher. "Now I know a T.A. promotion is not one of my options," she said. "I'm sure there is a black dot next to my name."

The last time I saw Leah, she got on my train looking well groomed and well rested. Her comp hearing had been held the previous day. The hearing officer had authorized payment for her operation and ordered the T.A. to pay her two thousand dollars in claims immediately, so she could meet her expenses. "The T.A. owes me a lot more. We're going to have to go back for another hearing for the rest of the money."

Just before I left T.A., Leah called me. She had resigned from the Transit Authority.

RIDERS
AND CONDUCTORS

Another very important factor in our lives was the cargo we moved: the riders. This was especially true of conductors. Between the stops, we were outside our operating cabs and exposed to the riders. At each station, we confronted the conflicting desires of those on the platform to enter the train and of those already aboard to get it moving. No matter what we did, some riders were angry with us.

Riders were unpredictable: as a mass and as individuals. We had no control over their behavior, yet we were held responsible for it. The supervision expected us to get in and out of the stations without delay, despite the fact that riders standing in our doorways literally prevented us from closing the doors. We were harassed and even threatened with discipline for running behind schedule, and "heavy riding" was not an acceptable excuse for a late arrival. Not only could we be disciplined if we were late, our breaks and lunchtime could be forfeited and our working day lengthened.

To be fair to the riders, it must be said that, during the years that I was a conductor, they were suffering from the most dreadful deterioration of service. Preventive maintenance had ended with the onset of the city's fiscal crisis of the mid-seventies. By the early eighties, the toll had been taken. Trains, switches, and tunnels were falling apart. Rarely inspected, rails broke, sometimes leading to derailments and often to stoppages in service. Flammable debris on the roadbeds was not removed, leading to track fires. These conditions created routine delays and, on an increasingly regular basis, disasters that threatened lives and brought service to a complete and long-lasting halt on an entire line.

In short, both sides had reasons to feel angry and hostile. Although neither was to blame for the problems, each side tended to direct this hostil-

ity toward the other. Policies formulated at a higher level set us at each others'
throats. The riders scapegoated us and treated us so brutally that this itself
became grounds for hatred.

The currency of interaction between riders and conductors was insult, as
the following examples show.

Problems such as broken trains and broken rails often led to "reroutes,"
sending trains off their designated lines, making express trains local, or local
trains express, in the last instance whisking astonished and angry riders past
their stops. Of course, we were supposed to announce route changes over
our P.A. system, but many P.A. systems didn't work. Even if the P.A. was
working in the conductor's position, it might not, and almost inevitably did
not, work in every single car. You often had cars in which some malfunction
in the car itself prevented the P.A. from being heard there.

Another problem was the conductors' sometimes not knowing of reroutes and finding out along with their astonished and unhappy riders. Some
motormen didn't bother to tell their conductors about changes. Many more
motormen tried but were unwittingly thwarted by P.A. systems that weren't
working.

This problem has since been solved by issuing radios to conductors as
well as motormen, so conductors can hear the orders changing the trains'
routes. But, back in my day, a conductor had to do a lot of guesswork.

Once on the No. 2 line coming north from New Lots, we were put on the
local track. No one had told me anything. I just figured it out and made the
correct announcements. Nevertheless, at Penn Station, a well-dressed, middle-
aged white guy got off and confronted me from the platform. "What are you,"
he taunted me, "too stupid to use the microphone?" Apparently, the P.A.
system had not worked in his car.

Once I hit a baby stroller with my doors. The man with the stroller had
waited until the last minute to get off and I was already closing. As soon as I
saw the stroller coming out the doors, I reopened, but I wasn't able to avoid
hitting the stroller. When the man got out on the platform, he screamed at
me, "You must be blind, stupid, blind! I ought to punch you in the face."

These kinds of insults were constant and typical, especially when the
train experienced mechanical problems. Once I had malfunctioning door
control buttons. They were sticking, and the doors were slow to open. One
rider, getting off, said to me, "You're a little slow, baby." It never occurred to

him it might be a mechanical problem, not human incompetence. I was even insulted and harassed after a rider broke my glasses and the train couldn't be moved, because I couldn't see, until a new conductor arrived. When I explained to the riders what had happened, the response was that I should carry spare glasses for just such an eventuality. One man offered me *his* glasses.

Riders constantly asked for directions, yet they often rejected the directions I gave. For me, this sometimes took a sexist form. One man said, "I don't like your attitude! You women conductors, you have an attitude."

A woman refused to believe the local did not stop at 20th Street and Third Avenue. "I'm going to ask a man!" she announced.

The riders never seemed to realized we had to follow rules, and they assumed we were doing anything we pleased. On the old equipment, conductors were allowed to sit in the seats opposite their operating cabs between stops, but were not allowed to sit inside the cabs. Once a guy sitting opposite my cab placed a pile of magazines on the seat next to him, which prevented me from sitting there. When I politely asked him to move them, he told me I could sit in the cab. I told him I wasn't allowed to. "How come there's a seat in there?" he asked.

"It's for the motorman," I explained.

Reluctantly, he moved the magazines. When he got off, he said sarcastically, "You sure have a hard job."

When the emergency brakes were activated, the motorman was required to inspect the outside of the train, and the conductor was required to go to the motorman's position and make announcements to the riders explaining the delay.

But once when I had done this, a rider complained that my announcements were making him and the other riders nervous. On another occasion, as I struggled to get through the crowded train, so I could return to my position and open the doors, people screamed at me for not being where they thought I should be. Although they would not let me pass, they were angry at me for not opening the doors.

When I worked on the No. 2 line on the P.M.s, early in my transit career, teenagers would regularly sabotage the trains. They would break into the cab of the last car and throw a switch or a circuit breaker, so the train would malfunction. Sometimes they would use the P.A. to babble obscenities throughout the train. Then, when I went to the rear car to "overcome the problem," they would make fun of me and blame me for breaking the equipment. A favorite theme was, what could you expect from a woman driver?

Riders could also cause problems for conductors, or for motormen, by complaining to the T.A. about us.

Once, during a rush hour, as I was closing my doors after a station stop at 14th Street, two white men in suits came hurrying toward me. I remembered they had asked me directions and boarded at Bowling Green. There was a Metro North strike on, and they probably weren't used to riding the subway. They said something to me about "missing glass."

As the train began to move, I figured out that the glass had probably fallen out of a door panel in one of my cars. It would leave a dangerous gap, because if some rider put an arm through the empty space as the door was opening, it could get badly mangled. I was therefore required to locate the problem and isolate that car, that is, get all the riders out.

So at the next stop, Grand Central, I attempted to do this. In the end, the entire train had to be discharged and go out of service. I had to write a G-2 about the incident, but, to my relief, no disciplinary action was taken against me.

The punchline to this story came about a month later, when I got a call from the Chief Trainmaster's Office. There was a "passenger complaint" about me. The two commuters who had told me about the missing glass had lodged a complaint about me because they thought I had ignored them. So I had to write a second G-2, referring to my first G-2. Since I was able to establish that I had taken proper action at the earliest possible time, I beat that one.

My greatest conflict with the riders was not complaints to management—it was assaults. Somewhere along the way, I started recording each attempted or successful assault on me by a rider. On the No. 4 line, I was assaulted on an average of twice a week. On the number No. 1 line, it averaged once every two weeks.

The assaults were almost without exception carried out from the platform as the train was pulling out and I was "observing the platform." Riders spit on me, threw things at me, or hit me with objects or even with their hands. Occasionally, this was retribution for something they imagined I had done, but mostly it was for amusement. Here was a chance to hurt someone—in my case, a white woman—and not suffer any consequences. All conductors suffered such assaults, and it was impossible to calculate whether I got it more often than the others.

I asked other conductors whether they were assaulted. "The school kids try to spit at me all the time," a young Hispanic man told me. "Once, when I was pulling out of Fordham Road, a kid ran up the stairs and threw a bag of flour at me. There was flour all over me, all over my jacket, and I had just gotten it from the dry cleaners."

One very senior black conductor told me how, while he was still on probation, he was knocked semiconscious at the Van Sicklen station. He didn't see who hit him, "I would have fallen on the floor, but an off-duty motorman caught me."

A conductor working New Year's Eve on the No. 1 line was hit in the neck with a dart at 110th Street. I witnessed kids on a staircase pouring something down on a conductor at Nevins Street as his train was leaving the station.

Lots of conductors related stories of how, when they were assaulted, they had pulled the cord, stopped the train, pursued and caught their assailants, and dispensed justice. I tried this—or couldn't resist doing it, a few times, and ultimately got in trouble for it. I never got to dispensing justice, but I did manage to get the cops involved a couple of times, though it never led to anything, as I'll recount later. It did seem to me that the assaults bothered other conductors less than they bothered me.

Once, I was hit in the face by something thrown by a kid at Kingsbridge Road. It hit me just above my left eye, under the brow. I pulled the cord to stop the train and ran after the kid. On the mezzanine were a bunch of cops and we actually caught the kid. Then, the cops took the kid's side, agreeing with him that it must have been an accident. Only at my insistence did the sergeant say they would give him a temporary juvenile record, which could be erased if he had no further trouble before he was seventeen.

Only once was I assaulted by a rider on my train. It was a very hot day on the No. 1 line, in a train with no air-conditioning. As we came out of the hole before 125th Street, I could almost see the riders lean toward the windows to catch a breeze. Yet even what air came into the slow-moving car was unbreathably humid.

My motorman did not have a working P.A., and I was trying to find out whether track work that would necessitate skipping the next stop had begun for the day or not. In order to find out, I decided to go out to the platform to get a look at the signal. My car was pretty crowded, so I had to twist and edge my way through the crowd.

When I came back to my car, right outside my cab was a short woman in a very advanced state of pregnancy, with a baby in a stroller. She and the stroller had moved directly in front of the door to my cab, blocking my way in.

"Excuse me," I said to her, bending my body a little bit to the right to signal what I hoped she would do. Instead, she raised her hands and placed them on her hips, elbows jutting out, so that now her left arm completely blocked my path. I shook my head in exasperation and simply pushed my body past her. As I closed the doors, she started cursing me. After we were out of the station, I explained, more for the sake of the other riders than for her, "I had to get by to get the train moving."

"I don't give a fuck if it goes or not," she said.

"Well, other people do," I said. She continued to curse, and her remarks got uglier and more obscene. I couldn't answer her in kind, but got angrier and angrier. Finally I said, "If you don't shut your filthy mouth, I'm gonna have a cop take you off this train!"

She spit directly up into my face, then smacked my safety glasses off my face, and went for my eyes. I grabbed her by the wrists and dug my nails as deeply into her skin as I could. She screamed and pulled away. I let her go and she backed off.

I had to make a complaint if only to protect my job. Tangling with a rider is no small deal, and I was very apprehensive. At the next station, my motorman called for police. When they arrived, my assailant was still there. Pregnant, with a baby in a stroller, she couldn't get away. I heard her say to the cops, "They just kept going by me, and I just decided I wasn't gonna let no more people by me." She didn't have the wit to make a complaint against me. I didn't think she had any idea what was happening.

I had to call Command and was told to write a G-2, but it didn't seem like I was in any trouble. But when I got back to work after my R.D.O.s, the dispatcher told me to call downtown. I was told that the next day, instead of reporting to work, I had to see "the Chief," the Chief Trainmaster, for a disciplinary hearing.

I went down the next morning. The Chief du jour was a thin white guy with cold, humorless blue eyes. At his order, I repeated my story, leaving out any suggestion that I did anything, even in self-defense.

After I finished, he said, "A rider who identified herself as Mrs. Wiggins called us and reported the incident. She gave us this statement."

According to "Mrs. Wiggins," the train conductor had been unable to close the car doors at 125th Street, because a pregnant woman with a stroller had been trying to board the train. In this fantasy, the train conductor left her position, walked to the doors, told the pregnant woman, "Get the fuck away from the doors," and slapped the pregnant woman in the face. The trainmaster said his office had called Mrs. Wiggins and that she had stuck to her story.

Potentially, this pack of lies could have cost me my job. Yet once I knew that I wasn't in trouble for any of the things I had actually done, I felt relieved. I explained why I'd left my position to get a better look at the signal, and that there had been no problem with closing the doors. My assailant had been on the train before 125th Street, not trying to board the train, and she was nowhere near the doors.

The Chief asked whether I had used profanity or slapped her at any point. I could answer truthfully and in clear conscience that the answer was "no" to both questions. I went on, "The woman who attacked me made a statement to the police. If you read the statement, it will tell you in her words what went on. You'll see it went just the way I said, not how Wiggins describes it."

I spent some tense minutes outside the office before I was called back in. The assistant train dispatcher told me, "Our finding is that Conductor Swerdlow behaved properly. The police report makes no mention of the incident alleged by Mrs. Wiggins to have taken place." But he looked at me like he was acting against his better judgement. When I got my paycheck the following week, I had been docked for the time spent at the hearing.

Riders had their hardships as well. They could be victims of crimes. They could be injured by the equipment. And their troubles became our troubles.

I have already related the shooting on my train during my first night on the road. Before I got off midnights, another rider was stabbed on my train, but he must have had his own legal problems, because he didn't stick around to wait for the police. I had a reported beating and robbery once, but, again, both the alleged perp and the victim disappeared before I could even get there. And two gangs once chose my operating car to wage a knife fight in. They also got off at the next stop but not before I gave up my tissues to stanch one victim's bleeding.

Once a well-dressed man came to my position at 59th Street during the rush hour to complain that his wallet had been taken. He hadn't seen the culprit. I thought of giving the motorman a long buzz and asking the man whether he wanted me to hold the train and call a cop. Immediately, I thought of the trouble that would bring to me, the pressure I'd come under, the explaining I would have to do for tying up the express track during the rush hour. So I merely shook my head sympathetically and let the train go.

One Sunday morning at 86th Street southbound, a rider came running toward me on the platform, "If you don't get a cop, he's going to kill him!" he shouted, "You got a pickpocket back there! He took the guy's wallet and now the guy's gonna kill him!" This put my choices in a slightly different perspective. I walked to the rear. I saw a tall, strong-looking, clean-cut black man who was very indignant. "He brushed up against me and now my wallet is missing! I want to search him! He's got my wallet!"

The object of his rage was a grizzled, old white man in a knit cap and threadbare coat. He was clutching a brown paper shopping bag to his chest. The alleged perp didn't leave the train as we waited for the police. He looked dazed and frightened.

At last the cops arrived. They searched the man and his shopping bag, but no wallet was found. I took a badge number, and our trip resumed.

After that, I noticed the same old man out at Utica Avenue and up at Woodlawn. One night, when I had finished work and was riding home, I saw him aboard. He was eating a banana. He looked very clean and didn't smell. As I passed him, I offered him some change. "Whaa?" he asked.

"I want to give you something."

"How much?"

"Fifty cents."

"No, no. If it were fifty dollars, or five thousand dollars, but not fifty cents."

When he looked away, I slipped it into his pocket.

When riders were injured by the equipment, it was a much more serious matter than when they injured each other, because for the first injury they might sue the T.A. You were supposed to ask them whether they wanted medical assistance and also to report it.

One way riders often hurt themselves was by riding between the cars. They did this most often when the trains were very crowded or very hot, or both. One very hot day, two young women, barely more than girls, were riding between my operating cars. We were outside on the structure, and it was much cooler out there than in the cars. They were in high spirits, laughing and singing. When I crossed over at Burnside, I said, "Young ladies, riding out here is dangerous. I would be very sorry to see you get hurt."

"Oh, but it's so hot!" they protested.

A few stops later, I heard a lot of screaming, but I thought they were just playing. When they got off at 167th Street, I noticed one of them had vivid welts on her calf and was limping. Foolish, I thought, to ride between the cars with a bad leg.

Then a little later, another rider, a young woman, handed me a piece of looseleaf paper with this written on it:

> Madam—The two girls that was on the train, I don't think you realized that one sure got very hurt on the right ankle. Remember you heard a loud scream. Well, that's what it was, that she definitely hurt herself bad. Maybe you told her already about being out there and so on. If she didn't listen to you then believe this, she sure will suffer. You should have seen her, she caught her foot between the train. That's what she gets if she didn't listen to you. I recognized all that action. I write all this because of stutter.

Even more dangerous than riding between the cars is the practice of boarding the train between the cars, either when the doors have already closed or when the cars are too packed to get through the doors.

One day as we were pulling out of the Fordham Road station, I saw a kid run up the stairs I had already gone past and try to jump between the cars to get on the train. Then I saw the riders on the platform turn and I heard screams. I caught a glimpse of legs kicking out from between the cars, then tumbling down. In a split second, before I could even think about it, I "pulled the cord"—yanked the emergency brake cord that hung above my right shoulder. The train halted. Over the intercom, I told my motorman, who happened to be the Great One, "Someone fell between the cars." Then I opened the rear section, left my cab, got out on the platform and started walking back.

I didn't know which cars he had fallen between, I realized as I walked on mechanically. How will I know? I realized I'd find the place because that's where the riders would be gathered. I looked up and saw the riders clustered—around the staircase!

"What happened?" I asked them.

"He ran away."

"His pants were torn off."

The most upsetting and haunting incident I ever had with a rider was not an accident or an injury. At least, not in a conventional sense. It was my hurting a rider who was obviously ill-equipped to take care of himself in order to protect myself.

I was working the late P.M.s on the No. 2 line. Out in Brooklyn, I saw two transit cops on the platform. They told me to hold my doors open. So I gave my motorman a long buzz and reopened. And I was damned sorry I had, because the cops put this big guy on my train. He had two shopping bags full of groceries. Blood was caked on his face where it had run from his nose and his mouth. He got in the car I was working in. "Now you've got trouble!" one cop told me gleefully.

The guy started scampering around the car. He was eating bananas out of his bags. He ate each in two bites and threw the peels on the floor. Most of the riders were leaving the car. I couldn't do that. I didn't know what was going to happen next. At Nostrand Avenue, as I was doing my station stop, my gift from the transit police came out to the platform and shoved his face, grinning, right into mine. "Hey! Conductor—" he began.

He had left his groceries on the train. I was sorry for him and afraid of him at the same time. Fear overcame pity. I closed my doors, and the train moved on.

The riders still left in the car were laughing. A couple of them approached me and told me solemnly that somebody had left their grocery bags on the train. "All I can do is give them to the dispatcher at New Lots," I said. By the time we got to New Lots, the bags were gone.

It was rare to have a really positive experience with riders, but it did happen. Once, on Christmas Day, I was working on a new train, an "R-62," when I heard a knock on my cab door. I opened it to see a little old man. His lively, clear blue eyes and luxuriant beard would have made him a good candidate for Santa Claus, but his clothes identified him as a Hasidic Jew. He needed directions to Flatbush and Nostrand.

Before Franklin Avenue, I left my cab to remind him that it was his stop.

He was reading a Yiddish newspaper and sitting next to a woman as little, old, and bright-eyed as he. They both thanked me effusively.

When they got off at Franklin, they came over to my position. The man said, "I'm happy to see a woman working here." I thanked him, but there was clearly something more they wanted to say.

She asked it, "Are you Jewish?"

I nodded, and they were completely delighted. "Good luck to you! Good luck!" they both exclaimed.

Go figure.

But my favorite rider ever was a white teenager whom I found sitting right opposite my cab. I didn't think he came from New York City: he didn't have that urban dead look. He started asking me questions, and I soon decided that he must be a buff.

"Are you from New York City?" I asked him.

"I used to be. My father was a motorman. He had a whole collection of photos and other historical things from the subways. He used to take me to the yard with him and we would 'okay' the train together. He would let me work the handles.

"Then, in 1977, he quit, and we moved out west. A few years ago, I came back with my mother to Rochester." He hated Rochester, "All the kids at school are into going to work for IBM and Xerox. And they mock me for wanting to go to work for the subway. I can't wait to come back to New York. I want to be a conductor." He wasn't interested in all trains, only in the subways. I told him about the new cars, the R-62s that were just starting to go on the road then. But he wasn't interested in these, either, "It's the old cars I care about. Do you think they'll still have them when I get here?"

I could picture him, a kid of nine at most, walking around the yard with his father. His father must have loved these cars to collect and save those subway artifacts. He had been sharing with his son what he loved most.

And suddenly, there had been no more trains. And then he had lost his father, too. Now, he wanted to come back to the only part of those happier times that he could come back to: the old cars.

We stopped at Brooklyn Bridge, where he got off to transfer. "Can I ask one thing? Maybe this wouldn't be alright with you, but could I just operate the door controls to close it up?"

Highly illegal.

"Sure," I said.

He got off. From the platform, reaching in the window of my cab, he closed down first the rear section and then the front. "That's the first time I've done that in eight years!" he exulted as the train began to move.

We waved to each other until I couldn't see him any longer.

For twenty years, T.A. has been ordering new equipment with cabs that are, or can be converted to, "transverse cabs." Old-style cabs were small cubicles occupying only one side of the car. Transverse cabs go across the width of the car. They enable the conductor to stay inside, away from the public, but they also enable the motorman to see and operate doors on either side of the car. They are part of a long-term program, undertaken in the fall of 1996, to eliminate conductors, beginning with several shuttle lines, and to implement "One-Person Train Operation" (O.P.T.O.).

When I came on the job, only a few lines in the other division, "B" Division, had transverse cabs. During my stint, the I.R.T. got the new R-62 cars that could be converted to transverse cabs. As these R-62 cars have been converted, the conductors are no longer visible. A significant number of cars in both divisions still have old-style cabs, but they will disappear in time, as will the job of the conductor.

As the prosperity of the 1980s enabled new rolling stock to be ordered, and a series of disasters put pressure on the T.A. to resume maintenance, service improved. In the new trains, doors were better constructed, and door panels didn't pop out. Newer cabs were harder to break into, harder for riders to sabotage. Today, all cars are equipped with air-conditioning, and it works most of the time. Moreover, transverse cabs eliminate storm doors at the ends of cars, thus making it harder for riders to ride between cars or get on or off the train from between the cars.

I didn't stick around long enough to find out whether rider hostility ebbed commensurately as service became safer and more reliable—but I'd be surprised if it didn't.

Today, however, the trend has reversed again. Cuts in federal, state, and municipal funding to the subways have led to cuts in maintenance and service all over again, even as the fare has risen. It took ten years for the maintenance cuts of the mid-seventies to devastate the subways, making them at best time-wasting and unreliable and at worst death traps. So if the past is any guide, the worst is yet to come.

TRANSIT WORKER
WIT AND WISDOM

Subway workers who had experience in other blue-collar industrial or service fields felt they had good jobs when they came to the transit system.

One summer day, three senior motormen were comparing the subways with other jobs. "It's not such a bad job," said the first. "My last job, I was a machinist." He held up his left hand. The last joint of his ring finger was missing. "Lost it on the press."

A second one contributed, "I worked in a bakery." Alluding to the hot summer weather we were having, he added, "You just think what it's like today inside a bakery."

Newer workers, with less stake in the job, less comparative experience, and none of the relative advantages of higher seniority, often saw the job differently. For example, one day, I overheard one young black conductor talking to another: "I wasn't born to be a conductor. You come into this world alone. You go out of it alone. It's time for me to do something for myself. Fuck their job. Fuck their pension."

A more complex view of the job was often expressed by the motorman, Angelo Gonzalez, with the comment: "This could be a good job but *they* make it bad, you know?" "They" might refer to riders, other workers, supervisors or management.

One day, I set out deliberately to question my coworkers systematically about their attitudes toward the job. No one found the job boring. They felt their families, neighbors, and friends respected them for their job, if for one specific reason: their income was perceived as high.

It should come as no surprise that subway workers were in it for the money, not for prestige or for meaningful work. One motorman had a degree in business administration, but found T.A. starting pay better than entry pay in his field. "All I want," he would say, "is a house and a car, and I'm going to get them." Another motorman had a degree in computer science from City University, but worked in transit for the same reason.

For subway workers, pay was the single most important standard for evaluating any job. Once a crowd of old-timers was discussing some line of work. One said, "I don't see how anyone could do it."

Another rejoined, "You'd do it. You'd do it if it'd put bread on the table."

This fit in with the attitude that the best survival strategy was to "go home and forget about" the job. When I was still in training, one of my break-in conductors advised me, "When you go home, forget everything that just happened. I take a nice hot bath."

Don't get too wrapped up in the job, then. As the graffiti in the cabs read, "In case of emergency: resign." Another, consistent graffiti read: "Ours is not to reason why. Ours is but to do or die."

It may not have been universal, but among many workers there was a strong conviction that a worker should never do one iota more than he was required to do. Once at the terminal I saw that someone had left a valise on my train and I took it to the Train Dispatcher's Office. A motorman asked me, "How long have you been on this job? I've been on this job fourteen years, long enough to know you never find nothing."

Once at Pelham Bay, the flagman was clearing riders out my train so it could be laid up. I spotted a homeless man still on the train and called to the flagman, "There's one in here."

A very senior motorman came by and admonished me sharply, "Shh! Don't say nothin'! It isn't your job, it isn't your business." When I went ahead anyhow, he added grimly, "Well, you'll learn. You'll learn to mind your own business."

It was universally understood that our employer did not care about us workers at all. The equipment first of all, the riders next (mainly because they might sue), and us last. I honestly believe this is a totally realistic assessment. As one of us said, "They don't care. They don't care about us. They don't care that we get hurt. Motormen, conductors, they get burnt in the cabs. They know about it. They don't care."

A story from a yard worker illustrates this perception, "This car cleaner, on probation, was warned about taking too much sick time. He was com-

plaining about chest pains and he asked if he could lie down. They told him
he couldn't lie down, that he could either go home or go back to work. They
had warned him about taking too much sick time, so he went back to work,
but he collapsed. To make a long story short, he'd had a heart attack. While
he was in the hospital, t.a. fired him."

When some high ranking t.a. official was coming to visit Woodlawn, we
found workmen in the dilapidated bathroom, trying to fix broken urinals.
The crews were very cynical about this, "It's because the Big Man is coming." "That's the way things are done around here. Everything is done for the
big shots, and nothing for the little guy."

One of my motormen, DiGangio, once told me, very indignantly, of the
special bubble-topped subway car used to transport VIPs around the system,
"And they sit there with bottles of liquor and drinks on the table, while if we
have a trace of alcohol in our blood, we could lose our jobs! They could have
the decency to hide it! It—it's like there are two classes! It's not fair!"

There were also adages to deal with the job's difficulties and injustices.
The final trip of a job was dubbed "the money-maker, because that's when
you earn your money." This was a recognition that, by the end of the job, you
could expect to be tired and worn out and have to push yourself to complete
it: "earn your money." (It occurred to me, however, that this could be an
interpretation of Marx's theory of surplus value: the first part of the working
day went to the boss as profit, and only after that did the worker earn his pay.)

Another byword that provided comfort in the face of frequent unfairness
was, "What goes around, comes around." Those who do evil will eventually
have evil done to them, and you and I don't have to do a thing to make that
happen. Very reassuring.

Despite the shared dislike of management, workers expected one another
to have an overall positive view of the job. One might complain about the
riders, the supervisors, or the equipment, but people who had been around
awhile discouraged complaints about the job in general.

"You came to the job, the job didn't come to you." This was a common
saw, addressed to anyone who expressed a general dislike of the job. As for
the prevalent conditions, another saying served, "Better days are coming."
Workers boasted, "I do my three trips," or two, or four. "I don't come here to
get dropped." This dictum wasn't 100 percent genuine; I never saw anyone
turn down a drop.

The work schedule held a vast variety of jobs. Each had its characteristics, good, bad, or a matter of taste. An easy job was called a "tit job," because working it was like a baby sucking milk. A tough job was "a workhorse." Once, Motorman Gonzalez, seeing me in a bad mood, was quick to ascribe it to my job. "It's that two twenty-one job. You don't get any breaks."

If you didn't like the job you were working now, within six months you would be picking a new one. And the practice of picking jobs by seniority meant that workers assumed that, at each future pick there would be more, and better, jobs for them to choose from. It was this underlying sense that things could only get better that made the pick such a preoccupation for subway workers. A couple of months after a new schedule (a "pick") began, they would begin asking each other when the process of picking new jobs (this process was also called a "pick") would start. Once it started, the ubiquitous transit worker conversational gambit was, "When do you pick?" If the worker had already picked, then the next question was, "Wudja pick?" This question was a guaranteed conversation starter until the new pick began, and the cycle renewed itself.

Another major feature of the job was getting in trouble, and there were complex and contradictory beliefs about rules and discipline. One of the things that complicated this situation was that there was a rulebook full of rules and then there were unwritten rules that were actually more important in determining whether or not a worker got in trouble. (I have written about them in an article appearing in the *Journal of Radical Political Economics*, Winter 1990.) The most important unwritten rules were don't hold up service and don't injure any riders (because they might sue).

This discrepancy between "rules" is illustrated by an anecdote one conductor told me. A trainmaster on his train told him, "Don't call Command Center when you have a problem. Use your discretion."

The conductor answered that the rulebook says, "Inform Command," and, "if I don't, and there's a problem, it's my ass, you know."

"So why was he saying that to me?" the conductor asked me, "Why was he telling me not to call Command, if that could get me into trouble?"

The answer to the conductor's conundrum is that the trainmaster was telling him to follow the unwritten rules, particularly, the ban on delaying service, which calling Command might do.

This was also the origin of another ubiquitous transit saying, "The rules are there to hang you." You could break a million rules and get away with it, but, as soon as you messed up the railroad, they took out the rulebook to find a rule you'd broken in order to discipline you. I heard some workers saying, "If you know your rulebook, you can stay out of trouble." Union reps were particularly fond of this saying. But a more common saying was, "In this job, you can try to stay out of trouble and still get into trouble."

Subway operatives perceived themselves to be "in the middle" between riders and supervision, and saw that as a potential source of discipline.

"I don't like the trains," a conductor who had picked construction flagging told me. "On the trains, you're in Catch-22. You're caught between the riders and the supervision. You can't please them both."

Once, a couple of motormen and conductors were talking. "You can't win" said one. "They—" the riders— "smoke pot and play radios right outside your position, and you can't do anything."

"You can do something, but *they*—" meaning supervision and management— "won't back you up."

A conductor told of seeing a guy swinging on the chains between the cars of the train. The conductor told him he couldn't do that. The rider answered, "I'm staying here. You'll have to get a cop to get me off." The conductor went back to his cab.

A listening conductor said, "Then if he falls, it's you that's in trouble. The only thing you can do is stop the train and tell Command Center you have a dangerous situation and you're not moving. Tie up the road. Then you bet they would stop blaming conductors."

Taking this to an extreme, a station cleaner told me that he'd had two experiences with people lying on the roadbed, "I had to run into the tunnel and flag down the train. I got a commendation. But I also was reinstructed that I'm not to go down to the roadbed! I'm to tell the clerk in the booth! And this was about the same time that it was in all the papers that a man was killed when he fell and they couldn't get him off the tracks before the train came. Telling the clerk won't stop the train!"

There was very strong agreement that all of us were bound to make mistakes. If I made a mistake, everyone reassured me that everyone, no matter how experienced, made mistakes. Once during my first year, I was carrying on about how many mistakes I had made. A senior man smiled at me

indulgently, "I've been here eighteen years, and I still make mistakes, too."
Once, when I was upset about closing the doors on a baby stroller, a motorman said to me, "Let's say you work in title five years. You'll close the doors
on mothers, children, old folks, cripples."

Every time I was in trouble, my coworkers said things to me like "A
caution is only a piece of paper," and "Unless you want to be a trainmaster, it
doesn't matter." Some people even claimed they wanted suspensions, "days
in the street" they were called, in order to get a little break from the job.

The job was considered dangerous; however, stoicism was the prescribed attitude. Once I noticed a conductor with a cut on his forehead. He
told me the train had lurched and he'd hit his head. "The train dispatcher
said if I wanted to report it, I had to go to the clinic. But I'd had a few beers
the night before and I was afraid they'd give me a B.A.T. [blood alcohol test]
You hurt yourself all the time on this job. The storm doors slam on you, right
on your funny bone."

But transit workers rarely talked about these things unless they were
specifically asked. Once a new and young conductor confided in me, "I froze
going across the structure. If my motorman hadn't come and got me, I'd be
on the side of a train right now." He asked me for advice. I was the wrong
person to ask, because I personally was terrified by the elevated structure.
When I asked a few other motormen, however, they were as much at a loss as
me. They all recalled how they too had fears at first. But no one ever talked
about that stuff. What is not discussed is just as much a feature of a culture as
what is.

Workers thought they had many rights that they did not have. They
believed that many laws protecting workers in private industry also
applied to us, like limits on cab time, mandatory lunch breaks, and disability
insurance. In fact, as public employees, we enjoyed none of these protec-
tions.

People felt they had a right to decent treatment, even if they didn't get it.
When the T.A. ended our practice of warming our meals on the heaters and
radiators, supervisors were advised to tell us, "There's no clause in their
contract for them to have hot meals."

Crews greeted this with indignation. The most frequent response was
"What do they mean, we have no right?" People clearly felt they did, indeed,

have a right to hot meals. Eventually, the crew room got a microwave oven, paid for by the crews.

The saying that best summed up the norm for how subway workers should act toward one another was, "You got to work together." This meant avoiding controversial subjects, like race, religion, and politics. It meant that even if you had a yelling brawl with a coworker, as I did upon occasion, bygones should be bygones as soon as humanly possible. It meant you weren't supposed to finger the other person in your crew, "Get your story straight together." Your story was supposed to be the same, and one that let both of you off the hook.

These attitudes were clearly useful for adapting to the injustices and difficulties of the job. They also formed part of a broader array of attitudes and practices that had the same effect.

While I was working for the Transit Authority, between 1982 and 1986, there was scarcely any collective action by subway operatives in response to what they took to be unfair treatment by management. The main reason for this, in my opinion, was that there was no leadership to coordinate such a response. The union officialdom was not interested, and no alternative leadership had yet developed.

There was constant talk of a "work-to-rules." There was skepticism over getting workers to follow it. Riggs the Radical, a motorman at Woodlawn, actually tried to organize one.

The most widespread action during this time came about as a result of a media and management attack on train operators that scapegoated them for a rash of derailments actually caused by policies of deferred maintenance.

For about two days during the summer of 1983, train operators carried out a widespread slowdown without any unified leadership. What coordinated the action was widespread media exposure, the headlines in the major tabloids about "cowboy motormen" and management's crackdown on "speeding motormen" who were taken out of service and given suspensions. The tabloid headlines produced universal subway-worker anger and indignation, and management policy produced a unified response: since speeding led to discipline, the motormen would go slowly, very slowly.

This slowdown was an important exception. Resistance was widespread, but it was isolated and individual. Still it was definitely there in uncoordinated acts that took place all the time in different arenas. Workers resisted unscheduled trips especially; because they felt they were unfair, they booked sick or sabotaged trains. Some workers got on their trains at the last possible minute, or ignored holding lights, enhancing their break time. Or they "dogged it," operating slowly in hope of getting to the terminal so late that their next trip would have to be dropped. In these and other ways, workers struggled to increase their control over the pace and amount of their work. These tactics were discussed and passed along in stories and rumors.

One story, probably embellished and possibly even apocryphal, involved a conductor working "the Deuce" on New Year's Eve. The train got up to 238th Street, the stop before the terminal, when the dispatcher told the motorman over the radio, "We're having signal trouble. Change ends. You're taking it back to Flatbush." The conductor went to the last car of the train, which would become the first one going back to Flatbush, and kicked out the motorman's vision glass. That was the end of that trip. The person I heard the story from concluded with a heartfelt, "And I would have done the same thing!" Sabotage was seen as a legitimate response to perceived unfair treatment.

Though employees often resisted, they more often accommodated. For example, employees often improvised from materials at hand to improve working conditions. Because the seats in the cabs of the old trains had all had their padding ripped out, a few motormen carried cushions. Others improvised with newspapers. Some ripped down large advertising placards in the cars and used them to sit on. To wedge open cab doors, conductors had special ways of folding the placards or the metal bands that held them in place. Placards also served to hold in place the catch that kept the storm doors open for conductors who wanted a cooling breeze in summer, and even to hold shut windows in broken frames or cab doors with broken locks. Also useful for these purposes were wads of the postcards attached to the subway advertisements for trade schools and their ilk.

A few subway workers had perfected the technique of using a shoe slipper to do some of these things. (A shoe slipper is a flat wedge of wood that looks rather like a baseball bat run over by a steamroller.) There's one in every cab. Its official function is to slip a train's power shoe back on the third rail if it should be dislodged, but in four years on the job, I never experienced, or heard of, one being used this way. It was widely touted, on the other hand, as a tool of self-defense, and nicknamed "the conductor's American Express Card: don't leave the terminal without it."

I could never learn the knack of wedging a door open in any of these ways, so I carried rubber door stop in my bag with me.

A few workers were even more ingenious. Mark Goniea once left his radio key, which is used to lock the motorman's radio into the cab, at home. He improvised a web of string which could unlock a radio from its bracket.

The improvisation of tools became a money-making sideline for some workers. One conductor at Woodlawn made side sign-turners. These signs on the sides of subway cars tell the train's origin, destination, and route. Since trains routes changed over the hours of the day, conductors had to adjust the signs. The improvised sign-turners made this otherwise arduous job much easier. This conductor and other subway workers made unique devices with attractive handles, and sold them for four dollars each. After asking one of the "manufacturers" about the cost of his materials and the length of time he worked on them, I ascertained that his profit was just under nine dollars an hour.

The examples above are almost all obsolete now. Cab doors need no longer be wedged open. Most windows are in good shape. With air-conditioning, no one has to wedge open a storm door. Even the need for sign-turners has dwindled to almost nothing. The T.A. furnished workers with sign-turners for the "R-62's," but future trains will have side signs run by computers like those already in use on buses and some subway lines. However, I believe that the subway workers' propensity and ability to improvise tools and technology to make their work easier will persist in other ways.

Transit workers related to each other in ways that helped them to release the tensions of the job. As one conductor explained it, "We come in off the road and we come in the crew room, we want to joke around, forget the things that happened on the train. It's better than brooding about it."

Crews kidded each other about the difficulty of the work. "Leaving already?" "Half-day today?" "Working hard or hardly working?"

I found the teasing witty and amusing, especially when I was not the object. For example, this exchange among very senior, very dignified black workers: three are teasing the fourth, who is lying down, dangling his foot over the back of the bench on which he is lying. One taunts, "If you'd get your ass home when you leave here, you wouldn't be so tired. But you've got to go out finger snapping, break dancing." After that, they made fun of him for eating peanut butter.

When the T.A. cut the number of workers who cleaned trash from the roadbed, a rash of fires broke out. This contributed to the stress crews experienced on the job. Their response was to joke about it. One motorman complained, "It used to be if you banged in a fire, Command asked, 'Can you see the signals, motorman?' and if you said yes, Command said, 'Then take a deep breath, motorman, and proceed according to rule thirty-seven Nancy.'" When federal inspectors arrived to investigate the fires, crews joked about the "Welcome to New York" fire that T.A. had set especially for the inspectors.

The heavy circulation of rumors on the job was a response to the job's great uncertainties. There was no written union contract available to us, and management and supervision had almost unlimited discretion over our work. Disciplinary penalties were not set by rule and could be extremely harsh. Our rights were nebulous, and union representation or even consultation was often unavailable. Changes were taking place in T.A. policies. There was once a rumor that a conductor named Jones (there must have been two dozen in the subways) had failed the B.A.T. and subsequently fingered twenty-eight conductors who he said would fail it, too. Another rumor had a different conductor being taken out of service for making the announcement, when he had holding lights: "This train is being held by supervision," an announcement most conductors used. There were always rumors about the pick, an obsession of subway workers anyway, that it would be held only every year, every two years. There was a rumor that if one member of a crew did not report, the other would be put "on board," meaning she or he could get any job that started anytime within her or his usual eight hours of work. There were always rumors that people would be forced to work on their R.D.O.S.

I heard rumors about myself. Years after I had had a shooting on my train, I heard the story of the woman conductor who had a shooting on her train on her first night on the road and had quit. This rumor clearly helped the men on the job feel superior to women employees.

Another rumor about me was that I when I was hit in the face, I left my train in pursuit of the culprit, and my train left without me. In real life, I had pulled the cord to stop the train so it couldn't have moved.

Another way to cope with the job's problems was to develop a fantasy about getting out. The lottery, and other forms of gambling, legal and illegal, clearly served that function and played an important role in the culture of the workplace. People discussed what numbers to play and how they chose their numbers, especially through dreams. The first time I heard a motorman announce, "I'm calling out, does anyone want anything?" I assumed it was for Chinese food or a Greek diner. Then someone called out a number, adding "Brooklyn, New York," and then another number.

Subway workers had well-established ways to respond to a coworker's illness or a death in the family. A close friend would place a notice on the sign-in sheets. The notice included the name of the person, usually the dispatcher or a worker whose job kept him in the terminal, who would collect the money for that fund. On the notice was space for the contributors to write their names and the amount they had contributed.

Workers did not resort to the fine arts to help them express their feelings about the job. They did not write poems or paint pictures. I did know of one motorman, however, who tried to write a song about his job, a statement of pride, a protest against deskilling, if you will, and a demand for recognition. The lyrics went like this (music accompaniment unavailable):

> We are engineers
> We are engineers
> Don't call us train operators
> (*Repeat*)
>
> This ain't no damn sewing machine
> And we don't answer no damn phones
>
> We put out those damn fires
> We walk all over those live wires
> We go down the road without desires
> We are engineers (*etc.*)
>
> We fix this old junk
> When it breaks down on strike
> The T.A. says we are train operators
> But I'm here to say today
> That we are engineers
> And we should get more pay!

Because we didn't have common weekends or vacation time, there were few official picnics, parties, or other social occasions off the job. There was one traditional social event on the job, the Woodlawn Christmas Party. Of course, informally, groups of transit workers partied and socialized together.

The two groups that subway workers had to deal with were riders and supervisors. I have already noted that they felt "caught in the middle," between the two—and with reason. The most common saying about riders was "You can't do enough for them." This summed up the workers' frustration and feeling of being unappreciated and unrecognized that the workers got from dealing with riders. I also heard variations on "Most of them are okay. It's only a few that make all the problems." There was also much speculation about why people seemed meaner on the subways than any place else, and riders' questions were repeated and ridiculed.

Humor was also used to cope with rider assaults on us. "You know," a conductor told me once, "the T.A. sends out these people. They take a look at your record, 'Hmmmmm. No one's hit Conductor So-and-so lately. You over there: Go over to Fifty-ninth Street.'"

The narration of justice triumphant and sweet revenge also helped to heal the wounds. A typical conductor story was how he stopped the train, ran, and caught his assailant. The next part varied. "So I took my slipper, followed 'em down the steps. Now they're all scared, 'Oh, man, don't!' Well, you know, downtown they frown on that," so to be law-abiding, the worker stops at scaring the daylights out of the culprits. The variation culminates with a savage beating, inflicted by the conductor, of course.

One of the most traumatic things that can possibly happen to a subway worker is a "twelve-nine," the code for a person under the train, and hence synonymous with critical injury and often death. Consequently, there are many stories characterized by irony and gallows humor about these incidents. Any time a twelve-nine occurs, all these stories are trotted out. A common one, probably apocryphal, tells of a motorman who has a twelve-nine on his trip out. Any motorman who encounters a twelve-nine is entitled to three days off to get over the shock and become calm enough to drive again (some motormen apply for and need more time). So this fellow is offered the three days, but refuses; he's tough enough, he's fine. En route back to the terminal, he has another twelve-nine, gets on the radio, "I want my six!"

The occasion of my hearing the following two stories was a twelve-nine on the No. 1 line, which marooned me in the crew room when service was halted.

"That reminds me," a conductor began the tale, "of one time out at Rockaway Avenue. A motorman hit a guy on the structure. He went into emergency, got out, and started looking under the train. Couldn't find anything. Soon the conductor got out and started looking, too. They looked under all ten cars. Command asked, 'You sure?' 'Sure, I'm sure,' the motorman said, 'I saw someone jump right ahead of me.' Finally, they gave up and went on.

"Well, it turned out the guy'd fallen through the structure. He'd been running away from these guys who wanted to kill him and he jumped on the tracks to get away from them. When the train hit him, he fell through the structure. They found him three blocks away. They said there was all pieces cut out of him and everything, but he was so scared he musta run a good three blocks before he collapsed. He musta felt if he could just get away from those guys, he'd be alright."

"Here's one," said a motorman, "There was this time they had this guy who was all cut up. They found everything except the arm. They looked all over the tracks and all over the train laid up in the yard. Couldn't find it anyplace.

"Finally they found out: the guy only had one arm."

Another story had no denouement: "One time a guy up at Dyre radioed Command, 'Command, I got a twelve-nine. I hit a cow.' They never found the cow. But the motorman stuck to his story."

On a different occasion, Motorman Gonzalez told his collection of twelve-nine stories. "That's the worst feeling in the world, when the train goes 'chow'! and your brake pipe needle goes all the way down to zero. Then you charge up again, and it's not someone pulled the cord—you hit something.

"One time, I found a shopping cart that kids pushed on the tracks. Other time, I found a cat. The worst time I had was when I went into emergency and someone says to me, 'A lady fell between the cars, you hit a lady.' I felt sick, I didn't even want to look. But it wasn't a lady. She had dropped a box she was carrying. And the box, well, it was a mess. She had bought a set of dishes. And she was sitting there, crying, 'It's spoiled! It's spoiled!'

"A trainmaster had to see the box. Came out to the train to see the box of broken dishes. They want to make sure you're telling the truth."

Once a motorman was very shaken up to hear another motorman declare over the radio, "I've got the body. Motor Instructor Tyner is looking for the head." It turned out the motorman had gone into emergency, gone down to the tracks, and found a giant stuffed toy bird with its head cut off. "Cowboy Motorman Crushes Baby Bird, details at eleven," he quipped.

And, of course, a dog on the tracks wasn't a twelve-nine, it was a "K"-nine.

These stories were bizarre. They distracted us from the realities of real accidents, which were gruesome and very upsetting.

The other group with whom we dealt was our supervisors. Our attitudes toward them were understandably complex and even contradictory. Any one of us was free to take a test for promotion to supervision. And all of our supervisors had once been "hourly employees" just like us.

It was often observed that our supervisors had it as tough, or tougher, than we did. Once the water cooler in the crew room was broken for many weeks. A motorman said, "The dispatcher says that someone is coming to fix it."

Another motorman said, "You can bet he's got water and lights up there."

The first motorman said, "They didn't have water up there for a while. They treat them as bad as they treat us."

"Worse," admitted the second motorman.

"But we complain more," added the first, "while they're always apologizing for the T.A.'s policies."

Workers often expressed the conviction that cooperation should be a two-way street and their dissatisfaction when supervisors did not recognize that. Soon after David Gunn became the new T.A. president, a neatly hand-lettered sign was posted on the wall of the Woodlawn crew room, signed by a dispatcher and a trainmaster. It listed obligations for crews such as "Crews on lunch must be prepared to jump ahead without question" and "W.A.A. crews must not leave the terminal without the permission of the train dispatcher." At the bottom was written, "Let's all work together and give good service."

A motorman commented after reading it, "First they tell us what we must and must not do. Then they ask for our cooperation."

We felt that our supervisors, especially the higher-ups down at Jay Street, had lost touch with the reality of our jobs and expected us to achieve the impossible. "Those guys should come back on the road once a year, and work the road for a week or two, because they forget what it's like, setting at a desk, get up and go to the bathroom, bottle in the drawer, no one buzzing around them, staring at them, asking 'em where'd they lose their time, spittin' on them. . . ."

Occasionally, they expressed the idea that supervisors were gratuitous: that we were the ones running the railroad. In this instance, it was expressed in jest: A motorman came into the crew room and saw both the terminal's dispatcher and assistant dispatcher back there. "Wait!" he cried in mock alarm, "Who's running the railroad?" Then, hastily, "No, no, never mind. It's running better this way! It's running perfect this way!"

When Mark got promoted to dispatcher, feelings about him were mixed. Some men approved, saying he would be a good supervisor. But another worker told me, "Your friend is a traitor."

Transit workers discussed social issues relatively rarely, whether because they were uninterested or they wished to avoid controversy, it was hard to tell. Most understood very well that the crisis of the deterioration of the subways arose from cuts in funding to mass transit. Many were angry that our union's leaders would not oppose Westway, a diversion of funds from mass transit to build a superhighway down the West Side of Manhattan. Some even criticized United States aid to Latin American dictatorships or the bloated military budget as diverting money from things like subways, and I'm not speaking here about people who were leftists.

Some workers were concerned about, and even active in, the anti-nuclear arms movement that crested in the late seventies and early eighties. Most workers were far more concerned about crime, and that was probably the most frequently discussed social issue. In those days, most of the trains we worked on were completely covered with graffiti, and subway workers were indignant about that. The remedies they prescribed included making the parents pay for it, making the kids clean it up, setting up a big farm upstate where the kids could be sent, or just meting out long prison sentences, which would be publicized on the front pages of all the newspapers.

Crime struck home at Woodlawn when Motorman Shaw's son was stabbed to death in a robbery. The headline in the *Post* said, "Ex-Grid Star Slain for $1." Naturally, a collection was taken, and everyone felt terrible. When Shaw came back to the job, after a week, each worker shook his hand and asked after him and offered condolences.

Shaw repeated to each one the whole story—exactly what had happened in detail. It was as if he were trying to get used to it. It usually ended with Shaw and the listener agreeing that the city was dangerous, full of people who will slit your throat for a nickel, and you had to be afraid all the time.

Shaw had always been very liberal, someone I could count on to back me up in arguments about social issues and politics. After this, however, he changed. He became obsessed with "law and order." "Did you read about those bank robbers in Oklahoma that shot four people?" he asked me not long after his bereavement, "I don't know why they gave them a trial. They got them red-handed. If they have a trial, they'll just get some fancy lawyer and go free."

But police were not popular, either, and police officers who used excessive force were considered just as much criminals as other lawbreakers. Even the most conservative workers felt, for example, that the police who killed Eleanor Bumpurs, an elderly black woman shot in the process of an eviction, had no business being on the force. The more liberal workers felt they should be prosecuted for murder.

Feeling was much more united around the affair of Bernard Goetz, the "vigilante," the white rider who shot and critically wounded a group of black youths who were trying to rob him. He was a hero to all subway workers, black and white, excepting only radical diehards like Riggs the Radical. On the television news we watched in the Woodlawn crew room, the young men who were shot were referred to as "the victims." The crew room erupted in indignation. "If he hadn't shot them," one worker cried, "he would have been the victim!"

While I was a conductor, the presidential election of 1984 took place, Ronald Reagan and George Bush running against Walter Mondale and Geraldine Ferraro. Not surprisingly, transit worker opinion was divided. Once, when a press conference with Reagan was appearing on the television screen at Woodlawn, it took a long time before the fifteen or so men in the crew room paid any attention to it. Most of them were involved in a very loud discussion around a card game.

Finally, a young Italian American motorman spoke up, "You know, I know a lot of people really hate him, but I'll say this for him. My family's in construction, and construction is booming. For years, construction was dead. Now there's more work than there's guys to do it."

A very senior black motorman agreed, "I know. There's more jobs for electricians than there are electricians."

A young black motorman with a college degree intervened cheerfully, "Personally, I can't stand the guy. But I must say he looks great. The job hasn't aged him at all." This led to a discussion of Reagan's appearance, which was much less controversial and therefore much more consistent with the crew room ethos.

Many of the discussions about the election also pointed up the workers' dislike and distrust of the media. They were cynical about the polls and the newspapers' endorsements of Reagan. But their dislike was more general. One motorman told how a *Post* reporter asked him what he thought about the plan to put motormen in uniforms. "I felt like saying, 'I don't like your newspaper.'"

An old-timer said, "It's a biased paper."

The people I worked with were exposed to leftist politics all the time by Riggs the Radical. They accepted Riggs, although they found him rather dogmatic and inflexible. Those weren't the words they used, of course. They would say something like, "That Riggs. Unless you agree with him one hundred percent . . . ." and then a shake of the head. Riggs made some inroads among the few white workers at Woodlawn, but the black and Hispanic workers steered clear of his group's activities.

Socialist ideas were discussed only among the workers who had been leftists when they came to the job, and there were quite a few of us, really. However, both black and white workers were willing to accept leadership from open socialists. As one white train operator said of a leader of the "old opposition," "Now, L. was a commie, but so what? He was trying to honestly change the union."

Subway workers' attitudes toward their union's top leaders, and sometimes toward the union itself, were negative. There was general agreement that it had to be changed. The question was how. It was usually agreed that, if you got involved in efforts to change the union, you could get yourself into trouble. And it was said that people were scared to get involved thereby. Never the person speaking—who was, of course, fearless—but, you know, the others.

People who became union staffers changed. Even officers changed, because they became dependent on the staff and higher officers in order to deliver favors to and defend their members. As one motorman said of the organizer known as "Take Your Days in the Street" Washington, "I knew Will before he was working for the union. He was totally different: night and day. I don't think he could have stayed where he is now without changing."

But there were many workers who wanted to get rid of the union altogether. There were discussions, and sometimes heated arguments, over whether we'd be better off without the union.

During the four years I worked in the subways, many important changes took place. The greatest changes took place in the structure of supervision and the introduction of new equipment. There was also a general "cleaning up" of the operation. More emphasis was put on appearances. Motorman were given uniforms. Mirrors were put up in crew rooms. Flagman had to start wearing uniforms. A lot of the informality of the job was jettisoned. Crew room food concessions run by workers were abolished. Flagmen had to stop treating the flagging shacks as, in effect, their personal apartments. The comfortable, cushioned chairs in the dispatchers' shacks were thrown out and replaced with hardwood seats.

It is interesting to note how transit workers felt about these changes. Generally, they weren't thrilled. But the new trains, the "R-62s" made in Japan by Kawasaki, really improved our working conditions. Any crew was happy to get one and vastly disappointed to get an old train, as shown by the names given to the old ones after the '62s appeared: "jalopies," "pintos," "tomato cans"; the '62s were "Cadillacs," "silver bullets," or "silver birds."

Yet the new trains were frequently criticized, too. When the bugs were still being taken out of them, one motorman, predicting they would never be fully implemented, called them the "sicky-twos." Very senior men criticized the brakes, "I don't like 'em because they don't let the motorman make a hard stop. The motorman is supposed to be in control of the train. He should be able to make a sudden, hard stop. The motormen don't have to be as good as they used to be. They are taking skill away from the motorman."

The new trains from the Canadian company Bombardier were called "R-62as." They were not so well made and had real drawbacks. Motormen complained that the brakes were hard to control, and conductors found their windows hard to raise and lower.

At the same time, the top officials of the M.T.A. and T.A. were reorganizing the supervision. They were taking some of the dispatcher positions, notably those at Command Center, out of the supervisory collective bargaining unit, and making them part of management. They were eliminating the Trainmaster position, which had been a civil service position with collective bargaining representation, and replacing it with "superintendent." Superintendents were not chosen on the basis of a civil service exam; they were just appointed by higher-ups, and they had no collective bargaining agent. Almost everyone was unhappy about this. As one dispatcher said, "It's going to be a mess."

Transit workers were in it for the money, although some might take pride in doing a good job and delivering good service. For workers with no dependents, who were mostly the younger ones, the money meant buying nice things and having a good time. For the others, it meant taking care of a family. Family values were extremely important to subway operatives. As Shaw once said to Mark, "You ought to get married. Family is the essence of life."

Family values significantly affected job performance. A family meant you couldn't play games and screw up. It was all very well to take a suspension if there was only one mouth to feed. But if others were depending on you, that was a different story. When one conductor's time was cut and he was sent home for leaving the terminal during his "w.a.a." everyone blamed him for being foolhardy. As Angelo Gonzalez said, "It would be one thing if he were a single man, but he has a wife and kids. A family man can't act like that."

Probably those with happy family lives never spoke much about them, so what got discussed were the heartaches and problems. But even many men who complained about their marriages were still enthusiastic about their children.

One Hispanic motorman told me, "At Christmas, I left home for a few days. One of my cousins called me up, 'Your little boy keeps asking for you.'

"I went to my home, I went up to the door, and I listened. And sure enough, I could hear him saying, 'Where's Poppy? Where's Poppy?'

"Finally I went in. He was so excited. He starts showing me everything, 'Poppy, look at this!'

"My wife and I drive each other crazy. But when you got kids, you love them a lot."

WHY I LEFT

W hen I look back upon my life, perhaps my greatest regret is that I didn't have what it took to stick it out in transit. I simply couldn't do the job. For one thing, I just couldn't figure out how to negotiate the T.A.'s crazy rules in time. For another, I couldn't take the physical rigors of the job or the constant verbal abuse a conductor endures. But the main thing was that I couldn't live with the constant expectation of being hit and spit on.

During the four years I worked for transit, I had an upper respiratory infection about once a month. The one time I tried working despite having a cold, I came down with bronchitis. Yet, I am not a particularly unhealthy person. In my present occupation, teaching high school for the New York City Board of Education, I rarely lose time to illness. During my rare colds, I usually work. I just put a box of tissues on the desk and share it with my students, who are often sneezing and wheezing along with me.

Not only that, but as a conductor, I had had a problem with my eyes that necessitated minor surgery, chronic and painful spasms in my neck, and even an infected finger, and with each of these afflictions, I also had some problems with the T.A., or T.A. rules led to further problems with my healthcare providers.

One morning, my throat was killing me and I was sneezing constantly. I was still a graduate student at Columbia, so I went to the student health service. Because I was still on probation with the T.A., it was important that I get "doctor's lines." "Doctor's lines" are a part of the form that T.A. employees must fill out when they miss work because of illness. The rule about when "doctor's lines" are required is: whenever T.A. says so. And the "lines" must be submitted within 48 hours of "resuming work."

That day, my usual doctor was not at the Columbia clinic, and I saw another doctor, who was clearly overscheduled and asked all the "transfers" to make appointments for the following week. And she did not want to give me "lines." "I'll tell you what I can do," she said, "I can write a note asking that they waive the rule."

I laughed and shrugged, "Okay. We can give it a shot. But the T.A. has thirty-five thousand hourly employees, not even counting supervisors. I doubt your note will cut any ice, but if that's all you feel you can do for me, we could give it a shot."

She finally did give me her signature, but she was not pleased, "I feel obligated to tell you as a patient, you know, that there is really no medical reason why you should miss work today."

I said, "I'm exhausted and dizzy. I work with machinery."

She said, "It's one thing if you need a break from your job. But I know I could work with your symptoms."

I replied, "If I had your job, I could work with these symptoms, too. But the subways are dusty. Often you can't get water to drink for hours. Often you have to stand without a break for hours—"

She interrupted, "I know you have bad working conditions. So you should fight for tougher occupational health and safety regulations. Still, you should be able to work with these symptoms."

"All I can do is hope that someday, somehow, you have a job like this one. That's the only way you'll ever understand what it's like."

I was too sick to work my job. And this professional woman, whose hardest physical exertion involved examining patients and writing, in a well-ventilated and well-heated office, didn't understand why.

During my last year with T.A., I developed serious neck pain which has never completely disappeared. By that time, I had gotten my degree at Columbia and was going to H.I.P. (Health Insurance Plan, an HMO) for medical care. So when I couldn't move my head without sharp pain, I called and asked for an appointment. They offered me one ten days later. I had to cry and die to get one for that day. I waited the usual hour for the doctor, who said it was probably either a muscle spasm or a pinched nerve.

"It feels a little better each day I stay home from work," I said, "so couldn't I stay home until it's all better?"

"It doesn't make any difference when you go back," she opined, "since you have to go back eventually." She would only give me doctor's lines for that day.

I went back to work. I took over-the-counter painkillers that made me feel woozy and sick to my stomach. I was making a station stop when I saw a motor instructor at my position. He said, "Bad news. More harassment from supervision. Now Fairfax sent us out to tell you, you can't have the seat down in the cab." This applied to the new trains, the R-62s.

"But I can't work with the seat up!" Although I am a little over five feet, five inches tall, the P.A. mouthpiece on the new trains was too high for me to speak into. There was an extremely narrow step, perhaps two inches wide, to stand on. To keep my balance on this step when the train was moving, I propped myself from behind with the seat. And I was required to make announcements as the train was moving into the station.

The union could do nothing to help me, so I continued to operate with the seat illegally down—an extra source of stress.

As for my neck, I went to a chiropractor recommended by a friend. His adjustments, not covered by my medical insurance, and the exercise regime he prescribed brought relief.

While I was with T.A., I also developed an eye ailment. (I have to say that I never had such a problem before I worked in the subways, and I haven't had any such in the ten years since I left. But that could be just a coincidence.) One day, I was gazing at one of the ads in my operating car and found I couldn't read the print. When I shut my left eye, I could. I shut my right eye and found my vision was totally blurry.

As it turned out, there was a growth on my left eyelid that had been pressuring my eyeball. It had to be cut out. After that, my doctor assured me, my eye would slowly return to normal vision. I was not thrilled, but treatment was clearly unavoidable. I made the appointment for the office procedure.

There was an awful, early spring snowstorm raging the evening I called to book sick for the procedure. The sick desk told me, "Rule 166(i) is in effect." This meant anyone who booked sick had to bring in doctor's lines. Then he asked me my ailment.

"Swollen and painful left eye," I said.

"Then you'll have to go to the clinic before you resume."

"Why?"

"Anything to do with any extremity."

I pictured my eye extended on the tip of a tentacle. "My eye is not an extremity."

"Or an eye. Or anything like that. Get a G-45 from any dispatcher."

I knew I was screwed. I wouldn't be able to read an eye chart until God knew when. I had only two days of paid sick leave remaining. If I had to wait to go back to work until my vision was normal in my left eye, it could take weeks.

A week after the procedure, I went to the clinic. They took me into a dark room for the eye test. The nurse said, "Cover your left eye and read the bottom line." That was easy. My right eye was my good eye. She told me to cover my right eye. I was sure she would tell me to read a different line, to make sure she was testing my vision and not my memory. But she didn't. "Read the bottom line," she repeated. I recited it from memory.

I was put back on full work, resuming the next day.

But my worst problem with illness and T.A. came when I got sick while I was on the job.   I had eaten something that didn't agree with me. My stomach was in knots. I had never used the toilets in the crew room at 137th Street. The cubicles had no doors and the stench made me gag. I told myself I could wait. Just one short trip and I could go home.

My train got rerouted out to Flatbush, Brooklyn. By the time I got to Flatbush, I felt as if I were going to pass out. I got off the train and walked to the dispatcher's office, and told him I felt sick. He told me, "You have to call Command."

The man at Command was nasty, "You weren't sick before you got rerouted."

"I need to get to a bathroom," I said.

"If you're sick, you can wait for an ambulance."

"If I can just have half an hour in a clean bathroom, I'll be okay."

"You can operate, or you can wait for an ambulance and go to a hospital. Or you'll be charged with insubordination."

If I went to a hospital, I'd spend six hours in a waiting room, then get dumped on the street in the middle of the night in an unfamiliar part of Brooklyn hours from home. Or I could be home in a couple of hours. I decided I could make it up to Van Cortlandt.

By the time we got back into Manhattan, I had violent cramps. I was sweating and between the stops, I sat down in the car. By the end of each station stop, I was getting faint. At Times Square I didn't make it through the station stop. Before I could even open the doors, I passed out. I came to, stood up and opened the doors, and sat down on the floor again. A platform conductor came over and called a transit patrolman. The police officer escorted me to the dispatcher's office at Times Square.

"Do you want an ambulance?" a motor instructor asked me.

It was the only way I could avoid disciplinary action, but I was too sick to care about discipline. "Please, I need a bathroom. A clean one. With privacy," I pleaded.

He took me two stops to 96th Street. The minutes seemed like ages. Every part of my body seemed to be in revolt. I felt like any moment I might lose control of my bowels or throw up.

When I emerged from the toilet the motor instructor told me I had to call Command. On the phone, I explained as best I could what had happened. "You mean, if you can't get to a ladies' room, you pass out."

"When I'm sick to my stomach, and I can't use a toilet for ten hours, yes, I do."

"I don't accept your explanation. I want you to see the Chief Trainmaster on Monday."

"I don't see how fainting is reprehensible. If the T.A. had decent facilities for women—"

He laughed, "Next you'll want powder rooms."

My hearing with the Chief Trainmaster was set for ten days after the incident. The "Chief" read me the desk trainmaster's report. It accused me of changing my explanation from illness at Flatbush to nausea at Times Square, of laughing while on the phone with him, and of refusing medical attention.

I gave my side of the story, and repeated my complaint about the facilities at 137th Street.

The "Chief" told me I would have to get accustomed to using the crew room facilities. I was not given any discipline, it was merely noted on my record that I had been "verbally reinstructed," and I was docked for the time of the hearing.

A few times I was injured on the job. Once, it was only my glasses that were injured. Because I couldn't see without them, and T.A. had neglected to provide me with the prescription safety glasses I had requested, I got a few days off on compensation.

Another time, there was an explosion in my cab, and I got a few days on "light duty" until I could hear normally again. My "light duty" was to stand on a platform during a G.O. on the Flushing line, giving directions to riders diverted from their normal routes. Presumably, when they asked me questions, I could answer helpfully, "What? Speak louder! I can't hear you! I have temporary hearing loss because my cab exploded!"

But my real difficulty with compensation occurred when I fell down the steps to the crew room at lunchtime. It was during my first year as a conductor, and I was working on "the Beast," the No. 2 line, on the P.M.s. Sunday evening, during my first trip, I was going down to the crew room when I lost my footing and started tumbling down the stairs.

It felt like a bad dream. I kept expecting to stop, but I just kept rolling. I was afraid of hitting my head, but I never really whacked it, just rolled it against the steps. After what felt like a very long time, I stopped. I sat up. People around me were asking whether I was alright. I thought I was, except that my knees were scraped and raw.

My motorman, seeing a chance to get a trip dropped if I were too badly injured to work, exclaimed, "We've got to report this!" Grabbing my forearm in a powerful motorman's grip, he led me back up the stairs and all the way to the opposite end of the platform, to the dispatcher's office.

I was put on light duty for about another week. The conductor in the compensation office told me, "Don't have any more accidents until after your probation" —as if a person could choose whether or not to have an accident— "otherwise the Safety Department will start investigating you."

The Safety Department never investigated me, but instead of getting my compensation check, I got a notice from the T.A. that they were controverting my claim. I called the union. They told me to go to the T.A. Compensation Office.

I ended up going to a private lawyer. He took the case on contingency: if I won, the comp judge would order the T.A. to pay his fee. If I lost, no fee would be involved. But he assured me that I was definitely covered at the time of my accident.

"Then why is the T.A. disputing it?" I wondered aloud.

"Because they're idiots," answered my lawyer.

I had to wait a long time for my hearing, because the T.A. asked for, and received, several postponements. At last it was scheduled for a date almost six months after my accident had taken place.

When I received the notice, I panicked: I was supposed to be working at that hour. How was I going to get off work? First, I had to fight with the Crew Dispatcher's Office to get them to relieve me after my first trip. Then, on the day of the hearing, I had to fight to persuade the dispatcher to let me leave, even though it was noted on the crew sheet that I was to be relieved.

At the hearing, my attorney asked me a number of questions. Then the T.A. attorney asked me only one, whether the stairs on which I'd fallen were inside or outside the turnstiles.

"Inside," I answered, because indeed they were.

"I rest," said the T.A. attorney.

My attorney also rested.

"Case established," said the hearing officer. I had won.

On the ride uptown, I caught Conductor Neely's train. We shared a rueful laugh over how the T.A., without a legal leg to stand on, had put me through so much.

"I had my own troubles with comp," he told me. "My train was standing at two-three-one [231st Street], making a station stop. There was a garbage train behind us. The motorman saw our train, but in the dark, he thought we were a lay-up in the middle track. So he keyed by the automatic and saw the green signal that was in front of our train. He thought that signal was for him, wrapped it around, and wham! I went to the hospital. Two riders went to the hospital. And the garbage train motorman—"

I laughed, "I bet they fired his ass!"

"He's a yardmaster now."

My next check was short. By now, I realized why. Of course, T.A. hadn't paid me for the time I took off to attend the hearing. Then, I was furious. They forced me to take time off from work, just to get back what they owed me.

When I politely explained and asked for my pay, the woman in charge was nasty to me. So I ranted and raved at her. "Don't get so excited," she said, and she got on the phone and ordered timekeeping to pay me.

But my biggest problem, and the largest contributing factor to my leaving T.A., was that I was regularly assaulted while "observing the platform." These assaults were so regular—they took place on an average of twice a week on the No. 4 line and once every two weeks on the No. 1 line—that each station stop became a stressful event. No wonder I developed spasms in my jaw and neck.

WHY I LEFT   219

My worst experience connected with an assault happened when I tried to apply the traditional conductor remedy: stop the train and chase the assailant.

It had started out as a typical day. A kid tried to hit me on the first trip down. A rider complained the car was too hot, so I reset some switches, just to placate him. "There," he said sarcastically, "was that so hard?"

At 176th Street, a woman ran up the stairs just as the doors were closing, and got into the front section. My indication in the front section didn't come in, but I couldn't see anything blocking the doors, so I didn't reopen. Then I saw a man carrying a stroller with a baby inside coming up the stairs. I reopened the front section. The woman, who had just gotten on as the doors were closing, stuck her head out the doors. "What's wrong with you?" she shouted at me.

At Mott, the woman and the man with the stroller got off the train and came over to my position. "What's wrong with you?" she repeated to me. "Couldn't you see we were together? Couldn't you see the baby?"

The train started to move. She pulled her arm all the way back and as I tried to move out of the way, threw a bottle straight into my face. It bounced off the left side of my face and broke on the platform.

I completely lost my self-control. I pulled the cord to stop the train, reopened the rear section, and jumped off the train and ran after them. The woman had disappeared, but the man, burdened by the stroller, was easy to catch up with. I was screaming for the police. "You're scaring my baby!" the man yelled. "Shut up and leave us alone! Stop bothering me!"

I followed him down to the No. 2 train platform. As I ran, I wiped my hand over my head and face and examined my hand for blood. I didn't see any, but I was nearly hysterical anyhow.

The No. 2 train pulled in. The man with the stroller dashed into the rear car. I couldn't follow him onto the train, so I stood in the doorway, waving to the conductor and still shouting for the police. The vaulted station had superb acoustics, so my cry echoed everyplace.

A big man got out of his seat and came over to me, "You're making me late to work!" And he pushed me out of the doorway and onto the platform with so much force that I almost fell down. The doors shut. I went running up the platform toward the conductor. He saw me, realized something wasn't right, and reopened. It was the conductor who had recently had the Goetz shootings on his train, so he was understandably edgy. In a couple of sentences, I told him what had happened. He grabbed his shoe slipper and ran to the end of his train with me.

When we got to the last car, both men were gone. A woman pointed up the steps, "He went that way!"

I went, but saw no one, except a cop. I explained to him what was up, and gave a description of my assailants. Then I went back to my train. There was a motor instructor at my position. "You know, of course, that I have to take you out of service," he told me.

I was too wiped out to have much of an immediate reaction. Going to my cab to get my belongings, I saw my R-62 key was gone. A rider had stolen it. My motorman, Angelo Gonzalez, appeared. The motor instructor ordered him to go back up front. "I'm just doing my job!" my motorman snapped, but he left.

Suddenly the conductor from the No. 2 train appeared, "The police have the guy. They need her to come identify him."

My train was being discharged. Someone said, "No wonder the train broke. It's a lady driver."

The transit officer was on the mezzanine, snapping and unsnapping a pair of handcuffs. He had the man with the stroller. "I didn't do nothin'!" said the man with the stroller, "*she* threw the bottle."

"Actually, I didn't see which of you did it," I lied, hoping he'd finger her. And he did. He gave her name and address.

Then the motor instructor took me down to Jay Street to see the Chief Trainmaster. I waited half an hour in the hot hallway. I was hungry, tired, and feeling extremely sorry for myself.

In the hearing, I admitted immediately that I had left my train.

"Did you make threatening gestures to the rider?"

"Did you pursue him?"

They were looking for something to pin on me.

"All I did was call for the police."

"You did not secure your train."

"Yes, I did. I pulled the cord."

The Chief looked at me, "I'm inclined to give you a reprimand. But in view of your clean record, I'm merely giving you a caution."

I wasn't mollified, "Excuse me, but what rule have I violated?"

So they went through the rulebook and found one forbidding a conductor from leaving the train except in cases of emergency.

I said that it was an emergency. "Well, if you wish, you may appeal it," said the Chief Trainmaster. And that was that.

I wanted to appeal, but the union reps were determined to talk me out of it. "The way you acted," one said, "you're lucky if they don't send you for a psychiatric examination."

The other rep, "Take Your Days in the Street" Washington, showed how he got his nickname by telling me, "I'm dealing with a case right now of an employee who was given a ten-day suspension, appealed it and was demoted, appealed it again and was dismissed."

I asked how much time I had to decide whether to appeal. "Three days. But if you don't accept the discipline now, you have to have another hearing, even if you decide not to appeal it. And the trainmaster will probably increase your discipline."

I signed the caution. My crime was recorded as "causing inconvenience to the riders."

I went home, crying the whole time. I called Dave Stone. He was sympathetic. He didn't fault me for failing to "take a stand." "You take a stand when there's a chance of winning. What's so amazing is that every time you go down to Jay Street, everything is up for grabs. There's no set standard for what infraction rates what discipline."

"I held up service. That's what I was punished for. A rule would only have been a pretext."

He was disgusted with the union reps. "They're doing management's work for them."

Back at work, everyone had heard something about what happened to me, piecing together my motorman's story and snippets of radio transmissions. As I sat at the crew room table and told my tale, it was immediately passed on to the cardplayers at the next table and out to the switchmen and board men lounging on the veranda.

One of the cardplayers looked over to me, "Were they both adults?"

"Yes," I answered.

"You're in the wrong line of work! You should have been a cop!"

The T.A. was wholeheartedly vilified for persecuting me on top of my assault. The crew room perception was that it had been an actual emergency.

A few old-timers asked me, "Did you pull the cord?" When I affirmed that I had, they were speechless. They'd expected me to say no, so they could nod wisely and advise, "Well that's what you did wrong." The transit-worker wisdom was that once you pulled the cord, you were free to leave your train. Since I had, they could find nothing reprehensible about my behavior. The charge of "inconveniencing the riders" was repeated in sneering and disgusted tones.

Nothing ever happened to the rider who threw the bottle at me. Months later, she menaced me on my train, and spit on me at Boro Hall. I reported the last incident to transit police, saying I had the name and address of my assailant, and I could identify her. They told me they couldn't do anything unless I got an order of protection and then she violated it.

So on my R.D.O.s, I went downtown to get an order of protection.

I went to the address the transit police had given me and started asking around. I was told to put my name down and take a seat in the hallway. "Is this where I get an order of protection?" I asked a court officer.

"This is where you begin the process."

After waiting an hour, I was interviewed. "Why didn't they simply arrest her?" I was asked.

"They said they couldn't. They said if I got an order of protection, then, if she bothered me again, I could have her arrested."

"They just passed the buck," he told me. "We can't give you an order of protection unless it's either domestic violence or you've been in the hospital. What we can give you is a summons, and you can serve it on her to appear in court. You can go to the precinct she lives in and have the police escort you to her home."

A tantalizing prospect.

Because the last shot (of saliva) she'd taken at me was in Brooklyn, they said I'd have to go to court in Brooklyn. I waited for the summons. They were having trouble with the computer. After two hours of waiting, I left without the summons. I gave up.

After that, I decided to be very careful about observing the platform after my train started to move. If I saw anything I didn't like, I'd best take my head in and pull up the window. But I knew that if I did that, it was only a matter of time before I would be disciplined and even lose my job. I had to get out of T.A.

One Friday, when I got back to the terminal, the dispatcher said, "I'm afraid I have bad news for you. The superintendent wants you to write a G-2 about not observing the platform at Grand Central."

I had the old cornered feeling. At Grand Central, I was sure I would have been trying my best to observe the platform properly, because this was a favored hangout of the road supervision. I remembered seeing someone threaten me with an umbrella on my way uptown, and my zipping up the window in response, but I didn't think it had happened at Grand Central.

I was sure this was a harassment campaign because it happened while I was running for convention delegate. Now I would lose my job, lose my home, end up on the street, et cetera, et cetera. I went home in tears and called Mark. "I've been being so careful! I haven't been hit in six months!"

"Well, you will be now!" cackled my sympathetic friend. "Better get yourself some handy wipes. You're going to be monitored, probably three times in the next couple of months."

By Monday, I had resigned myself to buying handy wipes and observing every platform for three car-lengths. On my first trip down, a rider got up to the platform just after the doors closed. As the train began to move, he lunged at me. All my good resolutions about observing the platform deserted me. I threw the window up. A second later, wham! his briefcase hit my window—it could have been my face. I was shaking.

There was no solution to my dilemma.

I received a notice that, without a hearing, I was being given a two-day suspension for the Grand Central incident. I decided to appeal. I was very nervous the week before the hearing. My coworkers were, as always, very supportive. One advised me, "Don't take the job so seriously. They aren't going to fire you."

The car cleaner sympathized, "They are getting to be a little like slave drivers around here. Like with us, when we get our fifteen-minute break, we can't sit down. They say, 'Lean against the wall.' We're not robots!" She agreed with my decision to appeal, "What they want you to do is not appeal anything."

The hearing was in a room that could have been a movie set for a Gestapo interrogation room. Grey concrete, cold lighting, utilitarian furniture. The union rep arrived. He read his copy of the disciplinary notice: "On May 20,

1985, you were observed by supervision at Grand Central Station. You (1) failed to observe the platform 3 car lenghts (*sic*) (2) sitting down in the cab."

I explained to the hearing officer how many times I'd been hit, and how good my record was.

"But no one actually hit you this time."

"No, but he did hit the window. I think it was with an umbrella."

The hearing officer considered. "You know you are supposed to observe the platform. It's an important part of the job."

"I know. And I do, unless I see someone about to hit me."

He said, "I find the charges not sustained." He smiled. "The superintendent will be angry!"

After this, I seriously examined my options. Ever since I came on the job, supervisors and even coworkers had been encouraging me to go down to Jay Street and apply for one of the clerical positions they filled with conductors.

I spoke to Dave and told him all my woes, though not my decisions about the future. He dismissed it all as "light stuff," which actually relieved me. But then he said, "If I didn't talk to you now and then, I'd never know what it's like to be a New York City transit worker."

"What do you mean by that?" I asked, "You may have meant it to be humorous, but it sounds pretty snotty to me."

"I mean it sounds like a different job."

It was the same job. But Dave could do it, and I couldn't. Now I'm a high school teacher, and I see people who can't do that job, while I can. Different people have different capacities. I had to find a job I could do. On my R.D.O.'s, I looked for jobs. I found little out there.

While Mark had been a conductor, he had worked down at Jay Street, so he had connections down there. He spoke to a few people, and within a week I got a call to come down for a typing test and interview.

I found the guy who interviewed me at Jay Street very patronizing, "I know you're nervous, although you're trying to hide it by reading that book."

I was nervous. But the purpose of the book was to divert me, not mislead him.

He gave me a lecture on the theme, "You can't get sick when you work here," and I shouldn't expect it to be easy.

Then he took me into the work area. A group of white guys in ties made comments. "Eat your hearts out," said my interviewer, "she's A Division."

Then he led me to an antique typewriter. Needless to say, it was completely nonelectrified. "You can practice," he said.

In practicing, I discovered (1) the wreck had no right margin; (2) just because I hit the key didn't mean the letter would print.

When my interviewer returned, I told him about these flaws. He tried to set the right margin. When he was done, it not only didn't have a right margin, it didn't have a left one either.

"Just ignore that," he instructed me. He gave me a sample to copy, "You have five minutes."

"What should I do when I finish?"

"Oh, five minutes will be up long before you finish."

To reach the paper, I had to hit the space bar four or five times at the beginning of each line. This cut my speed and my concentration. But I was still able to finish the sample and start it over again in the five minutes.

My interviewer took it, "From a quick look, it looks like forty-two words a minute, and that's before I count the errors."

It didn't make sense. I'd typed the entire sample once, plus the first two lines a second time. He hadn't expected me to finish it even once, and now he was saying my time was too slow! Obviously, he had no idea what he was doing. He thanked me for coming down and said he'd call me. But by that time, I had decided this was worse, not better, than the road. I was relieved when I never heard from him.

Weighing my options, I decided to pick over to Van Cortlandt, where I hadn't worked for two years, because assaults were less frequent there. During the last week of the old pick, I was spit at on the No. 4 line and had another assault on the No. 6.

But I couldn't help feeling sad as I left Woodlawn. Jasmin and I reminisced about the "Old Woodlawn," with the bachelor quarters in the flagging shack, and Gus, the flagging conductor who had the food concession, in his undershirt in the crew room, boiling a big pot of hot dogs on the hot plate.

On my final trip, I felt sad. I looked out over the hilly vistas of the west Bronx. What I remembered best was Mark. The first day we had worked together, how messed up the road had been back then! He had been such a colorful character, the Motorman Par Excellence, full of quirks. And I had tried so hard to be his idea of a good conductor, to please him. I remembered the times he'd helped me or diverted me with stories and pranks. I remembered the rainy Saturday when he caught sight of a violet umbrella lying in the west pocket. He hopped down to get it, and, there in the rain, in the pocket, he opened the umbrella and started to dance.

I had dinner with Mel Stockman, who had been my pollwatcher in my disastrous run for convention delegate. He said to me, "I don't think Dave is all that perceptive. I don't think he realizes how burnt out you feel."

I said, "Let me guess. You told Dave, 'Marian is very burnt out,' and he said, "Marian is always very burnt out.'"

"Yes," said Mel, a little surprised, "That's basically how it went."

"Well, at least I'm perceptive," I said.

We had held a *Hell on Wheels* meeting for Rapid Transit people one evening. Of all our contacts, only one showed up. We'd waited almost an hour and then gave up. "It just goes to show again," Dave said, "in New York, never schedule anything for August."

I wished I could believe that was the only drawback. The overwhelming defeat of the contract in Rapid Transit had shown that there was great dissatisfaction in that department of the union, but we still couldn't draw any members to a meeting.

The atmosphere at our conductors' division union meetings, however, had definitely changed. At one, a conductor made a motion that the union provide twenty-four-hour stewards in all terminals and abide by a 1980 divisional resolution that all shop stewards be elected. After discussion, the motion passed unanimously.

Members were now standing up and speaking their minds. The officers and the organizers were silent. We were spared their long-winded anecdotes. We had the feeling that at last it was our meeting. We talked and talked. We felt good. We felt listened to. I felt good, too, but my mind was skeptical. The motion would not be implemented.

During one of my many visits to the union hall about the train operator pick, Lawson, who was now recording secretary for the local, told me that the union was trying to get the names of train operators who had been through the chemical car wash, so they could follow up and discover if any of them had experienced health problems. If these people ever needed workers compensation, restricted duty, or a disability retirement, they would have a basis for arguing that any such problems were job related.

I typed up an explanation of this proposal. My original intention was to post it on one of the clipboards for bulletins in the train dispatcher's office, but I decided to take it around to people myself.

During my lunch, I approached several A.M. train operators, but none had been through the chemical wash.

"Never have and never will."

"I wouldn't go through the wash for anything."

But George Hoffman said he'd been through and wrote his name. Then I approached the board man. He and I had rarely had anything to say to each other. He did say he had been through the wash. I explained what I was doing and handed him the paper with the typed explanation. He read it and handed it back, looking at me as if I were trying to con him, "And get stuck in the booth?" he said, "uh-uh."

I tried to explain to him that this was, in fact, his best protection in case of such an eventuality. He was unconvinced. "It won't go anywhere," he said, "you can't beat 'em."

Hoffman, who had been listening to all this, took the paper back from me. "Maybe I'd better take my name off," and he carefully scratched over his name until nothing was left except a big, solid smudge.

I was shocked, "Mr. Hoffman! I thought you had more sense than that. He doesn't even know why he's afraid! And now he's scared you, too."

A conductor who was watching, said, "They're not afraid. They just don't care."

When I told the story to Jasmin Joyce, she commented, "That's why the union's in the shape it's in."

The trouble wasn't only with the bureaucrats. The workers themselves were not yet ready to do anything.

Working at Van Cortlandt again meant I was closer to home. I could walk to work in less than forty-five minutes, ride home in less than half an hour. Although there were about 50 percent more stops in a day at Van Cortlandt than in a day at Woodlawn, the attempted assault rate was much lower.

Still, working with the old equipment had drawbacks. It produced a different kind of fatigue from working the No. 4. The new equipment on the 4 line left me lethargic after work. After a day on the No. 1's old trains, I felt as if I had been grabbed by the ankle and whacked against a brick wall: bruised and strained all over.

I had to go back to stepping out of the cab between stops again. I had forgotten how much I hated being "looked over" by some of the men on the train. It made me feel as if sewage were being poured over me.

The state of the equipment was another hazard. Broken windows in many cabs that either didn't close or took both hands to close; p.a.s that made awful, piercing noises; the cabs with "backward doors"—doors that only opened out from the cabs; you had to close them during a station stop so they wouldn't swing into some rider. There was no door handle inside the cab, however, only a little vestigial bit of metal, which was hard to get enough grip on to move the catch. Sometimes I got stuck inside the cab. Other times, I lost my grip just as the door opened, and the movement of the train smacked the door into a rider.

But the worst part, I found, was the "running time," the amount of time in the schedule for the trip. It was cut much closer than on the No. 4 line. So you were always rushing, always worrying.

It had been almost two years since my doctoral thesis had been accepted and I received my degree from Columbia. I had applied for college teaching positions all over the country, and had even had a couple of interviews for temporary vacancies. Then, in March 1986, I was invited to interview for a tenure-track position at Buffalo State College.

Dave Stone happened to be on my train a few days before my trip up there. He asked me whether I would be going to the Friday rally for the meatpackers of Local P-9, who were on strike.

"I don't think so," I said glumly, "I have to go out of town."

"Oh," he said, with his usual emphatic brusqueness, "where are you going?"

"Buffalo," and feeling that wasn't exactly self-explanatory, I continued, "I have a job interview there."

"Oh," he said. He didn't look very happy. "Buffalo in March. Should be lovely."

The interview went well and it looked as if I had a good shot at the job. I was torn by the possibility of leaving New York, and of leaving transit. I kept telling myself, "It's an offer I can't refuse." Yet I was crying all the way back to the city.

I really love the people I work with, I thought. We go through so much together and we understand one another: the way I shake my head and the conductor across the platform whose name I don't even know shakes his head and nods, and then I nod back, and no words are needed.

I remembered the high hopes I'd had only a few years earlier when I had become a conductor. How strongly I felt about it, how excited I was. I loved my uniform. I was going to *be* a transit worker, to be in the union, go to the meetings.

And now, what lay ahead? What goals could I set? Publish or perish?

I felt I had been lucky to have met Dave and was lucky to be working with him. I didn't want to give that up.

Dave asked me how the interview had gone.

"Unfortunately, very well. A couple of people told me, off the record, that if I want it, I have it. And it's an offer I can't refuse. How can I rationalize turning it down?"

He said, "I don't mean this as a guilt trip, but the only reason to do it would be politics."

"Yes, politics. And that's the reason I came down here in the first place. But I really can't take this job anymore. It would be easy to blame it on whoever wasn't supportive, but I'm just miserable down here."

"Well," said Dave, "there's nothing we're doing down here that's worth someone sacrificing their health, physical or mental. It's a rough job. A lot of people on this job spend half their time devising ways to make some extra income. Part of it is for spending, but part of it is for saving some money to get out of the T.A. Or else people try to go to supervision. In our cohort, or the one after us, everyone is trying to get out or go to supervision. No one is planning to stay the thirty years."

I said, "I'm not going to say I'm leaving because I've realized nothing could be accomplished in this period or because I was wasting my time, because it's not true. I think this is worthwhile and, in the long run, it's likely to bear fruit. Ron told me that on New Year's Eve, Ivan got drunk and said, 'We're doing important work.' And I think he's right, it is important work. I just can't stand the *job* anymore."

The next time I visited Mark, he held out his hand, so that it was obvious there was something in it, but I couldn't see what, "Here," he said, "here's something for you."

It was a ring, gold, with a wide band of blue running around the center.

He admonished me not to wear it on my wedding finger and not to "brag about it" to Jasmin Joyce. He said he was giving it to me because "you've been through so much lately.'

A few days later, I got a "firm offer" from Buffalo State. I accepted.

I told Joyce, "I feel good I'm getting out of the job, but I feel bad about the people I'm leaving behind. I feel like a slave in the South planning to escape, but I have to leave behind all my family and friends and never see them again."

Joyce looked at me as if I were a bit off. "A lot of the people here think this job is Paradise," she said.

THE MORE THINGS
CHANGE . . .

D uring the four years I worked as a conductor, many things appeared to change on the subways. New trains were brought in, with air conditioning and reliable public address systems. The motorman and conductor could communicate privately by intercom on the newer trains. Things look better, from the crew rooms, to the trains clean of graffiti, to the motormen in their spiffy uniforms.

Our union leadership also changed. In place of fat old John Lawe, we had skinny, middle-aged Sonny Hall. For years, I had heard from many workers, including old oppositionalists and even some of the folks around *Hell on Wheels*, that Sonny was different. He was militant. He was just biding his time until Lawe passed the torch to him and then, well, the union would really change.

But my experiences in the last few months at T.A. left me convinced that, for employees, there had been no essential changes, not in our job and not in our union.

O ne day, one of the officers from the motorman's division visited Van Cortlandt terminal. I said to him, "We need more room than just a bulletin board for union business. And on the little space we have, look what the union reps put up! Management bulletins!"

"It's the union's job to inform the membership," he said.

"If it's *our* job, how come the union doesn't give members copies of the contract?" Union officers always answered our complaints that we had no copies of the contract by telling us that it was management's responsibility to supply them. "I've never heard of any other union where the membership doesn't have a copy of the contract."

"What other union do you know about? The bottle-suckers union?"

A senior motorman went up to the rep and said, "I've never heard of a union where you don't see a copy of the contract before you vote on it!"

Then a young, new conductor went to him, "It's been a year since the contract started, and we still haven't seen it. That's too long."

When Sonny Hall became president of Local 100, he came to our conductor's division meeting. He spoke about grievances, "Grievances have to be processed promptly," and picking, "We never pick anymore under protest. We will grieve a pick until it goes to the arbitrator.

"We have to stop fighting," he said, "It doesn't matter whose fault it is. It has to stop."

A white guy from my training class got the biggest hand of the evening when he said, "I think we have to consider job actions."

Sonny Hall replied, "What we used to do when management got obnoxious, there would be a reaction. What we've got to do is get our act together. I thought we could do it in months, a job action, but now I see we are too divided."

Another conductor said, "We should slow down as a solution" to the suspensions for P.A. announcements.

But Sonny said there would be no slowdowns. "We could not do anything that might alienate the public."

I spoke about getting out information. "The supervision came into our crew room and tore our union notices off the lockers. We do have union bulletin boards, but some of the union officers use them to post management bulletins. They stamp their name on management bulletins and post them on the union bulletin board. Too many of the members already feel that the union is too close to management, and this doesn't help the situation."

This made Sonny angry, "No union brother is *ever* to post a management bulletin."

The very next day was the inauguration of the long-awaited Rapid Transit union shop steward classes.

They showed us a movie, *Inheritance*, about the history of the Amalgamated Clothing Workers Union. Its leitmotif was that union members were "immigrants and the children of immigrants." Looking around the room, I saw maybe one in five people who fit that description. An unfortunate choice of introduction, but one that revealed the organizers' lack of intelligent planning.

The officers spoke. One opined that for a union rep, dealing with management was, first and foremost, a question of psychology.

The guest speaker at the second steward class the following week was George MacDonald. MacDonald had run against President John Lawe in 1979, along with Cherry and Lewis. After the election, he had become a union staffer, in charge of health and safety. This was the first time, in almost four years active in the union, that I had ever seen him.

For an hour he talked about right-to-know laws, which involve industrial products and have very limited relevance for subway operatives. Then he opened up the floor to questions and people began to ask about the things that were relevant to them. A few people in sequence asked about noise. MacDonald insisted that the noise to which we were exposed did not violate federal standards. Dave Stone pointed out that, according to federal law, we should all be tested for hearing loss annually.

MacDonald answered that ten thousand members of our local had been given hearing tests in the past year.

Everyone was incredulous. "Who?" "New people?" "Bus operators?"

"I assume most of them were subway workers," said MacDonald.

"No one I know." "Not me." "Not us." People were shaking their heads. It was clear that MacDonald had no idea what was going on and took on trust whatever T.A. told him.

When I got the floor, I explained that the reason we couldn't win workers comp cases for our cardiovascular problems was the lack of research linking these problems with our working conditions. He interrupted me in the middle to ask for the "next question." Very indignantly, I pointed out I wasn't finished. "What is the union doing to encourage research on hypertension?" I concluded.

MacDonald replied, "We got one hundred thirteen thousand dollars for training," but of research, he said nothing.

The next time I saw Vinnie "Turn Around" Torrelli, he was in a swell mood. "Marian, Will Washington is our new Veep! We're gonna see a lot of changes now, Marian. The old guy, Lang, used to really sit on us. I was always getting called on the carpet. You wanna be a steward? You shouldn't have a problem. I was always sticking up for you. I wish you'd stick up for me once inna while."

A few days later, Washington presided over the A Division schedule meeting. It was a litany of job cuts.

But after a few questions, someone made a motion to adjourn. In response, someone called out, "Vote!"

The chair said, "We don't have to vote on that," and the crowd surged toward the exits.

A woman in front of me protested, "We don't even vote on the pick? What did we come here for, anyway?"

When I described this to Dave Stone, he said, "I guess that's what Sonny means when he says we don't pick under protest any more. We just don't protest."

Afterward, Vinnie got hold of me, singing the praises of the new, militant Washington. I was more skeptical, "It's true there's a new direction around here, but it's coming from the top. Some people—like you, Vinnie—have wanted it all along. Others are going with the flow, for the sake of their careers."

"Marian, you know what I need now? Three things. An organizer's job, a son, and a gorgeous blonde."

"Vinnie, eventually you'll be an organizer. Fifty-fifty you'll get a son. And tell your wife to dye her hair."

(In retrospect, I should have kept quiet. Vinnie was never "made," and his first child was a girl.)

I had thought that the prospect of leaving the job soon would make it more bearable. The opposite was the case. Once I wasn't planning to rely on it for my long-term livelihood, the job became almost intolerable.

One day, at lunch, my motorman came in and sat down beside me. "We have to take a train to the wash," he said.

I went cold with horror, "You're kidding!"

It all ran through my mind. Washington, in front of the pick meeting, explaining to us how the union had held up the pick to get "c.w." noted in front of all the jobs that went to the car wash, to establish that the wash was *not* part of w.a.a.

"But they can't," I protested, "We're not a wash crew!" I headed for the train dispatcher's office.

"Oh, hello, Miss Swerdlow. Did your train operator tell you—" began the train dispatcher.

"You *can't* send us to the wash! It's not fair! If this job went to the wash, I wouldn't have picked this job! I don't want to be going home at twelve at night!"

The dispatcher said I would go to the wash, or go to the Chief. I called the union. It was a quarter to five and no one was answering the phone.

I went to the wash, all the way down to South Ferry, where they routed us onto the loop at into Bowling Green. From there we went up the East Side, all the way to the Bronx. This was about a two-hour trip. The train wash itself took less than half an hour, and then we took the same route home. I cleared three hours and forty-eight minutes late.

The next day, I booked sick and went down to the union. I found the new, militant Washington. When I explained the situation, he hit the ceiling, "Write it up! I'll take it right to Davis—" the line superintendent for the No. 1.

I wrote the G-2 right there on the spot. Washington took it with him. Another rep opened up the rulebook and showed me the section on "Working Conditions for Road Conductors." It included "laying-up trains and bringing trains to the terminal."

"The wash is neither of those," he said, "it's not a put-in and it's not a lay-up."

The T.A. had made a mammoth blunder that had, in large measure, produced my predicament. For a number of years, they had been building a lead—a track leading from the elevated structure of the No. 1 line—down into the 207th Street yard, where there was a wash. This lead was about seven minutes running time from the Van Cortlandt terminal. But it was still unconnected to the tracks on the structure. About ten feet of track remained to be laid. There were many hot rumors explaining its unfinished state. The most credible was that it was too steep and would have to be completely rebuilt.

I posted a copy of my grievance by the watercooler over the weekend.

The conductor who worked my 225 job on my R.D.O.s, said to me, "I saw your grievance. They sent me to the wash, on Friday." At first, he didn't want to grieve it, but when I told him they were planning to send every crew two or three times a month, he changed his mind.

Another conductor was also being sent, but he didn't want to grieve. "I could use the money. As long as they don't send me on Fridays."

I heard they were sending the drumswitchman, because he had too much trouble walking to get around on the platform.

I called Washington Monday morning and asked him if he had any news. He said he was going to call the superintendent immediately, "I'm going to step on them." I called Washington back a couple of hours later and he told me he'd just spoken with the superintendent, "I don't think you'll have any more hassles."

I went to work with a sense of cautious optimism. But at the end of our last trip, I heard, "Arriving crew, see the dispatcher."

The dispatcher said, "You're taking the next train to the two-thirty-ninth Street yard to the wash. Everyone's got to go. If you don't go today, you'll go tomorrow. But everyone's got to go."

My motorman and I both said that tomorrow would be better.

"Okay," said the dispatcher, "You'll go tomorrow. Even if you book sick, two twenty-five crew will go tomorrow."

The next morning I booked sick.

Most other workers agreed with me that it was wrong to send someone who had finished three trips on a five-hour trip to the wash. However, there was another sentiment was also heard, "It's easy money for a conductor." "They pay you, don't they?"

I answered, "Suppose someone threw a brick at you and knocked you out, but left five dollars pinned to your shirt."

My next day back at work, the weather was as hot as hell, and for our last trip we got what one motorman called "the Microwave," an old train. I went into the crew room and prepared to go to the wash. In the bathroom, I took off the tee shirt I wore under my uniform. I soaked it in water and put it back on. That cooled me off.

My motorman came into the crew room. "Did he say anything?" I asked him.

"No," he replied, "But—I couldn't tell you this because we didn't have an intercom—but I heard on the radio, all Broadway washes are going to Westchester yard."

We looked at each other and swallowed hard. This was an even longer trip than the 239th Street yard we'd gone to before. We sat and waited as the minutes ticked by. I felt like the defendant awaiting the verdict.

At last, the train dispatcher called for "three-oh-one crew." My motorman and I understood and breathed sighs of relief. We were reprieved, or at least granted a stay of execution.

I went home feeling slightly crazed. Going to Westchester yard and back was usually a five-hour trip. They also expected the crew to exit the wash by an elevated lead to the yard and go over this rickety set of boards—you couldn't call it a bridge—to the tower. I dreaded doing that in the dark.

I had 225 job eight more times before the pick ended. I had decided that if I were ordered to go to the wash, I would quit on the spot. The next night, after our last trip, I sweated out the minutes. I didn't want to quit. I still needed the pay. I watched the clock, barely daring to breath, until 7:45 P.M. I was safe.

My motorman told me that the dispatcher had told another conductor that he would never tell me beforehand when I was going to the wash, because of the way I carried on. I laughed, "Wait until the next time he sends me and I quit. Then he'll really be freaked out."

But my motorman looked unhappy. "After you quit, they'll send me every night. The only reason they don't send us more often is because you raise such a stink when they do."

The following Wednesday, they did send us to the wash at 239th Street. At least it was a shorter trip than the one to Westchester yard. We were not sent again, but Broadway washes continued to go to Westchester yard. The final week of the pick, I got a cryptic letter from Washington dated July 21. It referred to my "grievance of June 30th," and read in part, "I have spoken to supervision in the area and they have informed me the practice you mention will be discontinued."

But when?

It was too late to mean anything to me. But my motorman had picked the job again, before they had started sending us to the wash. I posted my grievance and a copy of Washington's letter in the crew room. I would be gone, but maybe this information would encourage crews who were sent to Westchester yard to contact the union.

In the middle of June, the T.A. unilaterally canceled the Fourth of July pick. Ordinarily, the subways run on a Saturday or a Sunday schedule on holidays no matter which day of the week they fall on. So, at the same time that workers pick their jobs, they also pick which jobs they will work on each holiday during that pick. If a holiday falls on their R.D.O.s, they get it off. If they have sufficient seniority, they can pick the day off. Everyone else works the job they pick for that holiday.

So when the T.A. ordered everyone to work the Fourth of July as an ordinary Friday, the old-timers, who had picked to be off that day, were all mad as wet hens. They were all over the place denouncing the arrogance of the T.A and the impotence of the union. The union was taking it to arbitration. But everyone knew that wouldn't work. T.A. would say "emergency" and "needs of the service." The *Hell on Wheels* position was that "the union must win back our rights over scheduling."

A week before the holiday, another bulletin came out, rescinding the cancellation of the pick. It stated that if there were not enough volunteers, people would be called to fill jobs in inverse seniority order.

With my four years, I never thought I'd be called. But three days before the holiday, I got a phone call from McAllister, "Marian! The sheets came out for Friday! And it looks like they gave jobs to everybody who has Friday off! They got pages and pages. They got Husband down for a job, and he's got seventeen years in title and *never* works any overtime!" McAllister also said he had called the union and asked, "What can they do to me if I don't report?" The organizer told him he would be AWOL.

I was horrified at the unlimited power T.A. claimed over me. They could make me work past my eight hours, or on my day off, and penalize me if I refused. My time was not my own, it belonged to them, not only when I was on the payroll, but all the time. I took my leisure only by their leave. I felt like a prisoner.

I booked sick "until further notice" the Wednesday before the Fourth of July, and I didn't come back until July 5.

I admired the way many of my coworkers responded to the T.A.'s attempts to force them to work on an R.D.O. or a day they had picked off. Many simply didn't report. "Why should I look at the sheets?" one asked rhetorically, "I never work an R.D.O." Another asked, "What can they do to me for not working an R.D.O.?" Others got doctor's lines.

A week later, T.A. had done nothing.

"Nothing yet," said Dave.

My motorman had gone down to the union and wrangled with the rep, who convinced him that he simply had no choice except to work. I heard that one man went down to the union and cursed them all out. I also heard that the union officers were hanging up on people.

Dave, with his customary lucidity, observed, "Given the union's strategy, there was nothing they could do. Its strategy is to fight it all the way up to arbitration. Well, the arbitrator had ruled that the T.A. could call people if they needed them."

A week after that, there were rumors that the T.A. was closing in on the people who didn't report. But it never came to pass. T.A. had gotten more than enough crews for the day. As Jasmin Joyce told me, there were "crews on top of crews." No intervals had to be dropped for lack of a crew, so there was no need to find a scapegoat to "hang."

I began telling people I was leaving. Everyone wished me good luck. One said, "You're too intelligent for this." But clearly, people did *not* feel that this was the worst possible job. They all assumed I'd make more money. Once they heard I would be taking a pay cut, they couldn't understand why I was leaving. When I explained how short my hours would be, they were more impressed. A few, but not most, said things like, "It's good to be getting out. Things are getting worse here. You can't do this for thirty years."

Jasmin Joyce called me. "I *used* to be a conductor!" she hooted, "I did it. I resigned." She told me whom to see down at Jay Street.

Friday morning I did the same, resigning effective August 2, 1986. When I got home, I called Mark. He was feeling bad. He told me he was getting more withdrawn working midnights. They wouldn't give him his birthday off. With that, he was really upset. "Yesterday, I couldn't decide whether I should go downtown and shoot them, or shoot myself, or both."

I couldn't imagine what would be meaningful to me in life after I had left transit. As we were laying out issue 9 of *Hell on Wheels*, I couldn't believe I was leaving *this*. It was the best thing I'd ever do in my life.

My final day, I'm sitting on the platform, reading *Shirley*, by Charlotte Brontë, and they make me do an "amenities check." I speak over the P.A., while another conductor walks through the cars to make sure the speakers are working. I get the brilliant notion to read the novel over the P.A., instead of just repeating "P.A. check," 'til death from boredom.

The R.C.I., a young guy, perhaps Hispanic, looks at me kind of funny. He makes a call on the MAG. Then he asks me my name.

I feel a pang of anxiety. But it's my last day.

A few minutes later, I hear the train dispatcher calling, "Flag, flag."

She makes light of it, "Someone made a complaint, and it went all the way down to the superintendent. Someone said that someone was reading the Bible, or something communist, on the train."

"I was reading a novel, a nineteenth-century English novel."

"Well, the superintendent said just to remind you that all you're supposed to say is 'testing, one, two, three, four.'"

I didn't tell people it was my last day. I didn't want to face the fact that it was ending.

Weeks later, I was still feeling I would be back. It felt very open-ended, as if each day was only an R.D.O. I felt as if that evening I would be making sandwiches and cleaning my gloves, and the next morning I would wake up and put on the uncomfortable, ill-fitting uniform. I would walk up to the terminal, walk through the parking lot, up the stairs, over the rickety bridge and over the tracks, greet the car cleaners, and go into the shabby office to sign in.

I remembered my first day, when I wondered how I could know for sure which train was supposed to be mine.

After four years, I knew the answer: you couldn't.

AFTERWORD

Fifteen years after I became a subway conductor, women are commonplace in both the conductor and train operator titles. Now probably one in every seven to ten subway operatives is a woman. Most of these are still black women, however, with few white or Hispanic women choosing to take these jobs.

To the eye, it appears that much has changed in the decade since I left the transit system. My friend Jasmin Joyce often laments, "The subways have been yuppified!"

The dilapidated crew rooms and shacks of our day have been spruced up. The primitive, unisex toilets, which gave the job the feel of "roughing it," have been replaced with decent, separate facilities. There is air-conditioning. The crude but sturdy benches on the Woodlawn veranda are gone, for no one has to go outside anymore to catch a breeze.

Recently, I took a nostalgic trip up to Van Cortlandt, where the crew room is raised above the elevated station. Its grimy and dull exterior has been covered with what looks like giant leggo pieces, in white and bright red.

Crews have undergone a corresponding makeover. When I came aboard, motormen wore anything they pleased. The favored getup was a torn fatigue jacket and dirty jeans. A group of motormen could be indistinguishable from a group of homeless men, except, of course, the motormen carry tools and a radio.

By the time I left, motormen had been officially renamed train operators. They were being told they must dress in a uniform of pin-striped overalls, which made them look like farmers up early to milk their herds. Apparently that was not the look T.A. had in mind, because soon the uniform changed again to essentially the one conductors had always worn: light blue shirt and dark blue pants.

By far the biggest change has occurred in the equipment. Gone are the porthole windows from World War II. Gone are the R-27s with their backward doors. Gone are the fuses: everything is switches now. Gone are the door control panels with handles: everything is buttons now. On the newest trains there aren't even any drumswitches: the conductor "drums up" the door control zones by simply putting a key in the door control panel. The side signs are turned with a neat little T.A.-issue sign-changer, so there is no need for the folk art of the homemade sign-turner.

The R-62 series of cars, introduced on the road while I was still working for transit, had cabs that could be converted to "transverse" cabs: cabs that span the whole width of the car. And in the last decade, the conversions have begun. The purpose of the transverse cab is to make the conductor superfluous by allowing the train operator to reach either side of the train to operate the passenger doors. But during this countdown to the demise of their title, conductors enjoy the private little world of the transverse cab, no longer required to step out of the cab between stops and "observe your operating car," as we had been. Conductors no longer need to prop cab doors open with wads of coupons or bands from advertising placards. This is just as well, because the coupons and the bands no longer exist. Subway advertising has been yuppified as well. The placards are larger and glossy, and often a whole car is devoted to one upscale advertiser such as a fashion designer or a telephone company.

The new cars allow much less noise and dirt in. The walls are graffiti-resistant. So the subway operative's job has become cleaner and quieter. When we went down the road, it was an adventure. We never knew what we were operating: a train that wouldn't start, a train that wouldn't stop. Doors that wouldn't open, doors that wouldn't close. Broken windows, broken brake pipes, broken rails. We never knew whether we would have to dump the load, or dump the train. Today's crews have trains that work. They usually come and go on schedule.

"Ah, these guys have it easy!" Jasmin says as she looks at the green-bulb starting lights alongside the amber-bulb holding lights. We used to have only one color, amber, to signal both keeping the doors open to hold the train and closing the doors to shut the train. We used to have to figure out, from where we were, which of these opposite orders the illuminated bulbs represented.

Today's conductors have radios, too, so they don't have to wonder why their train has come in on the local side of the platform instead of the express, or vice versa. They are no longer the last to know when their train heads up an unexpected route or skips an expected stop. We often didn't know what was going on, and we weren't protected in some transverse cab: we were right out there where angry riders could get at us.

Closing our doors on a crowded platform was an ordeal then. The doors on the old equipment did not work well; it was difficult to get them closed and locked even without a thousand riders pushing, pulling, and leaning on them. Today's conductors have the help of platform conductors, complete with safety vests and flashlights, to herd riders in, keep the rest away from the doors, and to swing the flashlights as a signal to the road conductor that the doors are clear and can be safely closed. Of course, all this luxury has its price. First of all, there *were* platform conductors in our day, too. But they weren't on the platform. A platform job was a form of early retirement. A platform conductor found a nice, quiet place to retire to for the day, thoughtfully leaving a little more room for the riders on the crowded platform. And this with the connivance of supervision: no one came looking for you, unless there was a twelve-nine or something unfortunate like that. The other price to be paid is signaled by the appearance of platform conductors with flashlights in preparation for the day when it will be the train operator who will be closing the doors, the road conductor having gone the way of the dodo bird. And that lone train operator will need all the help she or he can get in determining whether the doors in the rear car, two city blocks away, are clear and safe to close.

Even where actual things remain the same, the Transit Authority, obviously having boned up on George Orwell, has changed the names of things. A motor instructor is now a "train service supervisor," and Command Center is now "Train Control Center."

Yuppifying the crews is one thing—the Transit Authority wants to yuppify the riders. Ten years ago they gave conductors "courtesy classes," and now they want the riders to be polite! To this, I say, "Lots of luck." They want the riders on the platform to stand aside and let exiting riders off the train before pushing on. Paradoxically, they have paired this minuet with orders to the conductor to close the doors in forty-five seconds. This will only inspire those outside to crowd on even faster, to beat the forty-five-second deadline, for fear of being left on the platform—and the hell with the guys struggling to exit.

One of the major locations T.A. chose for this quixotic experiment is the Fulton Street platform of the No. 4 line. There T.A. has drawn orange boxes, which riders are supposed to avoid, and black arrows, which indicate where exiting riders should walk. The choice of location is ironic, because in this station, only a couple of years ago, a rider blew up a train. He was transporting a homemade Molotov cocktail and had intended to get off the train there, before the bomb exploded somewhere in the underriver tube, probably deep-frying everyone on the train. His goal was extortion of money from the T.A. by threat of further attacks. Everyone is lucky his timing was off. This guy, of course, was a pervert—certainly not a typical rider. But neither is the typical rider going to daintily skirt the orange box or obediently follow the black arrows. The typical rider is somewhere between the miscreant with the bomb and the Emily Post clone T.A. is fantasizing.

T.A. is also trying to sweet-talk the riders into accepting a new form of payment to replace the subway token: the Metrocard, a credit card–sized plastic item with a magnetic strip. More yuppification: plastic replacing metal. But you can't fool New Yorkers. We avoided it like the plague. We knew, intuitively, it couldn't be good for us. The more T.A. pushed it with cutesy-poo ads and dippy promotions, the more suspicious we became. And rightly so: down the path lies a sliding scale of fares depending on distance. However, as soon as T.A. built a free transfer between buses and trains into the card, riders took the bait.

So things look different. But how different below the appearances are subway workers' lives?

Is the job safer? Just before I began working for Transit, a motorman, Jesse Coles, was killed when signals failed. About two years ago a train operator on the Manhattan Bridge died in a similar accident. A midnight man, he was just coming back from his R.D.O.s. Like me and many other midnight workers, on his R.D.O.s, he spent his days awake and slept at night, so he could be with the rest of humanity—in his case, his wife and children. After spending his last day awake, with only a few hours rest before returning to work, he apparently nodded off there.

Two things should have saved him. When he dozed and relaxed his pressure on the controller, its "dead man" feature should have been activated, releasing his train's emergency brake. This didn't happen. His train went through an automatic signal, which was red because there was a train right ahead. The signal, when red, was supposed to "trip" any train going past it, that is, activate its emergency brakes. And it did, but that didn't save the train operator either.

It didn't stop the train in time. After the fact, after the man was dead, it was discovered that the stretch of track governed by the automatic signal was not long enough to stop a train in time to avoid a collision with a train ahead. Many years earlier, when trains were lighter and slower, that length would have been long enough. But equipment had become faster and heavier, and thus harder to stop. Yet T.A. didn't care enough about the safety of train operators, or riders, for that matter, to assume the expense of relocating the signals so that they protected longer stretches of track.

It is management policies like these that keep the subway jobs dangerous and stressful. Another source of stress is an increase in the harassment of and disciplinary action against employees. People are suspended for such minor infractions as being "out of uniform," although this may mean nothing more than a missing hat or tie, or wearing the wrong color shoes or sweater. A late report, failing to book sick in a timely fashion, not making announcements, and other violations that don't affect safety or service may be grounds for lengthy suspensions. More important offenses, such as hitting a timer signal or being AWOL, which once evoked suspensions, are now grounds for termination.

The main reason for the increase in suspensions, or "days in the street," is that the union leadership agreed to allow employees to "work off" days in the street at 70 percent of full pay. That is close to working *a day without pay* for every three days in the street. Let's say a worker is given three weeks in the street. To avoid losing three weeks' pay, he or she works for three weeks at 70 percent pay, and the T.A. gets almost a week of work for free! It is easy to see why this would lead to an increase in disciplinary suspensions. And it's also easy for workers to see that the union leadership that agreed to this doesn't give a damn about them.

The increase in firings also stems from the Transit Authority's plan to "downsize." The T.A. has been shrinking its workforce for years, mainly by attrition. From 1990 to 1997, the number of hourly employees in the subways, buses, and maintenance shrank by 10 percent, from about 35,000 to about 31,500. Now T.A. would like to exploit the introduction of "one-person train operation" to cut workers even faster. To get around the "no lay-off" provision in the current contract, the T.A. fires people.

Subway workers' discontent with their leaders has increased along with the arbitrary discipline and dangerous conditions. What has changed since my days there is that now subway workers have a viable alternative to the sell-outs who hold the top offices. The little shop rag, *Hell on Wheels*, which was nothing more than a subdued light in the eyes of Dave Stone when I met him fifteen years ago, has burgeoned into a vital rank-and-file caucus, which has the potential of making history in the United States labor movement. (For an account of the growth of the rank-and-file movement by two who led it, I recommend "Hell on Wheels: Organizing among New York City Subway and Bus Workers" by Steve Downs and Tim Schermerhorn in *The Reformation of American Unionism*, edited by Ray M. Tillman and Michael S. Cummings, forthcoming from Lynne Rienner Publishers.

Success has not come easily. *Hell on Wheels* remained static for a couple of years after I left transit. Then, in 1988, its activists organized a "New Directions" slate for localwide offices. The election results surpassed even their most optimistic expectations, with their presidential candidate garnering 3,065 votes, or 22 percent, against Sonny Hall. Successful runs for delegates to the International Union Convention and victories in elections for divisional and workplace offices followed.

In the next localwide elections, at the end of 1991, the "New Directions" candidate for president received 4,954 votes, or 33.5 percent, against Sonny Hall. "New Directions" won all the Executive Board races in the conductor-tower and united motormen subway divisions and the track division, and all the divisional offices in the subway divisions, as well as some in the maintenance division.

This leap in the showing of the rank-and-file candidates sparked a wave of militancy in the union. Shortly after the election, when a new pick was posted in "A" Division, the R.D.O.s had been "built into" the jobs. Crews' long-held right to pick their R.D.O.s by seniority was being taken away. Soon, subway riders were crowding the platforms and waiting thirty minutes for a train during rush hour. Train operators were crawling along, observing speed limits, and making time-consuming checks of every possible defect, real or imaginary. Conductors became paradigms of courtesy, holding car doors open for old people edging up the stairways, despite the pleas of the straphangers already packing their cars. It was a real slowdown, the kind we'd been dreaming about for years at Woodlawn. When our seniority rights had been threatened by train operators being forced to pick miscellaneous back in 1985, all we'd done was go down to the union hall. Our leaders first stonewalled us and then double-crossed us. In 1992, the workers were ready to take matters into their own hands. And they won a real victory. The pick with the days off built in was taken down from the pick boards and the right to pick days off was restored.

So workers were ready to resume the offensive when Sonny Hall, his reelection safely behind him, unveiled a tentative contract at the end of January 1992. A thirty-eight-month contract, with a wage freeze in the first year, and part of its total 7.7 percent increase conditional on gains in productivity, it also introduced a "copayment" for health care costs.

A "Rally and Speak Out" against the proposed contract was called by *Hell on Wheels* and "New Directions" slate activists. Thousands of workers crowded around Jay Street on February 12, despite the bitter cold. As one speaker after another ripped into T.A. and the union leaders, the crowd spontaneously set off toward the Brooklyn Bridge. The marchers surged onto the bridge, forcing off traffic, chanting, "No justice, no peace!" Once in Manhattan, they jumped on the subways and "pulled the cords," stopping the trains and tying up rush hour service.

The contract was voted down by a margin of two to one.

The following month, the Hall leadership came back to the members with what was essentially the same pact. But they had found a new way to push it down the members' throats. They told members that, if the proposal failed, their medical and health benefits would be cut off, a serious hardship for all transit workers, but especially for those with families or medical problems. The contract referendum ballot itself carried a further threat. Instead of simply offering the alternative between accepting or rejecting the contract, it offered accepting the contract or . . . binding arbitration!

This time, the contract passed overwhelmingly.

After the dust settled, the activists around *Hell on Wheels* and the "New Directions" slate decided conditions were ripe for them to form a permanent organization. The "New Directions" Caucus was born in fall 1992.

At the same time, many members had drawn a lesson from their defeat in the contract campaign: voting no, demonstrating, and holding job actions were not enough to get them a decent contract. To achieve that, they would need new union leaders. They had to wait two years, until the end of 1994, to make their next attempt to get them. The result was the closest race yet, as the "New Directions" slate got more than 7,000 votes, almost 45 percent, against Hall's successor, Damaso Seda.

Seda soon proved to be so hopelessly incompetent, and so disliked by the members, that Hall, now international president, engineered his removal. With only the Executive Board's approval, and no localwide election, Hall replaced Seda with Willie James. The fact that James was the local's first black president was clearly seen as an advantage in a run against the black-led "New Directions'" slate.

James, under Hall's close control, has run the local with his sights set on the tough election campaign looming at the end of 1997. In a surprise move, he settled the new contract in fall 1996, a year before the old one was set to expire, to give members time to forget a rotten deal before polling time came around again.

With this contract, the Hall-controlled leadership sank to new lows. It agreed to allow five hundred jobs held by union cleaners to be given to people on "workfare." The only crumb that the union members received in return was a promise that no cleaners or any other T.W.U. members would be laid off for the life of the contract. (And even that promise did not cover provisional employees and could be revoked in the case of a "financial emergency.") As the union cleaners left their jobs, however, they would be filled by nonunion workfare recipients.

This contract passed very narrowly, and mainly because of the union leaders' heavily played threat of lay-offs should it fail.

"New Directions" has been assaulted with everything its opponents could muster. Some of its leaders have been hit with spurious disciplinary charges, leading to long suspensions with the threat of firing hanging over them. Some were cleared, but at least one lost his job. Some have been offered staff positions and taken them, despite fears that this would change their thinking about how to change the union. Others have been red-baited. "New Directions" has been the target of anonymous leaflets and attacks, as well as forgeries in its name.

Stakes were high in the T.W.U. Local 100 elections of December 1997. As early as March 1996, Willie James had offered lucrative staff jobs to some

"New Directions" leaders. They accepted. By the time of the election, they had defected to his side.

James' campaign literature was predominantly negative. The former "New Directions" members, in particular, filled their literature with red baiting and outrageous distortions.

James made a promise that sounded nice but impossible. He promised, if elected, to deliver to the membership a pension plan, paid entirely by T.A., that would allow retirement at full pension after twenty years at age fifty. Currently, employees who started after 1976, which includes most people on the job, must contribute 3 percent of their annual salary to the pension fund to retire after thirty years, at age sixty-two, or 5.2 percent to retire after twenty-five years at fifty-five. James' promise seemed a cynical ploy, a clear case of pie in the sky at a time when public employers everywhere are reducing, rather than increasing, employee benefits.

The greatest fiasco of James' campaign was his choice of the slogan, "Devour the meatballs!" It was featured superimposed upon a photograph of a meatball hero sandwich. The buttons had to be taken out of circulation after Italian American transit workers objected to what they saw as an ethnic slur.

"New Directions," in contrast, ran a more dignified campaign. Its slogans were "Take back the power!" and "What difference will 'New Directions' make? All the difference in the world." It pledged to reduce union-staff salaries and benefits and to have vice presidents and staff reps elected from their divisions, "to end the gravy train that separates officers from membership." It vowed to "be in the field, meeting with members, picking their brains, organizing actions, and winning victories." And my experience with these folks leads me to believe they meant every word.

During the campaign, "New Directions" members became increasingly convinced that James had done more than negative and deceptive campaigning. They believed there was evidence that James was violating the rules governing union elections, such as those banning the use of employer and union resources on a candidate's behalf.

Despite the no-holds-barred assault on "New Directions," James' victory was narrow, with only an 800-vote lead out of 18,500 votes cast. "New Directions" increased both its total and its proportional support, garnering almost 2,000 votes over its 1994 total, and increasing its share from 45 to 48 percent of the vote. Its slate, headed by Tim Schermerhorn for president, won the majority of subway-worker votes. "New Directions" also won 20 of the 36 seats on the Local's Executive Board that are directly elected by the membership. However, the James slate prevailed among bus drivers.

Immediately after the returns were counted, "New Directions" began the process leading to the filing of a request for a Department of Labor investigation of the election. Its members were convinced James' victory was the result of fraud, not the support of the majority of the voting members. Besides violations in campaigning, many believed that the election, which was conducted by the Local 100 Election Committee, all of whose members were appointed by James himself, was actually stolen, that is, that the ballot box was stuffed. One "New Directions" leader advanced this scenario, "It is possible for the Local leadership to know which members have never voted in an election," since past elections have also been run internally, and the names of those who voted were checked off of the lists, "they can hold back the ballots for those people who haven't voted in the past and wait to see if any call to say that they hadn't received a ballot and ask for a duplicate. Most don't. Then, a few days before the ballots are due, union officers or staff can fill out ballots in the names of these nonvoting members, complete with signatures and pass numbers, and mail them in. I don't know that this happened, but it could, and it would work." Allegations have been made that pro-James shop stewards intimidated many drivers into giving them their blank ballots.

This reminded me of something I overheard during a previous T.W.U. election. Votes were being counted at the union hall, and John Lawe, the International president, was strolling about with Sonny Hall, the Local president. Sonny said to John, "It's easy to be honest when you're winning."

The women and men of "New Directions" will not content themselves with a legal challenge to this election. They plan to keep building "New Directions" as the real leadership of the union. They believe that they were the ones actually chosen by the members to lead the union, and they intend to fulfill their responsibilities.

—December 26, 1997
New York City

GLOSSARY

A.M.S: Jobs that start between four A.M. and noon. The names given to all A.M. jobs start with the number 2, for example: 201, 202, and so forth.

A.V.A.: or accumulated vacation allowance, which doesn't clarify anything. These were days that workers could choose to save, instead of being paid double time for working holidays. Then, a worker could request permission to use them as days off at a chosen time.

BACK UP: I just want you to know that the only way to back up a train is for the motorman to CHANGE ENDS.

BALL: signal. To hit a ball is to go through a red signal, activating a trip that puts the train into an emergency stop.

BANG IN: report something over the motorman's radio

BEAKIE: an undercover Transit Authority supervisor, named for a man named Beake, a head of labor relations on the early subways.

BEHIND: *see* "ONE BEHIND."

B.I.E.: brakes in emergency: the emergency brakes of the train have been activated. This may be done by the crew, by the riders on the train, by the train hitting some unauthorized object on the track, or by the train's going through a red signal. *See also* EMERGENCY BRAKE.

B.O.: This stands for "bad order," that is, not working properly. It may also be used as a noun: a B.O. is a train that is not functioning correctly.

BOARD: a term with many meanings. A board job is a category of job for either conductors or motormen. The job sets a terminal and a reporting time. The worker signs in at that terminal at that time and basically waits until someone is needed to pick up a job or even a trip. If there is no job in eight hours, the BOARD MAN goes home. The worker usually puts in more than eight hours, counting the board time and the job, so board jobs are a good source of overtime pay.

BRAKE HANDLE: a motorman's tool, used to operate the train's brakes.

CALL LETTERS: When an interval leaves the terminal, it receives call letters, which are used to identify it on the radio, based on its terminal of origin and the minutes past the hour that it actually left the terminal. For example, the Woodlawn oh-five, the Pelham twenty-three, or the White Plains forty-eight. If a train leaves after its scheduled time, it may be called, for example, the White Plains forty-eight at fifty-two.

CHANGE ENDS: The motorman moves his position from one end of the train to the other, so that the train can be operated in the opposite direction.

CHARGING UP: a motorman filling the brakes of the train with air to make the brake system work. The motorman does this by installing the BRAKE HANDLE in the cab at the beginning of each trip.

CHIEF, THE: the Chief Trainmaster; *see also* SEE THE CHIEF.

CLEAN OUT THE TRAIN: to get all riders off the train, usually at a terminal, so the train may be laid-up.

CLEAR: to finish your job on schedule.

COMMAND, COMMAND CENTER: located at T.A. Headquarters at 370 Jay Street in Brooklyn, where supervisors oversee the working of the subway system as a whole on a continuous basis. The central supervisors are in contact with all motormen on the road and their supervisors via radio.

CONSTRUCTION FLAGGING: a category of conductor job. Construction-flagging conductors safeguarded work crews who were not from T.A. but from outside contractors (T.A. crews were from the track department, and they did their own flagging.) Their job was to set up the flags-green, yellow, and red banners outside or lamps underground that told motorman there were workers on the tracks, when to go slowly, to stop, and to resume speed. They also set up portable trips, so that if a motorman were heedless, the train would be stopped anyway. It was not a job for the faint-hearted because you could be up on the structure, in the middle of a bridge over the East River, or down in the hole dodging trains. But the stouthearted fellows who picked it loved it, because once you set up your equipment, you basically had a picnic.

CORD, THE: the rope in the cabs and in the cars that, when pulled, activates the train's emergency brakes.

CREW: a motorman and conductor working together on a train. Crews are identified by the numbers of their jobs. Job, and therefore crew, numbers have three digits. All midnight jobs begin with "1," all A.M. jobs begin with "2" and P.M. jobs begin with "3." So, for example, a dispatcher might announce at the terminal, "Two sixteen crew, that's you to go in the west."

CREW ROOM: a room in the terminal where crews have their lockers and may take their breaks and lunch. A real center of working-class culture.

CUT OUT: to take the power off a door motor, so the door remains locked and does not open, even when the other doors are opened, as in "cut out the door."

DAYS IN THE STREET: days a worker is suspended without pay for disciplinary reasons.

DEADHEADING: a crew riding on a train instead of operating one. Much preferable, but hard to come by.

"DEUCE, THE": the No. 2 line.

DIE ACROSS THE SWITCHES: when a train loses power and cannot take power while crossing a switch. Very bad situation. The train can't be moved, and the switches can't be moved either. Ties up the whole railroad.

DISCHARGE: evacuate the riders from a train.

DOUBLE: as in "work a double": working two jobs consecutively. A source of overtime pay, since everything over the first eight hours is paid at time-and-a-half.

DROP: When a crew doesn't have to make one of their scheduled intervals, it is said they've been dropped. They can usually go back to the crew room and prop up their feet and watch HBO. This is the best thing that can happen to a crew, although most deny it ("I come here to work!"), and it is only slightly less frequent than a blue moon. Not to be confused with DROP BACK.

DROP BACK: to take the train for your return trip that was your follower on your outbound trip.

DRUMSWITCH: the switch, on old equipment, that the conductor used to set up a cab so that the doors could be operated from it. It required a key to set it.

DUMP IT, DUMP THE TRAIN: automatically activate the emergency brakes of the train.

DUMP THE LOAD: evacuate the riders from a train.

"EAST, THE": A terminal usually has two tracks. Depending on the location and position of the terminal, one of the tracks may be known as THE

EAST, the other as THE WEST. These tracks are also called POCKETS, as in, "There's a B.O. in the west pocket." May also refer to the train in that pocket, as in "Flag, open up THE EAST," or "Two eleven crew, take THE WEST."

EMERGENCY BRAKE: Subway trains have an emergency braking system that may be activated in a number of ways: by the motorman releasing the controller (the "dead man" feature for stopping the train if the motorman should lose consciousness), by the conductor's emergency valve, a rope in each cab; by an emergency cord in the subway car; by the "trips" on the bottom of the train that are activated if the train goes through a red signal or hits an object on the roadbed. When the emergency brake is activated, all the air is released from the train's airbrakes, and the train cannot move. The first thing the crew must do is figure out why they are B.I.E. (brakes in emergency) if neither of them activated the brakes. The first step in doing this is for the motorman to attempt to RECHARGE the brakes, that is, fill them with air again. If they won't recharge, probably a rider has pulled an emergency cord, and the crew must find and reset the cord. If not, it may be a malfunction, for instance, a brake pipe rupture (very bad news, take out your overtime slip). If they will recharge, this is worse news: it means the train has been tripped either by an object on the roadbed or by going through a red signal. The motorman then must inspect the train by getting down on the roadbed and walking around the train to see what the train has struck.

EXTRA: a category of job for motormen and conductors. An extra job has a division (for example, Eastern-Queens) and a tour of duty (for example A.M.s), but the worker "floats" and may be assigned any job in his division and on his tour of duty. He finds out what his job is by reading the SHEETS or calling the Crew Dispatcher's Office at Jay Street.

EXTRA-EXTRA: People too new to have picked a job (i.e., during the most recent pick either they were not yet working, or all the jobs had been picked before their turn came) are EXTRA-EXTRA. They are like the EXTRA people, except that the EXTRA people picked their jobs, and thus chose their tour of duty and division, and the EXTRA people as far as possible are given preference over the less senior EXTRA-EXTRA people.

EXTRA SERVICE: a form of overtime, but one involving additional work within the eight hours of the job. For example, if one's job involves three trips to Atlantic Avenue, each scheduled to last 50 minutes, and on one of these trips, one is rerouted to New Lots, a trip scheduled for 80 minutes, one gets 30 minutes EXTRA SERVICE, which is paid at time-and-a-half. So one earns 45 minutes worth of one's hourly pay. Significantly, this is only given when one is sent off the route of the job one picked. It is not good for delays, or when a trip lasts longer than it is scheduled for, but still ends within the eight hours of the job.

FLAG: basically a means of communication. To flag a train means to signal the person operating from a position other than the front, how to move it. It can also mean to adjust the signs on a train to show the correct designation and other information. "The flag" is the flagman, a person who does the flagging. The "flagging shack" is a small shelter on the platform of an elevated terminal, where the flagman may stay while changing train side signs. *See also* CONSTRUCTION FLAGGING.

FLASH: as in, a signal flashed, suddenly turned red for no reason, with the effect of tripping the train, as if the motorman had gone through a red signal.

FOLLOWER: The train behind yours and its crew are your FOLLOWER. *See also* LEADER.

FULL SERVICE BRAKE: 70 pounds of air. (*See* HOLDING N POUNDS OF AIR.) Takes forever to release.

G-2: a memo written by a transit worker. Supervision orders G-2s written about any incident they wish. Also, G-2s were used in place of formal grievances. Workers also wrote G-2s to request A.V.A.s or similar things.

GAP STATION: a station with holding lights, which, when lit, are the signal to the conductor to keep the train's doors open. Thus trains are "gapped," that is, kept roughly equidistant from each other.

G.O.: general order. This is a preplanned change in subway service and schedule for any reason, but usually for repairs or construction.

GO DOWNTOWN: go to T.A. headquarters for a disciplinary hearing.

GO OUT BEHIND: *see* ONE BEHIND.

GUARDLIGHT: lights on the outside of the train car, one for each door panel. Generally, when the GUARDLIGHT is illuminated, the door is not closed and locked. A HANGING GUARDLIGHT remains illuminated when the doors have been closed and all the other lights are out. It shows the location of the door that is not secured. As long as there is a single

HANGING GUARDLIGHT, the conductor should not have INDICATION. If the conductor's indication light is off and there are no guardlights, it is possible that there is a burnt-out HANGING GUARDLIGHT.

HANDLES: the tools a motorman uses to drive the train; therefore, "having handles" means being a motorman. Handles can also refer to the handles on some older door control panels that conductors used to open and close train doors. On newer trains, these have been replaced with buttons. The advantage of door control handles was that a conductor could tell, from the position of the handles, whether the doors were open or closed.

HANGING GUARDLIGHT: *See* GUARD LIGHT.

HEADWAY: the amount of time between intervals. For instance, during rush hour, the No. 4 could have as little as four-minutes headway; after midnight, the headway might be twenty minutes.

HOLDING LIGHTS: amber bulbs at a GAP STATION. When lit, they signal the conductor to keep train doors open until they go out.

HOLDING N POUNDS OF AIR: The motorman stops the train by applying air pressure, measured in pounds, to the wheels to stop them. The more pounds of air, the longer it takes to release the brakes and start the train moving again.

HOLE, THE: the underground tunnels.

HOMEBALL: a signal at a track crossroads, or "interlocking." It governs not only whether a train may go or must stop, but also which of the possible tracks the train should take.

I.C.: intercom between motorman and conductor.

IN SERVICE: with riders. The opposite of OUT OF SERVICE.

INDICATION: A light in the cab that indicates when lit, that the doors of a section of the train, or of the whole train, are closed and secured. "Motorman's indication" is activated when the motorman installs his tools in his cab, right above the dial that shows the air pressure, and "conductor's indication," on the door control panel, is activated when the cab is made into the door control position, which is accomplished in various ways on different forms of equipment. *See also* GUARD LIGHT.

INTERVAL: An interval is a scheduled train trip. Each one has a name, based on the time it leaves its terminal, for example, the three-oh-two, which leaves at 3:02; the four-fourteen, which leaves at 4:14. As in, "Two oh nine crew, you're going out one behind on the four-fourteen."

ISOLATE A CAR: to seal off a single car of a train so it may not be used by riders, to get all riders out of it if necessary (and possible) and lock the storm and side doors so no one may board. The means of doing the latter vary with the type of equipment.

JOB: each working day, a subway worker has a JOB. If he or she works on a train, the job consists of INTERVALS, that is, scheduled train trips. The job also has a number (*see* CREW).

JUMP AHEAD: to go out on an earlier interval than the one you were scheduled.

KEY: Conductors and motormen used an array of keys to operate. There was a key to open the cabs and storm doors, and different keys, depending upon the type of equipment, to operate the other doors. Motormen also had a key to install their radios in the cab, and a "cutting key," to divide and combine cars in a train.

KEY BY: To go through a red signal without activating the train's emergency brake. This is accomplished by going very slowly, perhaps ten miles an hour. It is, nevertheless, an extremely dangerous thing to do, because a red signal usually indicates there is a train ahead.

KEY IN: On each subway car, two of the side doors, one on each side, have keyholes next to them, both inside and outside of the cars. One of the conductor's keys, turned in this keyhole, will open this door. To enter the train this way is called "keying yourself in," and you may naturally also key yourself out, and do so for others as well. Not to be confused with KEYING BY, a far more dangerous motorman prerogative.

LATE CLEAR: finishing work after your job is scheduled to end and also the overtime pay earned this way.

LAY-UP: an empty train stored on an unused track or in a yard. To lay-up a train means to take and leave a train in such a way. A train going back to the terminal or into service is called a PUT-IN.

LEADER: the train in front of you and the crew on it are your LEADER. *See also* FOLLOWER.

LIGHT: *See* RUN LIGHT.

LINE SPEAKER: a cross between telephone and public address system, used by dispatchers at terminals and gap stations, to communicate with one another.

LINE UP: the way the tracks are lined up at a switching point to route the train on one of the possible tracks. The motorman must call the towerman on the radio, or press a button, to ask for the correct LINE UP for the train's destination. If the tower gives the wrong line up, and the motorman doesn't realize it (*see* READ YOUR IRON), the train is going to go off its route and make a lot of riders unhappy, and they will blame the only innocent employee, the conductor.

MABSTOA: Manhattan and Bronx Surface Transit Operating Authority, a.k.a. "O.A." It includes most of the bus lines in Manhattan and the Bronx. The workers on these lines were in T.W.U., but they were not under civil service, and they had a separate health and benefits system. They definitely had work practices distinct from the subway workers and even the bus drivers on the T.A. lines in Brooklyn and Queens.

MAG: the magnetoelectrical phone system, used within the system. An ancient technology it is totally extinct outside THE PROPERTY.

MARRIED PAIRS: a form of train cars. The cars come in pairs, so each one, for example, has a motorman's operating position in only one of its two cabs. This build made them very vulnerable to problems. In addition, they were constructed flimsily, and their doors, windows, and seats were prone to breakage.

MIDNIGHTS: jobs that start between midnight and four A.M.

MOTORMAN'S VISION GLASS: *See* VISION GLASS.

MOTORS: the motorman's job; "to go to motors" is to become a motorman.

"NO LUNCH": If members of a train crew got less than twenty minutes in the terminal for lunch because of delays on the road, they were paid thirty minutes overtime for NO LUNCH.

NORMAL: running according to schedule.

NORTH MOTOR: the car on the northern end of the train, from which the motorman operates going northbound. The second north motor is the car behind it, and so on.

NOT IN SERVICE: *See* OUT OF SERVICE.

OBSERVING THE PLATFORM: a main feature of the conductor's job. At each station, after the stop has been completed, the doors closed, and the train started, the conductor must put his or her head out of the window of the cab and watch the outside of the train to make sure no rider is caught in the doors and being dragged by the train, until the train has moved three car-lengths.

OKAY: as in "okay a train," go to a LAID-UP train and do a standard series of checks to make sure it is ready and fit for service. Part of a motorman's job description; conductors may participate.

ONE BEHIND: when a crew goes out on the interval after the one they are supposed to make. There are also two behind, three behind, et cetera, ad nauseum.

ONE-TRIPPER: A job with one trip. Very unusual, desirable, and the province of the very senior.

OUT OF SERVICE: referring to a train, not in passenger service, a train with no riders. But also, when it refers to a worker, suspended from work.

P.A.: public address system.

PENALTY TIME: the time on a job that goes over eight hours. Desirable to people who want to make more money, because it is paid at overtime rate, time-and-a-half.

PICK: a term with various meanings, all of which are important in the transit worker's daily vocabulary. All are based on the right of transit workers to pick their jobs by seniority, approximately every six months. The period of time during which they hold these jobs is called A PICK. The process of picking new jobs, which lasts many weeks, is also called A PICK. And of course, it also serves as a verb, as in "What'd you pick?" Finally, if someone more senior than you picks your job, you lose it: you've been "picked out."

PLAT: a conductor's job, working on a platform. It is considered a good, high-seniority job, because you aren't on a train and for its potential for goofing off.

P.M.S: jobs that start between noon and midnight.

POCKET: *See* THE EAST.

"THE PROPERTY": T.A. premises. Nuff said.

PUT-IN: *See* LAY UP.

R.C.I.: road car inspector. A mechanic who is sent by supervision to trains encountering difficulties on the road. If he cannot "overcome the problem," he may take the train OUT OF SERVICE, a desirable result for the crew.

R.D.O.: regular day(s) off. A motorman or conductor's weekend. Must be two consecutive days. Days off are picked by seniority, with the most senior people picking one or both weekend days, and the least senior ending up with Tuesdays, Wednesdays, and Thursdays. The term may also refer to working on a day off for time-and-a-half pay, as in, "I work an R.D.O. each week because I'm paying off my mortgage."

READ YOUR IRON: a motorman's skill in looking at a switching point on the tracks and being able to detect which way the switch had been thrown, in order to be sure which way the train will go if it proceeds.

RECHARGE: filling the brakes with air again after an activation of the emergency brakes.

RELAY: to move a train from one track to another, to get it to a platform for a different destination; usually done at a terminal.

RESTRICTION: Injury or medial condition can excuse a worker from certain duties of the job.

REVERSER: one of a motorman's tools. When installed in a cab, it activates the equipment there so the motorman may operate the train from that cab.

RUN LIGHT: operate a train without riders. Presumably, those riders were heavy.

RUNNING TIME: the scheduled amount of time that an interval should take from its terminal to its destination. For example, the RUNNING TIME from Woodlawn terminal to Atlantic Avenue was fifty minutes.

"SEE THE CHIEF": to have a disciplinary hearing with the Chief Trainmaster.

SHACK: Structures on the subway platforms, both elevated and underground, were often called SHACKS (and indeed that is what they were). Thus the dispatcher's office was the "dispatcher's shack," and the often ramshackle shanty on the platforms of elevated terminals, where the drumswitchmen or flagmen took shelter, were called "the flagging shack."

SHEETS: daily information sheets published to inform workers and supervisors who is covering for workers whose absences are known in advance, due to promotions, jury duty, retirements, deaths, and DAYS IN THE STREET. Also, the records the terminal dispatcher keeps of intervals and crews, as in "They wouldn't know how to fix the sheets to go one behind." Also, the papers that motormen and conductors sign in on.

SIDE SIGNS: the signs on the sides of a train that show its origin, destination, and route.

SIX WIRE: the emergency broadcasting system of the subway radio system. When you put something "on six wire," it reached six places simultaneously, including Command Center, the police, and the fire department.

SKEL: transit-worker slang for a homeless person living on the subway.

SOUTH MOTOR: *See* NORTH MOTOR.

SPOTTED WHEELS: wheels with flattened areas on their contact surfaces. Naturally, they created problems both small—noise and vibration—and major—danger of derailment.

STORM DOOR: the two doors either end of the car, as differentiated from the six doors on each side of it.

STRUCTURE, THE: the elevated tracks above the street.

SUPPLEMENT: a work schedule supplanting the regular picked one, for example, to accommodate a G.O.

SWITCHMAN: a motorman assigned to a terminal to move trains not in passenger service. Switchmen are either very new: motormen in training who are not yet "road qualified" to drive a train in passenger service; or they are very senior: enough so to pick a job that mainly involves sitting in the crew room or the yard.

T.C.: transferring cars. The predecessor of W.A.A. However, a worker on T.C. could not be ordered to make a trip.

THREE-TRIPPER: *See* ONE TRIPPER.

TITLE: conductor was a title; motorman was a title. Seniority for picking was determined by the length of one's time "in title," that is, as a conductor or a motorman.

TOWER: a room from which signals and switches are operated by a tower operator. Dispatchers may also work from a TOWER.

TUBE, THE: *See* UNDERRIVER TUBE.

TURN: occurs when a train is on its way to the terminal; and supervision orders the motorman to CHANGE ENDS to take the train back in the opposite direction, usually because of problems on the road ahead. This is especially bad news on your last trip.

TWELVE-NINE: code for a person under a train. Not good news.

TWELVE-SEVEN: call for assistance code.

TWELVE-TWO: the code for smoke or fire.

TWO-TRIPPER: *See* ONE TRIPPER.

UNDERRIVER TUBE: any of the subway tunnels that go underneath the rivers, particular the East River between Manhattan and Brooklyn.

VISION GLASS: the window in the cab that faces in the direction in which the train is moving, hence the one the motorman uses. Hence, it is also called the MOTORMAN'S VISION GLASS.

W.A.A.: work as assigned. A period of time in conductors' or motormen's jobs when they are in the terminal, but can be used at their supervisors' discretion to do anything in their job descriptions, including making a trip.

"WEST, THE": *See* THE EAST.

WRAP IT AROUND: to drive a train as fast as it will go. The "it" refers to the motorman's controller, which moves in a horizontal circular path and controls the train's speed.